Charles Axtell
Fountain Hills, Az
May 20, 1999

AMERICAN
ORIGINAL

AMERICAN ORIGINAL

A Life of

Ray Robinson

New York   Oxford | Oxford University Press | 1996

Oxford University Press

Oxford   New York
Athens   Auckland   Bangkok   Bombay
Calcutta   Cape Town   Dar es Salaam   Delhi
Florence   Hong Kong   Istanbul   Karachi
Kuala Lumpur   Madras   Madrid   Melbourne
Mexico City   Nairobi   Paris   Singapore
Taipei   Tokyo   Toronto

and associated companies in
Berlin   Ibadan

Published by Oxford University Press, Inc.,
198 Madison Avenue, New York, New York 10016

Oxford is a registered trademark of Oxford University Press

Library of Congress Cataloging-in-Publication Data
Robinson, Ray, 1920 Dec. 4–
American original : a life of Will Rogers / Ray Robinson.
p. cm.   Includes index.
ISBN 0-19-508693-7
1. Rogers, Will, 1879–1935.   2. Entertainers–United States–Biography.
3. Humorists, American–Biography.   I. Title.
PN2287.R74R53   1996
792.7′028′092–dc20   [B]   95-31578

9 8 7 6 5 4 3 2 1

Printed in the United States of America
on acid-free paper

For Holly and Eva Marie

The secret source of humor itself is not joy but sorrow. There is no humor in heaven.   —MARK TWAIN

Contents

Acknowledgments

While preparing this biography of Will Rogers, I became acquainted with Will Rogers Jr. My research process was an enjoyable experience, but it was marred by Will Jr.'s death, by his own hand, in 1993. He had informed me several times that he was not in good health, but when I heard the news of his suicide, I was still not prepared for his making such a choice. In addition to being very forthcoming about his father, Will Jr. sent me his own videocassette of *The Ropin' Fool,* an early silent movie made by Will.

A number of other people made significant contributions to this book, offering their memories, insights, and advice. Jim Rogers, Will Jr.'s younger brother, a former pole-vaulter from Pomona College in California, was especially helpful, always talking candidly about his father. Will's coworkers in the entertainment industry, including Douglas Fairbanks Jr., Lew Ayres, Shirley Temple Black, Maureen O'Sullivan, Mickey Rooney, and Morey Amsterdam were gracious and forthcoming when I approached them for information.

Jonathan Alexander Dunn provided me with his master's thesis on Will's ranch, originally written in 1986 for the faculty of the Graduate School of the

University of Southern California. Jerry Beatty sent me a copy of an out-of-print 1924 book, *The Illiterate Digest,* written by Will in 1923. Mary Helen Evans gently prodded her father, William Edward McElhone, a former member of the Royal Canadian Mounted Police, to give me information about Will's ill-fated trip to Alaska.

Jeré Wineman, a longtime admirer of Will's from Columbus, Mississippi, sent along his child's scrapbook on Will Rogers. Lawrence E. Wikander of Williamstown, Massachusetts, enlightened me about correspondence between an apologetic Will and President Calvin Coolidge. Mary V. Dearborn of Norwalk, Connecticut, informed me of Will's relationship with Anzia Yezierska, the "Sweatshop Cinderella" of the 1920s. James Whitmore explained why he has been playing Will in a one-man show for over twenty-five years. Willard Hunter, a freelance writer from Claremont, California, put his notes on actor Joel McCrea and on Will at my disposal. Julian "Bud" Lesser described his youthful days as an "outsider" at Will's ranch. Nolan Porterfield of Cape Girardeau, Missouri, a biographer of Jimmie Rogers, the "father of country music," filled me in on Will's tour on behalf of the Red Cross.

I would also like to thank, for their willingness to answer questions, Greg Malak, Casey Tefertiller, Norm Bobrow, Sy Presten, Martin Quigley, Graham S. McFarlane, Dr. Reba Collins, Faigi Rosenthal of the *New York Daily News,* Andrew Sarris, Al Navis, Bryan Sterling, George Vecsey, Mark Sufrin, Warren Cowan, Donald Honig, Steve Robinson, Greta Walker, Louis H. Kerner, and the custodians of the New York Society Library; also, Richard Kornberg, the publicity representative for *The Will Rogers Follies* which played in New York for over two years.

My deepest gratitude to Sheldon Meyer, an admirable editor, to Joanne Curtis for retyping the manuscript with a minimum of miscues, and to my wife, Phyllis, who has endured endless requests with understanding, spirit, and love.

The following books were of considerable help in rounding out a fuller portrait of Will Rogers:

Will Rogers by Donald Day; *Will Rogers: His Wife's Story* by Betty Rogers; *Our Will Rogers* by Homer Croy; *Just Relax* by Will Rogers; *The Will Rogers Book* by Paul M. Love; *Will Rogers: His Life and Times* by Richard Ketchum; *Will Rogers: How We Select Our Presidents* by Donald Day; *Will Rogers: An American Life* by Ben Yagoda; *The Men Who Invented Broadway* by John Mosedale; *1600 Pennsylvania Avenue* by Walter Johnson; *The Little Brown Book of Anecdotes* by Clifton Fadiman; *Great Times* by J. C. Furnas; *Heywood Broun* by Dale Kramer; *Huey Long* by T. Harry Williams, *Ring Lardner* by Donald Elder;

Ring by Jonathan Yardley; *These Were Our Years* by Frank Brookhouser; *A Treasury of Great Reporting* by Louis Snyder and Richard B. Morris; *This Fabulous Century* by Time-Life; *Vanity Fair* by Cleveland Amory and Frederic Bradlee; *The Jazz Age* by Marvin Barrett; *The Year The World Went Mad* by Allen Churchill; *The Shadow of Blooming Grove* by Francis Russell; *From Harding to Hiroshima* by Barrington Boardman; *Witness to a Century* by George Seldes; *Knute Rockne* by Francis Wallace; *Moe Berg* by Kaufman, Fitzgerald and Sewell; *Loss of Eden* by Joyce Milton; *The Life That Ruth Built* by Marshall Smelser; *Bury My Heart at Wounded Knee* by Dee Brown; *Will Rogers: Courtship and Correspondence* by Reba Collins; *White House Fever* by Robert Bendiner; *Tom Mix Died For Your Sins* by Darryl Ponicsan; *Film As Art*, Museum of Modern Art Film Library; *Child Star: An Autobiography of Shirley Temple Black; Shirley Temple: American Princess* by Anne Edwards; *John Ford* by Tag Gallagher; *Rolling Stone* by Fred Stone; *The Campaign of the Century* by Greg Mitchell; *Take My Life* by Eddie Cantor; *Will Rogers* by Jerome Beatty; *Cobb* by Al Stump; *America's Dizzy Dean* by Curt Smith; *Fords: An American Epic* by Peter Collier and David Horowitz; *Red Ribbon on a White Horse* by Anzia Yezierska; *W. C. Fields* by Robert Lewis Taylor; *The Ziegfeld Follies* by Marjorie Farnsworth; *The Ziegfeld Touch* by Richard and Paulette Ziegfeld; *Will Rogers' Illiterate Digest* by Will Rogers; *Ziegfeld* by Eddie Cantor and David Freedman; *A Pictorial History of the Movies* by Deems Taylor; *The Long Count* by Mel Heiner; *Henry Ford and The Jews* by Albert Lee; *Herbert Hoover, American Quaker* by David Hinshaw; *42 Years in the White House* by Irwin Hoover; *The Triumph of Herbert Hoover, an Uncommon Man* by Richard W. Smith; *Goldwyn* by Arthur Marx; *Goldwyn* by A. Scott Berg; *A Puritan in Babylon* by W. A. White; *Coolidge, the Quiet President* by Donald McCoy; *Calvin Coolidge* by Claude M. Fuess; *Henry Ford* by William A. Simonds; *Schickel on Film* by Richard M. Schickel; *Myrna Loy, Being and Becoming* by James Kotsilibas; *The Frontier Years* by Mark H. Brown and W. R. Felton; *The Cherokees* by Grace Steele Woodward; *Cherokee Sunset, a Nation Betrayed* by Samuel Carter III; *Eleanor Roosevelt* by Blanche Wiesen Cook; *Righteous Pilgrim, The Life and Times of Harold Ickes* by T. H. Watkins; *The Hollywood Studios* by Ethan Mordden; *American Film Criticism*, edited by Stanley Kauffmann with Bruce Hentsell; *The War, The West and the Wilderness* by Kevin Brownlow; *The American Irish* by William Shannon; *American Demagogues* by Reinhard Luthin; *Memo from David O. Selznick* by Rudy Behliner; *Ford, the Men and the Machine* by Robert Lacey; *Louise Brooks* by Barry Paris; *The Nation Comes of Age* by Page Smith; *The Theatre Handbook* by Bernard Sobol; *Inside Oscar*, by Mason Wiley and Damien Bona; *FDR* by Ted Morgan; *Capone, the Man and the Era* by

Laurence Bergreen; *Hollywood Players of the Thirties* by James R. Parish and William T. Leonard; *Buffalo Bill* by Henry Blackman Sell and Victor Weybright; *Jack Dempsey* by Randy Roberts; *The Aspirin Age* by Isabel Leighton; *Brother, Can You Spare A Dime?* by Milton Meltzer; *A Pictorial History of Burlesque* by Bernard Sobel; *Ol' Diz,* a Biography of Dizzy Dean by Vince Staten.

AMERICAN
ORIGINAL

Introduction

n August 1935, Will Rogers, a one-man wrecking crew against pretense and pomposity, died in a plane crash in a remote outpost of Alaska. The newspapers of that day treated the sudden death of this American folk figure as a national calamity—rarely have so many spoken and written words of praise gushed forth about a departed private citizen. The Irish-born American tenor John McCormack accurately reflected the temper of his adopted land when he said that "a smile had disappeared from the lips of America and her eyes are suffused with tears."

Rogers wasn't a president, a crooner, a handsome screen lover, a victorious general, or a prodigious home-run hitter. Yet he had earned such eulogies through the seeming sweetness of his personality, his downright horse sense, his compassion, and a mischievous sense of humor; he rarely showed even a smidgen of ill will. He was an optimist in a world that had already seen millions of unemployed Americans shivering through the long winters of the country's most serious crisis since the Civil War.

From 1915 to 1935, Will had been America's foremost cracker-barrel philosopher, a congenial mixture of Mark Twain, H. L. Mencken, and the garrulous baseball pitcher, Dizzy Dean. Twain specialized in a contempt for the universe, while pricking the thin skins of the pious. Mencken put the "booboisie" down daily with his own acerbic brand of misanthropy. Will, on the other hand, projected kindness, even as he mildly scalded the hypocritical and the self-righteous.

Whenever Rogers was compared to Twain, he politely turned down the anointment. "There's one thing that ought to be eliminated in this country," he said, "and that's every time somebody gets a laugh of some small dimensions, he's called the modern Mark Twain." An earnest practitioner of humility, Will was having none of the comparisons.

Columnist Damon Runyon said Will was "America's most complete human document," and theologian Reinhold Neibuhr said Rogers "could puncture foibles which more pretentious preachers leave untouched." Others regarded Will as the "La Rochefoucauld of the Roaring Twenties." But the highest praise of all was attributed to an anonymous Washington observer, who suggested that "this country could never go to war unless Will Rogers was for it. He'd destroy the plans of the jingoes in a week. The people would believe him, and with him, would laugh the politicians into defeat." These designations would have brought howls of delight from Will, the "poet lariat" who regarded himself as something of an illiterate.

Some who disparaged Will, like columnist Mark Sullivan, thought he was little more than a clown, who made a joke only for the joke's sake. The dour Ring Lardner, a gadfly baseball reporter who authored the hilarious "Alibi Ike" and "You Know Me, Al," didn't see anything particularly funny about Will. As a matter of fact, he felt he could write a hundred words a day better than Will could, and for less money. (At the time, Will was getting about $350 a minute, to tell jokes, while thousands starved or sold apples on street corners for a nickel.) Homer Croy, who, like Lardner, had worked with Will, believed that Will's syntactical mistakes and grammatical slipups were often deliberately cultivated stage decorations. Still others deprecated Will as hardly more than a village explainer, a sort of nonstop blatherer and windbag, who managed to sell the notion that he possessed ultimate wisdom.

In that long-ago summer of 1935, I was a fourteen-year-old boy, a camper in upstate New York, when word of Will's death came first over the radio. Within minutes, the news spread miasmically from one camp bungalow to another. And within a few days, my parents sent me copies of The New York Times and the New York Sun, which reported what seemed like endless details of Will's sad demise. It had occurred as he was sharing a ride with his famous aviator buddy, Wiley Post. Post had only one good eye—the other, shielded by a patch, had become as familiar to the public as the unruly lock of hair that constantly intruded on Will's forehead.

To the kids at that camp, Everyman seemed to have died. Will was certainly not one of our youthful generation; yet, as a man of fifty-six, with a face as crinkled as a tossed-away love note, he had as much appeal for us as he had for our parents. He had, in his homely way, connected with all generations.

In his time, Will earned the gratitude of almost everybody, even us kids, by taking on everybody who was anybody—dictators, presidents, stuffed shirts, royalty, big shots, celebrities, gangsters, heroes, villains—the high and mighty. The list included Huey Long, Henry Ford, Herbert Hoover, Franklin D. Roosevelt, John D. Rockefeller, Warren G. Harding, Calvin Coolidge, Father Charles Coughlin (Will sat next to the demagogue priest at the 1934 World Series in Detroit), the king of England, Al Capone, the queen of Romania. He could sniff out the ripe smell of the mucker and the mountebank from miles away, but he preferred to leave untouched life's underdogs or those who had suffered in their daily struggles to put food on their tables.

Although he came close to being dangerously simplistic in his views (he never *really* said, "I never met a man I didn't like," which is universally regarded as his epitaph), Will would have been the first to admit he wasn't perfect. In the end, his decency and generosity always prevailed. W. C. Fields, who rode to fame, as Will did, as a headliner on the glamorous boards of Florenz Ziegfeld's *Follies,* nearly checked his dyspeptic nature when it came to Will. "The man's fakin' with that way he talks," mumbled Fields, from a hospital bed. But in his weaker moments, Fields couldn't help loving the guy.

For all of Will's good fellowship, he was not averse to engaging in unpleasant stereotypes about various groups. In his eyes, Mexican peasants had fleas; Italians invariably reeked of garlic; and Jews were, more often than not, "kosher lawyers," or "Yiddisher cowboys" who knew how to make more money than ordinary cowboys. Cowhands who worked with sheep were "woolies"—a derogatory term employed by cowboys. In many of Will's movies in the 1930s, black people, such as Hattie McDaniel and Stepin Fetchit, played embarrassingly obsequious roles, as a counterpoint to Will's paternalism. True, it was white Hollywood's vision of how Negroes behaved, but Will was a willing partner in such insensitive portrayals.

Some of these perceptions were not evil, however misguided they might have been. However, they did bespeak Will's failure to break loose from a common parochialism. That people blithely accepted his descriptions, usually with laughter, underlines the fact that Will always landed smack in the mainstream. He was always the sly naturalist, even though he posed as an iconoclast.

Born in the Indian Territory, in an area that is now Oklahoma, Will traded on the fact that he was a Cherokee. But he was really more Irish than Indian. He chose, nonetheless, to play up the Indian side and let the Irish run their revolution. He also had some Welsh blood and a spot of English blood, which would have made him about one-fourth Cherokee, by his own belated confession. That he was born on Election Day gave him an early start in working politicians over. But he never registered or voted in his life; nor did he ever bother very much about going to any church.

Will was a restless soul, constantly moving and on the run. His public pace—even his incessant gum chewing—was a frenetic one. He worked, walked, rode, and bummed his way around the world before he was twenty-five. Before most people could get oriented to the risky concept of flying, he was an enthusiastic advocate of air travel, something of an unofficial ambassador of wings. He handed out large gobs of cash almost indiscriminately, keeping few records of his largesse. When someone needed help, he was always there.

Three years before Will was born, John Ruskin, the English writer and critic, uttered these words: "There is no wealth but life." Though Will probably never heard of Ruskin, he certainly lived his own life with all due respect to this maxim.

What was at the root of Will's temperament and character? How much did his mixed heritage affect his behavior? Was he engaged in a flight from any personal demons or fears? Was he perpetually trying to prove to his tough, demanding father, Clem, that he wasn't a ne'er-do-well or an unemployable transient? How did he become the world's most incurably curious and friendly man, with such an insatiable appetite for people and far-off places?

James Whitmore, the veteran actor who has played the role of Will Rogers in innumerable one-man shows since 1969, has summed him up this way: "He was one helluva man for any time, a prescient fellow with all the right gut instincts. Like heliotrope, he always wanted to face the sun."

1

The Indian "Problem"

In 1926, during one of the many overseas jaunts that Will undertook as a roving reporter for the *Saturday Evening Post,* he got into a minor brouhaha with customs authorities because he had no birth certificate to show them. The explanation for such a bureaucratic failure was simple, according to Will: "In those days of the Indian Territory, there wasn't any such thing as a birth certificate. You being there was certificate enough—we generally took it for granted that if you were there, you must have been born at some time or other; . . . having a certificate of being born was like wearing a raincoat in the water over a bathing suit."

William Penn Adair Rogers was born on November 4, 1879, in a house located four miles northeast of Oologah, in the Cooweescoowee District of the Cherokee Nation, Indian Territory—in an area that later became part of the state of Oklahoma.

Oologah, the name of a not particularly well known Cherokee chief, was in the midst of cattle country, twenty-three miles northeast of what today is Tulsa. The area was a collection of small houses, made mostly of sod and logs. In later years, Will boasted to his Broadway audiences that his Cherokee ancestors had not arrived on the *Mayflower* in 1620, but that "they met the boat."

Nobody is certain of the origins of the Cherokee Nation. Their name may be derived from a corruption of "Tsalagi" or "Tsaragi," which means "Ancient Tobacco People."

Hernando de Soto, the Spanish conquistador and explorer, first encountered the Cherokees in the sixteenth century. They were then in control of a vast region in the southern Appalachians, primarily in the Carolinas, Georgia, Alabama, Virginia, Kentucky, and Tennessee. De Soto dealt harshly with the Cherokees until his death in 1542, even though they had reached a higher peak of civilization than any other Indian tribe. By the time Will was born, there were fewer than a hundred thousand Cherokees alive in the world, with perhaps half of them residing in Indian Territory.

White men branded the olive-skinned Cherokees as a "warlike" people, thus rationalizing their cruel actions against them. As a result, the Cherokees, taller and stronger than most of the white men they encountered, developed their own set of defenses, one of which was a remarkable ability to josh each other, even while they were under a constant threat to their existence. They exhibited an indestructible tribal vitality that no doubt prevented their early extinction.

Will once commented wryly about how he envisioned his own death: "When I die, my epitaph, or whatever you call it—those signs on gravestones—is going to read: 'I joked about almost every prominent man of my time but I never met one I didn't like!' I am so proud of that, I can hardly wait to die so it can be carved. And when you come around to my grave I'll be sitting there proudly reading it."

In 1809, Will's ancestors, the Vanns, purportedly carved an epitaph on a modest wooden slab in Georgia, marking the grave of James Vann, who had been murdered by his mother-in-law in a shooting episode:

> Here lies the body of James Vann
> He killed many a white man
> At last by a rifle ball he fell
> And devils dragged him off to Hell.

Along with their durable humor, the Cherokees were known to be highly adaptable, aggressive, and persistent, whether as farmers or warriors. These qualities helped them subsist on the land's corn, carrots, squash, and beans.

They seemed equally efficient at trapping and killing the abundant game that roamed the countryside.

For years the Cherokees resisted the white man's stubborn effort to convert them to Christianity. They were made to understand that if they were "good" on this earth, they would "go up." If bad, they would "go down." They were regarded—as were all Indians—by Spanish Catholics and British Protestants as "servants of the devil." The missionaries were convinced that the Christian gospel was superior to any Indian practice of religion, which included devil worship. Thus, all measures of persuasion, including force, were considered quite justified. However, very few of the Cherokees accepted the missionaries' concept of heaven and hell.

In 1760 the Cherokees pulled off a surprising political coup. Two of their chiefs sailed for England, where, on their arrival, they were royally received at Windsor Castle. With the help of an interpreter, a treaty was made with His Majesty's government, which, in essence, acknowledged the sovereignty of George II. The Cherokees had found that the British were more apt to respect treaty obligations than were the disrespectful frontiersmen, who were inclined to pay little attention to them. The pact with the British, however, caused the Cherokees endless difficulty with those fighting to organize the new American republic. As a result, even after the British ended their struggle at Yorktown, the Cherokees and other Indian tribes continued to harass the colonists. This did precious little, of course, to smooth over their relationship with the victors.

As the years went by, the German, English, Welsh, Scotch, and Irish settlers mingled increasingly with members of the Cherokee Nation, often marrying Cherokee women. There were also occasional marriages between Cherokee men and white women. But this interbreeding failed to produce the thoroughly harmonious climate in which the tomahawk could be permanently replaced by the pipe of peace.

Ironically, while the Cherokees came more and more to look, dress, think, and act like white men (some Cherokees, following the example of the colonists, took slaves for themselves, even white men's names), their relationships with the white community continued to be strained. In addition, the Cherokees had little regard for members of "lesser" tribes, such as the Creeks, Seminoles, Choctaws, and Chickasaws (whom the Cherokees viewed as being less educated), thus adding to their own turmoil and insecurity.

When it appeared that the white settlers' encroachment on the Indians' hunting grounds might be deterred by negotiations, the Cherokees agreed to sign a treaty with President George Washington. The pact spoke bravely of lasting peace between the Cherokees and the United States, specifically forbidding Americans to hunt on Cherokee lands. But it turned out to be wishful thinking, and marked the last time that an American president would legally express such a permissive policy.

President James Monroe, in the early years of the nineteenth century, emphasized that the Indians were not sufficiently civilized to have their own independent communities. This general philosophy, also propounded by Presidents Adams, Jefferson, and Madison, prevailed among those Europeans who had come to America with the belief that they had been ordained by destiny to be the dominant race and should therefore rule all of America and its lands, mineral wealth, and forests.

By 1819, the U.S. government had forced the Cherokee Nation into twenty-four treaties involving land cessions, and in 1828 the Georgia legislature unconscionably declared that it had jurisdiction over all Cherokee lands.

Just as every president had done before him, Andrew Jackson expressed benevolent intentions toward the Indians, while, in reality, he was their mortal enemy. He even encouraged the Indians to move to a vast western preserve. However, while urging the Cherokees to move beyond the Mississippi, he indicated he could provide no federal protection if they failed to do so. In a letter full of sentiment, but structured in deceit, Jackson wrote to the Cherokees that "where you are now, you and my white children are too near each other to live in harmony and peace. . . . Beyond the great Mississippi, where a part of your nation has gone, your father has provided a country large enough for all of you, and he advises you to remove to it; . . . there your white brothers will not trouble you, they will have no claim to the land and you can live upon it as long as the grass grows or the water runs, in peace and plenty. The land beyond the Mississippi belongs to the President and no one else and he will give it to you forever."

The great orator, Senator Henry Clay of Kentucky, who despised the backwoods President Jackson with all his heart, spoke out against removal of the Indians, referring to the "woes and injuries of the aborigines." But his stand drew only meager support from his fellow senators, who were not moved in the least by Clay's tearful remarks.

Only the Christian missionaries continued to demand serious consideration for the Indians, asserting that the issue was of a moral nature, not a political one. These Christian gentlemen and occasional bureaucrats would make hegiras to Indian communities, as they uttered words of endless sympathy and wrote reports that went largely unread.

On June 30, 1834, Congress decreed, in an "Act to regulate trade and intercourse with the Indian tribes and to preserve peace on the frontier," that "that part of the United States west of the Mississippi River and not within the states of Missouri, Louisiana or the territory of Arkansas" would be the Indian Territory. According to this law, no white person would be permitted to trade in Indian country without a license, and no white traders of bad character would be permitted to reside in Indian country. The military forces of the United States would be used to enforce such laws—or so the law stated.

First the *invitation* to move out had come. Now the Indians of five tribes— Cherokee, Choctaw, Seminole, Creek, and Chickasaw—were being asked to get out—no more, no less.

Traditionally, the American West is supposed to be a roughhewn, egalitarian democracy. In it every man is blessed with a plot of land and a glowing promise of ultimate prosperity. The legend goes on to say that every sodbuster dwells there in harmony with nature and with his accommodating neighbors. In this supposed nirvana, everyone pulls together for the good of one another and for a common purpose.

But the picture painted distorts the facts. Since the Indians were regarded as little more than ignorant and superstitious creatures by all but a handful of protesting Americans, the government had condemned them to virtual enslavement and isolation. Indeed, although the Indians were not, as some current revisionists insist, just innocents routed from Eden by rampaging white settlers, they were relegated to almost inhuman status. The policy that sent them west was rooted in lies and hypocrisy. The result of that hypocrisy evolved into a moral and environmental disaster in a land almost haunted by cruelty.

For a decade, until 1838, the Indians were subjected to oppression, theft, cheating, and double-dealing of such dimensions that many became resigned to their fate—removing themselves to an area that presumably might provide them with a surcease from their persecution.

Finally, in December 1835, the Cherokees ceded to the United States more than seven million acres of land claimed by the Cherokee Nation in the area east of the Mississippi River. In consideration of this concession, five million dollars was to be expended by the federal government, under the terms of the Treaty of New Echota. This decision, yielding to the white man's entreaties, was by no means popular with all of the Cherokees: Some of the seventeen thousand Cherokees felt keenly that they had been betrayed. For years afterward, they carried a grudge that caused an angry rupture in the Cherokee family. Only a minority of mixed-bloods, whose homes had been seized, set afire, or occupied by white men, supported the move.

At the outset, some two thousand Cherokees picked up their belongings and set out for the lands bordering on the Arkansas River, in the northeast section of the Indian Territory. These early arrivals came to be known as the "Old Settlers." The Rogers family was part of that group.

The general exodus of the Cherokees began in May, 1838, according to a precise schedule set down by the U.S. Senate. Ultimately, the episode evolved into one of the most shameful in American history. Some historians have compared it to the Nazi Holocaust during World War II. Technically, the purpose of American policy toward the Indians was to *save* them from extermination, while Hitler's aim was to kill off the entire Jewish population. However, during the 1830s, a surprising number of Americans, some of whom were even avidly antislavery, seriously pondered whether the "Indian problem" shouldn't culminate in the group's extermination.

The removal—now known as the Trail of Tears—cost the lives of an estimated forty-five hundred Cherokees, who were victims of disease, hunger and deprivation. The crude wooden markers on Cherokee graves that were stretched out for all to see, from the Appalachians to the Arkansas, represented an average of four or five deaths a day.

U.S. Army regulars supervised the exodus of fifteen thousand Cherokees, under the direction of General Winfield Scott. These army men managed to conduct themselves with a measure of decency. However, the Georgia volunteers, in their unseemly haste to dispatch the Cherokees, dragged many of them, young and old, from their homes, stripping them of their possessions, often at rifle or bayonet point. One of the volunteers, who later fought with Confederate troops in the Civil War, wrote, in comparing the horrors of the Civil War with the Trail of Tears: "The removal was the cruelest work I knew."

There were some vocal protestors against the harsh policies of the government, including theologians and John Howard Payne, the author of "Home, Sweet Home," who was jailed for his defense of the Cherokees. But, as the trail moved painfully through Georgia, Alabama, Tennessee, Illinois, Missouri, and then into Oklahoma, with only the aged, the sick, and the very young making the journey in drafty, ill-equipped wagons, the government failed to suffer any perceptible sadness of heart.

President Martin Van Buren, the successor to Andrew Jackson and, ironically, an opponent of any extension of slavery, commended the emigration. "It has had the happiest of effects," he said, even as people died daily from brutal treatment.

The purpose of crowding the Indians into the Indian Territory, where the rolling hills plunged into endless plains and the slate-blue sky merged finally with the red, clay earth, had always been twofold. One purpose was essentially punitive: to drive them from the area east of the Mississippi. The other was to put them on land that nobody wanted and was thought to be worthless.

Not until the white men began to fill up the vast expanse of fertile land, from coast to coast, did they cast their eyes on poorer soil. In the end, a few impoverished Indian tribes in the Indian Territory that became Oklahoma found themselves sitting on property of great potential wealth. The "undesirable land," with its hidden, rich oil deposits, became, in truth, more valuable than anyone had imagined. So it turned out, in much the manner of a sly Will Rogers joke, that the white man had outfoxed himself with his predatory policies.

In a short time the first settlers in the Indian Territory became the "Old Settlers." They labored on the hills and prairies to set up their own way of life, with stores, churches, mills, schools, farms, and wooden houses that replaced the makeshift tents and wagons of the Trail of Tears. Antagonisms between the Old Settlers and the new arrivals often heated up, coming precariously close to civil war between the groups.

But the Cherokees survived. By 1850 they had achieved a fairly stable society in a region filled with greedy frontiersmen trying to grab lands not assigned to the Indians, nomadic tribes, cattlemen, and boomers. In all, there were less than three hundred thousand Indians in the United States and its territories, most living west of the Mississippi, by the 1860s—a population that had almost been halved since the arrival of the first settlers in New England and Virginia. By that time the culture of the American Indian had practically been destroyed, even as the engaging, but largely false stories of the Old West had been written into myths and folklore.

2

Civil War

The Cherokees of Georgia—Bible readers, merchants, and farmers—were already cultured and educated people when Will Rogers's great-grandfather, Robert, the son of a British officer, settled among them around 1800. He was at once inducted into the tribe when he married Lucy, the daughter of an Irishman, whose wife was a full-blooded Indian. Will's great-grandparents had two sons: Robert and then John.

Cherokees who had Robert's blood ancestry were known as "white Indians," but this failed to enhance their relationship with the white community. When the removal to the west took place in 1836, Robert and his wife, Sallie Vann, the daughter of a prominent Cherokee family, joined John in the great migration.

A brawny, dark-skinned man, Robert settled near a Baptist mission in the Going-Snake District (in what later became Oklahoma), one of the nine districts that had been created in the Cherokee Nation West. Each tribe, established as a separate nation by a treaty with the U.S. government, made its own laws, supervised its own court system, and built its own schools. Half of the Cherokees could already read and write: Robert and John were in that group.

The tribal economic structure was largely supported by the interest from funds held in trust for the Cherokees by the U.S. government, so they did not pay taxes. The money was put to good use in the maintenance of good schools in the district. Robert and Sallie built a two-story, five-room log house, near the Arkansas border, and raised long-horned cattle and horses on a ranch that also grew fruit, wheat, and corn plentifully. By Cherokee standards, Robert was considered a rather prosperous man.

A first child, Margaret, was born shortly after the arrival of the Rogers family in the territory. Three years later, in January 1839, Clement Vann was born to the couple. But Clem scarcely got to know his father, for Robert died in 1842, presumably of natural causes, although it was rumored that he may have been killed by a Cherokee who resented his new-found affluence and abrasive temperament.

Clem's mother married William Musgrove two years after Robert's death. Musgrove was a skilled carpenter and black-smith, and also was part owner of a factory that processed chewing tobacco. But from the start, young Clem took a dislike to his stepfather. It was said, within the family, that on the day Musgrove married Sallie Vann, Clem refused to attend the ceremony and threw rocks at the newlyweds' buggy, not an auspicious beginning for the relationship between stepfather and stepson. In a later incident, Clem shot a bullet over Musgrove's head, causing the latter to grab his pistol, only to jam it while aiming it at Clem. There was, in short, a spiritual rupture between the two men that was never resolved.

Clem hated school almost as much as he disliked his stepfather. He was given an excellent opportunity to acquire a good education, at a Baptist Mission School and then at the Cherokee-sponsored Male Seminary at Tahlequah. But he was restless, and annoyed at the notion that he should spend so much time in the classroom. So, when he reached seventeen, he left the family ranch, where he had learned to become a skilled horseman and a handler of cattle, and set out for the Cooweescoowee district, located near the Verdigris River. There, with a bull, twenty-five longhorns, several horses, and two Negro slaves, Houston and Rabb (given to him by his stepfather), Clem set up a trading post, on land that he claimed as his own.

Under Cherokee law, all land was held in common by the tribe; thus the thousands of acres in the virgin area were fair game for anyone with sufficient zeal and enterprise to work them. Clem did just that. The two slaves did the farming, while Clem, astride his horse, roamed far and wide to establish his demesne near a trading post once occupied by Osage Indians.

Now the owner of a two-room log house and a business that was doing well, Clem found the area to be the fulfillment of his dreams. He had settled on rich prairie land, which was as thick with bluestem grass as it was with quail, prairie chickens, and wild turkeys. There was also enough game—panthers, wolves, and deer—to satisfy an adventurous young man like Clem.

All that was missing from Clem's life was a wife to share his prosperity. But soon the nineteen-year-old Mary America Schrimsher, from a family that was as relatively well off as Clem's, reentered his life. Clem had known her during his brief period of skirmishing at the school at Tahlequah, where Mary had attended the female seminary. She had now moved into the Cooweescoowee country and she renewed her old friendship with Clem. In short order, Clem proposed marriage to her, and the tall, slender, black-haired young woman accepted. Physically and emotionally, the two were very different: Mary was witty, light-hearted, vivacious, and a churchgoing Methodist. With her broad face and narrow cheekbones, she looked in every way like an Indian. The light-haired, blue-eyed Clem, on the other hand, was a driven man, inclined to rough talk. He was not concerned much with any religion, and one would not have expected that he would appreciate Mary's finer qualities, including her love of dancing, books, and music. Also, as an Old Settler, Clem was part of a group that had been at odds with Mary's friends, most of whom had suffered the indignities of the Trail of Tears.

One day in 1859, Clem and Mary rode off, from Mary's home in Fort Gibson, behind a team of horses, to seal their marriage at Clem's ranch. There was little reason to believe, considering what opposites they were, that the marriage would be successful. Yet they got along well and by the end of their first year of marriage, their first child, Elizabeth, was born.

The long, dark night of the Civil War now loomed over the land, abruptly ending Clem's happy existence. Nominated by the Republican party on an antislavery platform, Abraham Lincoln went on to win the presidency. Determined to preserve the Union, Lincoln, within a year, was faced with the secession of eleven Southern states. In April 1861, the war erupted when Confederate troops fired on Fort Sumter, the fortification at the entrance of the harbor to Charleston, South Carolina.

Living close to the Kansas border, where northern soldiers were stationed, Clem and Mary could not escape the angry ripples of war. Kansas, a pro-Union state, had already become a seething battleground, with frequent raids in the state emanating from the Indian Territory. The Indians were badly torn in their loyalties. Mixed-bloods, such as Clem, who had owned slaves and had often conducted themselves much in the style of southern gentlemen, were quick to rally to the side of the Confederacy. At first, John Ross, the principal chief of the Cherokee Nation, sought to preserve the neutrality of his people. But the role became increasingly difficult to maintain, as the Confederacy made its case to the Nation by stressing that in the past the North had treated the Indian tribes poorly—therefore, where was the logic in going over to Mr. Lincoln's side?

In October 1861, the Cherokee Nation officially formed an alliance with the Confederacy. Despite this, many Cherokees still clung to support for the North. Within Clem's own household, Rabb chose to join up with the Union, while Houston, his brother, fought with the South. Whether or not a Cherokee fought for either side, there were few of them that didn't possess firearms.

After a year of the war, Clem, uneasy about the safety of Mary and his child, sent them back to her parents at Fort Gibson. Accompanied by a trusted Negro slave, they rode along a dusty, hard prairie trail for more than fifty miles. Trying to soothe the child, Mary and the slave took turns holding her. The difficult trip took its toll on all of them—but they arrived safely. However, Elizabeth, weakened by the journey, died not long afterward.

Mary didn't remain at home for long, for the family felt that it would be prudent for her to move along to Texas with her sisters. Clem had no trouble deciding about his own course of action: He enlisted, as a lieutenant, in Company G of the Cherokee Mounted Rifle Regiment, under Colonel Stand Watie, a fearless and colorful advocate for the South, who became one of the most celebrated Cherokee figures of the period. Watie's brother had been murdered more than twenty years before the war, presumably by an enemy belonging to John Ross's clique. Watie, it is said, had been marked for assassination, too. But he was never an easy target for his foes.

During the war, Watie's men engaged in innumerable raids, mostly against pro-North Cherokees and occasionally against northern troops. In 1864, at Cabin Creek, in Indian Territory, Watie's fighters, including Lieutenant Rogers, pulled off a daring act at dawn. They seized a federal wagon train carrying a cargo valued at over a million dollars, and they did it with such alacrity that it was rated as one of the Cherokees' most glowing military accomplishments, in an otherwise disastrous war for them. As a result of this coup, Watie was promoted to brigadier general, the first Indian to win such a distinction, while Clem was promoted to captain. (Previously, in 1862, Clem had been selected as one of three delegates to the Cherokee Confederate Convention, signaling that he wanted more out of life than ranching and business. But, obviously, he had chosen the wrong side in the internecine war.) Watie, unrelenting in his commitment to the Confederacy, fought for several more months, even after General Robert E. Lee had surrendered to General Ulysses S. Grant at Appomattox. When Watie finally gave up, the last Confederate general to do so, he offered his brigade to the Union.

With the war over, it remained for Clem to rejoin Mary and restructure his life, under ground rules imposed by the victorious North. The federal government, now presided over by President Andrew Johnson (who had succeeded the slain Lincoln), declared that because of their support of the Confederacy, the so-called Five Civilized Tribes (including the Cherokees) should forfeit their lands. But a compromise was soon reached, with the United States taking only the western part of the Indian Territory. Indians were no longer permitted to have slaves. In one treaty between the Indians and the government, it was stated that the Indians should attempt to unite in a territorial government that would become a state. Oklahoma (meaning "red people") was advanced as a possible name for the state. But it would take another half-century before Oklahoma came into being.

Clem, at the age of twenty-six, discovered that he had lost everything. His slaves and cattle were gone, his land was now a wilderness, his house was destroyed. But he did have a new daughter, Sallie, born in 1863, plus his indomitable nature. He wanted to get back to ranching as soon as he could— but he needed money for that; so he hired a Cherokee youth to farm his land in Fort Gibson, and he went to work for a store owner named Oliver Lipe. For two arduous years, he drove a six-mule freight wagon from Kansas City to Sedalia and on to Fort Gibson.

As a result, he accumulated enough funds to go into partnership with Lipe's son. He also traded for cattle, which he shepherded back to his new ranch in the Cooweescoowee District, not far from his original land. Clem had chosen this rich grazing land wisely. In the tradition of the Cherokee, one was free to occupy, and improve, any land that he selected, as long as one didn't intrude on property already claimed by somebody else.

Clem had staked his claim in an ideal area. One could see for miles on this land without fences, near the Caney and Verdigris rivers. The winters rarely nipped the fingers; the summers were glorious. Grass was sweet and plentiful, perfect for fattening Clem's cattle, which were always marked with the CV

(Clem Vann) brand. He bought the steers in adjoining states, then shipped them in the fall to the growing markets in Kansas City and St. Louis. Before Clem put up his barbed wire (supposedly the first to be installed in the Indian Territory), the two rivers provided a natural barrier to prevent the cattle from roaming. And with the coming of the railroads, shipments could be facilitated.

Before long, Clem owned thousands of acres, employed enough helpers to keep his cattle in line, and was selling his steers—up to five thousand a year—at four dollars a head.

Despite his new-found prosperity, Clem worked harder than ever. Ambitious and a tough bargainer, he still believed that a man should start the workday early and end late. There was very little on his ranch that ever escaped his keen eye. But he was still proudest of one thing: He could sit a horse as good as any man—and better than most. Years later, when he would recollect his days with Papa, Will Rogers said: "Papa could get more out of a horse than any man I ever knew. Riding along with Papa, I could never keep up with him. We'd start out in the morning, side by side, but the first thing I knew, my horse was lagging behind and I'd have to kick him in the sides to catch up. Papa could ride all day long and his horse would never be out of a fast walk or a dog trot, while I'd be in a lope half the time tryin' to keep up. At the end of the day I'd be plumb played out and my horse in a lather but Papa never tired and his horse never turned a hair."

Several years after the war, Clem brought Mary back to the ranch, where he had constructed a two-story, white longhouse that stood at the foot of a rocky hill and looked toward the Verdigris valley, a mile away. The nearest "big cities" were Coffeyville, Kansas, some forty miles to the north by wagon; and Fort Gibson, Mary's former home, fifty miles southeast in Indian Territory. Friendly neighbors came to pitch in as the impressive building, with its portico and two stone chimneys, went up. They helped to hoist heavy walnut logs that had been cut from the river bottom and that workmen had hewed and seasoned in two years' time.

In all, there were seven rooms, four open fireplaces, porches upstairs and downstairs. The house was weatherboarded outside and plastered inside. In the rear of the house were a dining room, a kitchen, and a bunkroom, all used by cowboys employed on the ranch. The dominant feature downstairs was the big parlor, which included one of the fireplaces and a grand piano, perhaps the only one in the Indian Territory.

By the time the house was completed in 1875, it qualified as a true frontier showplace, with its handmade lace curtains; walnut furniture; a picket fence garnished with a gallimaufry of southwestern flowers; and a stone walk leading from the front gate to the porch.

The delicate hand of Mary Rogers was in evidence everywhere, her grace and old-line southern elegance providing all of the tasteful touches. She injected her own warmth into the house's every nook and cranny and she loved having visitors. But strangers, too, were welcome, as they passed through the area. Friends and neighbors joined in the gaiety, with square dancing and songs becoming seductive elements in the merriment.

With the soft voice, calm demeanor, and good manners she displayed to all, Mary had become the perfect host for this homestead. It was said that she was loved by all, while the blustering, sometimes bellicose Clem might have turned people away if he had not had her with him. Curiously, in spite of his militant nature, Clem rarely spoke to anyone about the recent bloody war, and his own role in it. These were memories he was content to bury. Losing was something he didn't enjoy—and he had been on the losing side.

Many spoke of Mary as a missionary for the poor and for those in any kind of difficulty. She would often volunteer to bring food to the sick, either by horseback (she was a good rider, although not up to the level of Clem), or by buggy.

By 1878, seven children had been born in her fine house—five girls and two boys. However, disease often cut off young lives in those days and, despite the general good fortune of the Rogers family, three of Mary's children died in infancy. Only Sallie, Maud, Robert, and Mary survived before Will arrived in November 1879.

Childhood

By the time of Will's birth, Clem had made a considerable name for himself, not only as rancher, cattleman, and businessman, but also as a significant dabbler in the politics of the Cherokee Nation. When he was thirty-eight, Clem won election to a judgeship in the Cooweescoowee district for a two-year term, despite the fact that he had had no formal legal education and had to rely on his own visceral reaction to the law. Two years later he was elected to a seat in the Cherokee senate, which met once a year. Subsequently, he won that office three consecutive times, a tribute to a man who was as diplomatic as a drunk at a ladies' tea party. The voters must have sensed Clem's ironlike integrity, preferring that perceived quality to the usual duplicitousness of other politicians. Although Clem was once accused, without proof, of taking a bribe in return for supporting a bill favorable to certain cattlemen, his reputation remained spotless. Without question, he regarded dealing with his brood mares, riding the trail, or engaging in the calf roundup in the spring as preferable to politics. Yet, he sought an involvement in local affairs because he had proved to be a tough but fair bargainer with other people.

By some calculations, not necessarily accurate, Clem was rated as the third richest man in the territory when Will was born. What is clearly known is that he was handling as many as five thousand head of cattle a year by 1879, buying them in Texas, fattening them on his own bluestem grass, and then guiding them to St. Louis, which was then the principal market.

Clem and Mary were both forty years old when Will—the last of Mary's eight children—was born in his parents' bedroom. Clem was not at Mary's bedside at the time, for he was away on another of his seasonal roundups. With Clem still absent, the little boy was christened William Penn Adair Rogers, after Colonel William Penn Adair, a full-blooded Cherokee, a lawyer, and member of the Cherokee supreme court, who had served as a soldier at arms with Clem during the Civil War. Mrs. Adair happened to be a guest at Clem's ranch when Will arrived, so it's conceivable that she had some input in the naming of Mary's son after her own husband. But Mary didn't have any difficulty with such a choice, for she shared Clem's feeling of admiration for Colonel Adair.

The world, fourteen years after the Civil War, was a relatively peaceful place in 1879. Rutherford B. Hayes, a Harvard-educated lawyer and former Republican governor of Ohio, was the nineteenth American president, having won the post after a hotly disputed election in 1876, with Samuel Tilden as his opponent. Hayes made some strides toward civil-service reform and was interested in pursuing conciliation with the old Confederate states.

During Will's first years, Mary, not unexpectedly, watched over him with great tenderness. Since she had already lost three of her children, it was understandable that she doted on Will, but without ignoring her other children. Sallie, the oldest sister, was away at boarding school; May, the infant of the house before Will was born, was six years old when he came along; and Maud, with her sparkling blue eyes, was ten. Robert, a husky, vigorous lad of twelve, was very much like his father and had a predilection for the outdoor life.

The closeness of Will's relationship with his mother was something that he remarked about as an adult. He continually spoke of his mother's sweet, lilting southern voice, and clearly recalled how Mary patiently tended to the Negro helpers when one of them became ill.

"I could see her settin' in her chair, smilin' at me," Will would say, "and she would lift her hand to gray-streaked, black hair, which she wore in a knot at the back of her head." Mary enjoyed calling Will her "Willie," and that diminutive stuck among his family and friends.

Will was raised in an environment that was far removed from the harsh, legendary frontier. Clem's diligence had produced an idyllic boyhood for his son, who had only to ask for something and he would get it. He was deprived of nothing in a home that was classically indulgent. "There's plenty of mule in that boy," Clem would say, half-admiringly, of Will—but that didn't mean Will would ever be disciplined by anyone.

Growing up in such a rural nirvana, Will was on a horse's back almost from the moment he learned to walk. He got his first pony when he was five years old—a cream-colored colt, named Comanche, that Clem had bought from one of his former slaves, Huse Rogers. From the moment Comanche came into his life, Will didn't want to leave the horse's back; the two were almost inseparable. "Comanche was Will's heart 'til the day he died," said Spi Trent, a friend of Will's.

Not that Will didn't have early difficulties with Comanche. Since he was only a little guy, Will needed a pillow tucked behind him, under the saddle horn, and a cowhand would always have to swing him up onto the horse's back. Comanche was a lively animal and would rise up on his hind legs as Will struggled into the saddle. When Will came to dismount, Comanche would act up again, so someone would have to be around to get a grip on him. Mary never stopped worrying about Will; she would be alarmed and cover her face with her hands. While Clem stood alongside her in the corral, beaming proudly, she would say loudly to him: "Clem, you're going to get our boy killed!" But Clem knew the horse was gentle, if somewhat shy. He also knew Will was fearless. Years later, Will said, "I was born bow-legged so I could sit on a horse."

Not long after Comanche became his personal property, Will was permitted to go on roundups, but always under close supervision. Clem may have been an indulgent father but he certainly wasn't a darn fool.

A Negro couple, Uncle Dan and Aunt Babe Walker, were employed in the Rogers household, mainly to help Mary with her daily chores. But Uncle Dan, once a cowboy himself, taught Will all sorts of interesting tricks with ropes. They would spend hours together, with Uncle Dan demonstrating with the lariat, and then Will trying his best to imitate him. Will called it "cutting curlicues." Before long, Will was almost as skillful and adept at the art as Uncle Dan was. Will was just like all the other kids in the territory who loved their lariats as much as they loved their horses. Roping was an integral part of their lives, as it certainly was of Will's. After a while, there wasn't a moving thing that these youngsters couldn't lasso, whether it was a jackrabbit; a calf to be branded; or one of their own friends. Will probably could have done it in his sleep, and a day didn't go by when he wasn't honing his skills and practicing different throws.

Uncle Dan had twelve children, many of whom played with Will. The mix of white, Indian and Negro kids in the area near the Verdigris River played the mindless, endless games that formed such a large part of the simple, healthy life that they were privileged to enjoy. The summers seemed to go on forever, as did the ritual of the games. When the kids got tired of the games or riding their horses, they'd go over to the local swimming hole, jump in, and cool off. Sometimes the horses would jump in with them and the shouting children would grab onto their tails. Afterward there were always jackrabbits and prairie dogs to chase after, and they had little jokes they would play on each other and on their dogs, such as cutting off too much hair or painting spots on the creatures.

The riding, roping, frolicking, and unvarying blue skies provided Will with sweet memories of his youth—though he claimed he never remembered much about it at all—but there were other memories not as sweet: Malaria could result from mosquito-bites sustained in the Verdigris, and at times Will would shake like a wet dog from the chills. Mary then would mete out to Will and the others the calomel and quinine that was the preferred medication. It was always doled out to Will on the blade of a kitchen knife. "It had a terrible taste," Will would recall, "so you'd have to eat something real quick to take the awful taste away."

Will did not get to know his brother Robert very well, for when Will was only four years old, in April 1883, Robert died of typhoid. The tragedy left a deep imprint on the family. Robert, sixteen when he died, had returned to work too soon on the ranch, unduly taxing his body.

Mary grieved for many months after Robert's death, but Will, as the only boy in the family, now became the beneficiary of her attention and affection. If he had been spoiled before, as was generally acknowledged, now he might engage in any conceivable mischief short of a felony, without so much as a simple reprimand. Although Clem continued to have little patience with the stubborn Will, there were few times when he sought to discipline him.

In 1885 it was time for Will to have his first experience with education. Clem decided to send the boy to the Drumgoole School, a tiny, one-room log cabin located a few miles east of Chelsea—which was across the river from the Rogers ranch.

Will's older sister, Sallie, had just married Tom McSpadden, the son of a white missionary, and they lived a few miles from Drumgoole. Will was sent to live with them, in order to be close to the school. Each morning, Sallie packed off the six-year-old to Drumgoole on his horse, tying a lunch box firmly to the saddle. But Sallie was always suspicious of just where Will might wind up, for it was clear to her that he despised school, with its day-to-day routine and its endless drills. (At the time the fee at Drumgoole was a dollar a month for a child.)

When he grew up, Will retained few positive memories of Drumgoole. He recalled: "The school stayed with such books as *Ray's Arithmetic* and *Mc-Guffey's First and Second Reader.* We had geography around there, too—but we just used it for the nice pictures of the cattle grazing in the Argentine and the wolves attacking the sleighs in Russia. It was all Indian kids that went there and I, being part Cherokee, had just enough white in me to make my honesty questionable among all those Cherokees. There must have been about 30 of us that rode horseback or walked miles to get there. We got to put on horse races and that made me lose interest in what we were really there for. I could also run pretty fast, so they nicknamed me 'Rabbit.' I could never figure out whether that referred to my speed or to my heart."

After a year at Drumgoole, Clem decided that his son wasn't learning much of anything, except how to avoid attending; so he was enrolled at the Harrell International Institute in Muskogee, a girls' Methodist boarding school that had been attended by his sister, May. Will was allowed to enter Harrell because the school's president, Reverend T. F. Brewer, had a son who was eight years old, just like Will. It was envisioned that the two boys could room together in the midst of all the young ladies. ("I felt like Custer surrounded by all the Indians at Little Big Horn," Will once said.)

But the experiment was a crashing failure. Will spent most of his time yelling at the girls, trying to play tricks on them and arguing with his teachers. He was by common consent a darn nuisance. By mutual agreement between Clem and the school authorities, Will was removed from Drumgoole. Not long after that contretemps, Will came down with a bad case of measles.

However, the worst was yet to come in the Rogers household. In 1890, Sallie and Maud developed typhoid fever; then Mary Rogers became ill and was put to bed. At first it was thought that Mary, too, had contracted typhoid, but the ailment was finally diagnosed as amoebic dysentery, or flux. A Negro boy was sent to fetch Clem, who was on a business trip some sixty miles away.

Clem at once sped to Mary's side, driving his team of horses from sundown to sunup, with a lantern tied to the tongue of his buggy. The family doctor, A. L. Lane, arrived to find Mary practically pulseless. He indicated that there was little anyone could do, although Clem kept wagons continually on the move, bringing ice to the ranch from nearby Coffeyville.

Finally, on the morning of May 28, 1890, Mary died, at fifty-one, leaving her son Will with nothing but pleasant memories of her. Years later, Will said he never got over his mother's death. He always felt deprived of her presence, her friendliness, gentle manner, humor, and easy way with folks—all traits that Will himself seemed to have inherited from her.

"My mother's name was Mary, and if your mother's name was Mary and she was an old-fashioned woman, you don't have to say much for her. Everybody knows already," Will said about her, years after Mary's death. Whenever he spoke of her, tears invariably welled up in his eyes.

Mary was buried alongside her son Robert and the three infants in the ranch's family cemetery, which was marked by a number of twisted cedar and grape myrtle bushes, enclosed by a rusted iron fence.

In the fall the saddened little boy was sent to still another school, this one being the Presbyterian Mission School at Tahlequah. While Will was trying to settle down, Clem was chasing after the notorious Dalton boys, who had run off with some of his horses. It soon became clear that Will's distaste for classrooms was lingering. Often his lack of discipline and his restlessness were interpreted by his teachers as downright carelessness and laziness. Whatever it was, Clem wasn't pleased. So he proceeded to take Will out of Tahlequah and enter him in the Willie Halsell Institute at Vinita, about forty miles away in the Indian Territory.

The institute called itself a college and was coeducational, with most of the kids coming from Will's home area. The chief characteristic of Vinita was that it was muddy and deserted, a place with no curbs, pavements, or sewers. At the school the boys' dorm was on the top fourth floor; the girls' dorm, on the third floor. On the first and second floors were the classrooms. In today's terms, it was something of a private boarding academy, perhaps the equivalent of a modern junior high school.

At Halsell the students continued to call Will "Rabbit"—a designation that had more to do with the size of his ears than with anything else. Surprisingly, in Will's first term at Halsell, he made it onto the honor roll, even though he was still demonstrating only minimal interest in his studies. He continued to show a preference for his dad's cattle and horses, while pursuing his piano playing, and a bit of oil painting. However, the lariat in his hands had now become an appendage to his lanky body. Although many of his schoolmates showed a propensity for picking fistfights, Will's good nature generally precluded such involvement, even when he was goaded.

By the end of his third year at Halsell, Will seemed actually to be enjoying the place. "I sure have lots of fun up here," he wrote to his friend, Charlie McClellan, whose father was white, and who had remained at the Tahlequah school. "We have dances and do anything we want to," he wrote. What Will enjoyed most of all was talking, just plain talking—certainly a harbinger of things to come. He showed a special affinity for elocution, earning a commendation at commencement exercises. Indeed, *The Vinita Indian Chieftain* reported that "the recitation of Willie P. Rogers was rendered so well that the judges decided he was entitled to a medal."

During this same period, fifty-three-year-old Clem was remarried to a woman named Mary Bibles. She was not much more than half Clem's age and for some time she had been known as Clem's housekeeper, filling in for Will's departed mother. Will never did take to her ill-conceived surrogacy, but it was unlikely that anyone else could have replaced his dear mother in his eyes. Will rarely spoke about Mary Bibles and, from all accounts, didn't pay much attention to her.

Though Will had happy memories of Halsell, Clem again decided to switch schools for the boy. This time, he was sent to Scarritt College, in Neosho, Missouri, another private boarding school, just outside the Indian Territory. Scarritt, run by the Southern Methodist Church of Neosho, was eighty miles from Will's home, which was now called Oologah.

With his sisters having married and gone from the ranch, Will spent more time with Clem; and although the father drifted into the habit of giving the boy almost anything he wanted, the relationship still wasn't ever a warm one. Homer Croy, a biographer of Will Rogers, wrote that Clem was able to do all these things because the family was "rich." But, at the time, it was unlikely that Will fully appreciated how well off he was, compared to other Cherokees in the area: Will was one of the first in the Indian Territory to own a bike, and he could have one of Clem's horses for the asking.

In 1893, Clem took Will to the Chicago World's Fair, along with a trainload of cattle. There Will, an impressionable lad of fourteen, saw, for the first time, the legendary Buffalo Bill. With a cast of five hundred, Buffalo Bill and his Wild West show were the darlings of the fair. Over six million people came from all over America and Europe to see the forty-seven-year-old scout and master showman, who hailed originally from Le Claire, Iowa, about one hundred miles upstream from Mark Twain's birthplace. Buffalo Bill's "Congress of Rough Riders of the World" was bound to attract Will's attention. But it was a group of Mexican vaqueros—led by a red-sashed Mexican, Vincente Oropeza, who billed himself as "the greatest roper in the world—that really seized Will's imagination. As a matador, Oropeza had developed a number of spectacular tricks with ropes, including writing his name, one letter at a time, in the air, with his lasso. It appeared as if Oropeza could rope anything that moved. It wasn't long before Will was trying to do the same, especially with the girls at school.

The Rogers family, already prosperous by local standards, benefited additionally when the federal government issued a Cherokee payment of $8.5 million for land known as the Cherokee Strip. There was much excitement in Claremore when the federal paymasters arrived in the area, with money in hand, and names on sheets of paper. Each Cherokee, including the children, received $265.70, certainly a goodly sum, especially for those who had little to begin with. For weeks, Indian families celebrated the event, turning it into a field day for peddlers that offered every conceivable type of merchandise— stoves, jewelry, musical instruments—often on credit. Will joined other youngsters in the general merriment—a strange midsummer holiday that included a medley of sideshows and enough fried catfish, chili beans, and ice cream to keep a boy's stomach in turmoil for days.

At Scarritt, things did not go as well for Will as Clem had hoped. Most of the boys at the school were not Cherokees—only three besides Will were. This gave Will, for the first time in his life, a sense of being excluded, even though all of the students lived close together in boarding houses, where they took their meals.

It also wasn't long before Will developed a reputation as the "campus cutup." He was initiated into the joys of drinking wine, and he continued to play practical jokes on the girls, who were discouraged from "going" with him because of his wildness. Whether or not it was Will's wildness or his Cherokee background that earned him this exclusion, at least one young woman, little Maggie Nay, turned down a date with him, probably his first such rejection. Obviously hurt and troubled by Maggie's refusal to see him, Will wrote her a rambling letter, charged with self-pity and confession. "My dearest friend, if you can not be my sweetheart," he began, "if your mother does not want you to go with me, why it is all right. I would hate to do anything contrary to her will. I know I drink and am wild and a bad boy and all that . . . I am an outcast I suppose, so of course dont do anything that will get you with a drunkard as I am . . . I was a fool trying to go with you anyway. I might have known you would have not gone with me . . . I am too far below you to write to you and then you do not want my picture, you want the one you are going with, not I . . . well I suppose you have heard enough of this *drunkard* that they call Will Rogers, so I will close hoping you all a merry evening . . . now please dont let anyone see this Maggie and I will not let anyone see your note. . . "

What was most remarkable about Will's letter, aside from the obvious pain being suffered by a sixteen-year-old boy, was his failure to use proper grammar and punctuation. On this he never changed; it became his trademark as a writer and columnist (incorrect spelling also marked his letters).

Will's trouble with girls was perhaps the least of his difficulties at Scarritt. His obsession with ropes and roping got him into continual trouble with the authorities. Every moment of his time was spent practicing with ropes, and he constantly came up with new targets to lasso and harass. The headmaster kept taking the ropes away from Will, only to see him find other ones, which he at once put to use. As he pursued his formidable skills with ropes, Will managed on one occasion to break off the arm of a drinking-fountain figure— a Grecian goddess bearing a stone pitcher on her shoulder.

But the ultimate crisis in Will's tenure at Scarritt occurred when a mare owned by the headmaster ambled onto the campus one day, followed by her colt. On a dare, Will lassoed the colt. In the excitement, however, Will lost his control of the rope, letting the colt loose. The frightened animal proceeded to tear through a nearby tennis-court net, jump over a fence, and run crazily through the streets of Neosho. While his schoolmates howled with delight, Will quickly learned that the headmaster failed to see any humor in the incident. The headmaster then decided that Scarritt had seen enough of Will Rogers and his ropes. Will was informed of his expulsion from Scarritt, and he immediately returned to the ranch to break the distressing news to his father. Clem did not take Will's poor marks, cutting of classes, and general unruly behavior lightly. While he mulled over his son's future, which seemed dim to him, other serious matters intruded to engage Clem's attention. In 1896, Matt Yocum, the husband of Will's sister, May, was suddenly shot dead by an intruder, as he prepared one night to get into bed. The murderer was never found, although there were suspects brought in from time to time. A few months later, Will Cheatam, a lively stable worker who had been dating the bereft May, was returning to his home—after spending an evening with her— when he was shot and murdered. Again, the assassin was never found.

Two such incidents were enough to cause the tongues to wag in Clem's neighborhood, and the local newspapers published unsubstantiated reports that Clem, himself, had been involved in both deaths. The enraged Clem sued the writer of the stories for criminal libel. Nothing came of the suit, nor were the killers ever apprehended. During the rest of his life, nobody ever heard Will talk about these deeds. In time, May married Matt Yocum's first cousin.

Meanwhile, Clem, hopeful that more extreme discipline might prove beneficial for Will, made up his mind to enroll him in the Kemper Military School in Boonville, Missouri. It was not unusual for undisciplined young men to be placed in Kemper, often in the hope that the school might instill in them a measure of respect for others and for learning. Some in the Rogers family— Maud's husband and Sallie's son—had previously gone there, and they were never as much of a problem as Will was to Clem.

The itch to keep moving—a restlessness that was to characterize Will's entire life—caused him to take a trip to Buffalo, New York, in the spring of 1896, when there was some promise of greenery in that usually frigid area. What he sought there is not clear by any means. But Will may have figured it was his chance to break loose a bit before being subjected to Kemper's stringent military regimen.

One day in that upstate New York region, Will stopped to gas a bit with a street beggar in front of a barbershop—this habit of walking up to folks for a spontaneous chat was another of Will's predispositions—and out of the blue came a great roar. Something went radically wrong at a nearby street excavation; there was an explosion and the barbershop collapsed. Several barbers as well as patrons were killed; others were grievously wounded. Had Will meandered into the shop, instead of talking to the beggar, he likely would also have been killed or injured. In talking about the incident when he got older, Will always felt that the time spent exchanging remarks with somebody he didn't know had saved his life. It was a happenstance that may have set the moral compass for the rest of Will's life.

When Will arrived at Kemper in January 1897, at the age of eighteen, he was decked out in flamboyant cowboy style, with a vest that "talked for itself," as one observer put it. He had on a flannel shirt, with a fiery red bandanna around his throat, and high-heeled boots with red tops and spurs. The horse-hair cord around his cowboy hat could have been used to hang a horse thief, remarked biographer Homer Croy. A dude in every respect, Will had fashioned a contrariness in his garb, in comparison to the drab military uniforms that were supposed to be worn by all hands at Kemper.

Many of the seventy-two students at Kemper were from the Indian Territory, and Will himself was known to other students as "Swarthy," a nickname that was rather strange, considering that many of the boys shared Will's muddy complexion. Will's first roommate at the school was one John Payne, otherwise known as "Hurt" Payne, which suggests that he was the local hypochondriac. Hurt always contended that Will wasn't a bad student but was a "dogie" at things like math and algebra, subjects that had as much appeal for him as a kick in the pants. However, Will did well in history, earning a grade of 100 one year, and in education. He excelled in anything that had to do with talking, encouraging some at home to think he should be a preacher.

Will exhibited a memory that at times amazed his peers, all of whose names he memorized after one meeting. When it came to reciting such orations as Patrick Henry's "Give me liberty or give me death"; Abe Lincoln's Gettysburg Address; or Brutus's speech that begins, "Friends, Romans, countrymen, lend me your ears," Will's performance was unflawed, though he often delighted in adding comic gestures or purposely putting the wrong emphasis on certain key words. A lifted eyebrow, a quirky turn of the head, or an exaggerated shrug of the shoulders would send Will's classmates into hysterics. The one thing Will couldn't talk his way out of was demerits. He had 150 of them, well earned, for any number of minor violations of Kemper law, which meant that his punishment was to walk as a guard for an hour at a clip. Even here, Will managed to turn the chore to his benefit, by choosing to march near the kitchen, where he asked the cook for food for "a vanishing American."

Military school had to be the most unlikely gestating place for someone like Will. He never dressed properly, was invariably late for class and constantly flashed an irreverence that irked his superiors and mentors. His favorite games were still those played with ropes. In one of them he would encourage his pals to get down on all fours and moo like calves before he threw a loop over them.

He enjoyed organized activities such as baseball and football, showing good coordination in these team games. But when it came to handling weapons, particularly his rifle (a sacred implement in military schools), he was inept and uncaring. One day, while on his first summer vacation from Kemper, he was showing off some of the moves with a rifle that he had learned at school. Plunking the rifle on the ground so forcefully that it went off by mistake, Will was grazed by a bullet that left a scar on his forehead, which he carried for the rest of his life.

Despite being all thumbs at the manual of arms and looking like a clown in his uniform, Will enjoyed his stay at Kemper. Even if he did cling precariously to his school career at Kemper, he delighted in amusing others and never took matters too seriously.

4

Roamin' Free

Will often tried to sum up his career at Kemper: "I spent two years there, one in the guardhouse and one in the fourth grade. I knew more about *McGuffey's Reader* than McGuffey did."

One of Will's best pals at Kemper was Billy Johnston, who hailed from the Texas Panhandle. Billy loved to spin yarns about the wonders of ranch life in Texas, all of which appealed to Will's chronic wanderlust. Since he was perennially on the verge of expulsion at Kemper and wasn't managing the details of military life in a very exemplary manner, Will made up his mind to call it quits at Kemper in 1898. An added inducement to leave Kemper, without first consulting his father, was that Will had no idea how he could break the news to Clem.

"There has always been lots of curiosity about whether I jumped or was shoved out of that place," Will wrote, years later. "Well, I can't remember that far back now. All I know is that it was a cold winter and old man Ewing's ranch on the Canadian River near Higgins wasn't too warm when I dragged in there."

At the urging of Johnston, Will had embarked for Higgins, Texas, where he sought employment on the ranch of W. P. Ewing (the old man he refers to), who was a friend of Clem. Young Frank Ewing, the son of W. P., was a friend of Johnston's.

W. P. Ewing wrote at once to inform Clem that Will was "settin'" there on his property and that he didn't know just what to do with him. Clem wrote back that W. P. should put Will to work doing something, anything, to keep him busy and to put a few dollars in his pockets. "See if you can get any work out of that boy; I can't," complained Clem.

For several months, Will stayed on the ranch, a thirteen-thousand-acre property. He turned out to be a pretty good ranch hand, too. When Ewing offered him thirty dollars a month, after a trial run of a month, Will turned it down on the grounds that he had come only to visit! For a while, he also drove a delivery wagon for a grocery store in town; then he went on a cattle drive to Medicine Lodge, Kansas, with Frank, four other hands, a cook named Aaron, and thirty horses. Aaron was a rather hot-tempered character, who had a reputation for getting into knife fights. It was said that he had killed a couple of men in such brawls. On the six-week drive to Medicine Lodge, Aaron made some complaints about Will's behavior toward him, but Will didn't back down. "You haven't got nerve enough to fight," Will growled at him. "If you have, come on out here." Aaron never took up the challenge. Will might even have surprised himself at his courage, for he'd never been a fellow who liked fights—jokes, and kidding around, but not fights.

The Spanish-American War had just broken out. Will didn't know an awful lot about it or why American fighting men were involved in Cuba. But the idea of enlisting in the Rough Riders of Colonel Teddy Roosevelt and Colonel Leonard Wood appealed to him. Heck, he loved riding horses and he had never seen Cuba—it might turn out to be quite an adventure. When he went to Amarillo and tried to join these cavalry volunteers, made up mostly of cowboys, ranchers, and a bunch of blue blooded students from prestigious eastern colleges, he was told that he was too young. Teddy Roosevelt helped to make his reputation with the charge at San Juan Hill; but Will's reputation would be made in other, less bellicose ways.

However, going back to school, any school, simply wasn't in the cards for Will. His rejection of further education fostered the myth about him that he was essentially an illiterate who couldn't spell his own name, and who had had only a meager education. The fact is that up 'til now, Will had had a perfectly good education, even if he didn't cotton to it much. But as time went on, it didn't hurt Will's image, carefully nurtured, that he was a nature boy who had just sprung from the prairies and ranchlands without a smattering of learning.

What Will was doing now—living on horseback (he had his own little yellow pony, named Comanche), with a bedroll and a saddle of his own, riding seven days a week; breaking and training horses; rounding up and branding calves; buddying with the weathered, veteran cowhands—was what he truly loved more than anything else in the world. Sure, it was tough work for a boy of nineteen, and summer months in Texas were scaldingly hot, with dust clogging your lungs and getting into your hair and your face; and you didn't get to bathe much, and you slept on the ground, more than was good for your back. But in his bones, Will felt this was the perfect existence— nobody to tell you what to do, how to dress, what to say, or what to dream:

All I had was a few dollars and the clothes on my back [Will would say, years later, in a romantic glow, about one especially rugged winter on the range]. So I bought an old horse that had been eating loco weed, and he was just as spooky as they made 'em. . . . It was still pretty cold and somebody around the ranch gave me two old comforters—we called 'em "sugans." The cook gave me a sack of grub. I rolled it up in my sugan and tied it on behind my saddle. Late one evening I rode up to a drift fence that was going in the direction that I wanted to go and I'd been following it for almost fifty miles. About sundown I rode up on a line camp where there was a windmill and a well. I didn't see anybody around, so I watered my horse and rode off a couple of hundred yards, found some grass for my old horse and started to make camp for the night. I staked out my horse with a long rope, ate my jerky and biscuits out of a paper bag, rolled up in my sugans and went to sleep. Pretty soon I woke up and the rain was hitting me in the face. I'd never seen such lightning or thunder in my life. A bunch of big ranch horses that had become frightened at the storm had come aflyin' down the drift fence; they hit the rope that my old horse was tied with, turned somersaults and fell all over the place. When it would lightning I couldn't see my horse anywhere and I knew he'd broken loose and run off with the others. I dragged myself out of there, and when I got back to the line camp I began hollering, 'Hello, hello!' I thought that maybe the man that lived there was away and his wife was just afraid to let me in, so I said, 'Lady, I'm no thief or burglar, I'm just caught out in the rain.' Nobody answered, so I opened the door. It was nice and warm in the room. I found a table and laid down on it and soon fell asleep. Next morning the sun was shining bright and I found there wasn't a soul in the place. It was a one-room shack used as an outpost for line riders. Plenty of grub was stored there and over in the corner was a nice bed and plenty of good blankets. I knew that my old horse had run away, so I started out to get my saddle and outfit and bring 'em back. But I hadn't gone very far when I saw this old jug-headed pony grazing around as good as ever . . .

This was typical of the kind of experience that Will relished. He might have stayed forever, doing that sort of thing, living out there with his horses and nature, if it hadn't been for a third incident that almost cost him his young life.

He had returned briefly to help Clem on the Rogers ranch, but that brought him little contentment. So he lit out for New Mexico. While he was in Deming, he got together with a fellow named Billy Connell, and the two of them were asked to accompany a trainload of cattle to San Luis Obispo, California, where the William Randolph Hearst ranch was located. After the cattle had been delivered, Will and Billy figured they would go down to San Francisco to see the sights. They arrived there and checked in at a small rooming house. Billy was still so charged up that he wanted to go out to see what was going on in the saloons and dance halls. But Will, dead tired, preferred going to sleep. Before retiring, he blew out the light, which was different from the kerosene lamps he had been accustomed to. With the flame extinguished, gas began to pour into the room.

In the morning they had to come and get Will out of bed, where he had almost expired from gas inhalation. The doctors had a nasty time trying to revive him. When the main doctor on hand was on the verge of giving up on Will, some medical students grabbed the chance to practice on him. When they finally managed to bring him around, he was a weakened and chastened young man.

"They just happened to light on some nutty remedy," Will related. "But it was just bull luck. No regular doctor would have ever thought of it. So I came to, to everybody's surprise."

The dastardly gas, of course, had gotten into Will's system and he was in bad need of some rest and convalescence. A ranch hand was sent by Clem to pick up Will when he got back to Oologah. Clem took one look at his pale son and shipped him right off to Hot Springs, Arkansas, to use the baths to recuperate.

In a few months, Will had recovered sufficiently so that he could run after girls in order to play his innocent practical jokes on them. The crude pranks were reserved for his male friends, for he would take the harness of somebody's horse, then put it on backward. He would change the wheels on wagons, so the big wheels were up front and the small ones in back. After committing such a prank, he was invariably good-natured enough to help a fellow fix it. However, as a great lover of animals, Will would not countenance playing any jokes on dogs, cats, or horses. Cruelty to animals around the ranch was out, as far as he was concerned. He objected to people who cut off the tails of their horses. "Don't they know it hurts 'em?" he'd say. "What good does it do?"

On his return to Claremore, Will found that Clem now expected him to run the ranch. In 1899, Clem restocked the ranch with cattle and gave Will a number of other animals. He even provided him with an assistant, Spi Trent, a cousin who lived in Fort Gibson. The two young men tried to take hold of things. But Will discovered in due course that life around the ranch was much different from what it had been when he had been at home before. Now there were no big cattle drives to anticipate; there wasn't the usual talk about branding and roping; and the place was run down, without the elegant touch of his mother, who had been dead for almost a decade. Even the breakfasts of toast and tea didn't appeal much to him, for he preferred the hearty fare of preserves, creamy gravy, hot biscuits, and beans that were served to him in "the old days." The Illinois couple hired by Clem to do such chores didn't realize that Will and Spi considered such tea breakfasts effete.

One way to put up with things, Will thought, was to move away from the ranch with Spi, close enough so that it would be easy to come in to work the place, but sufficiently away from the premises so that they could conduct themselves in the way they wanted. With the help of a black friend, Hayward, they built a one-room, twelve-foot-square log cabin, perched on a hill near a little spring just a couple of miles from the ranch. Will wrangled horses there and Spi did the cooking. When it was built, the cabin had no windows—oops, the boys just forgot—so they punched holes in the mud between the logs so they could have some fresh air. There were few amenities in the cabin—two boxes that served as chairs, a stove, two lanterns, and a double bed.

Whenever Will needed some money, he knew he could sell one of his animals. But more often than not, the farming aspects of his job were irksome, so he often hopped on a train to get away to places like New York and to the states that surrounded the Indian Territory.

For a while, Will doted on Spi's cooking—three times a day he could get his navy beans and "anyone could ride in and find the big old iron kittle full to overflowin' with them." It wasn't precisely Will's idea of the rugged cowboy life—but it was as close to it as he and Spi could get. Of course, there were always plenty of activities in town to keep him busy when he wasn't working on the ranch or just lazin' around the cabin.

Will liked to get himself all "duded up" for his dates with young women in the area. He probably could have been elected the flashiest dresser in the Cherokee Nation, with his derby hat cocked over one eye, and a bow tie around his neck that was as big as his nose, which was of considerable size. There were the bonneted McClellan girls, Mary and Pearl, who sort of took to Will. And there was Kate Ellis, whose father ran a small hotel in Ooologah. Belle Price and Mary Bullette also found him pleasant company, because he was a pretty funny fellow and always the center of attention. They admired his endless tricks with ropes and his riding ability, even if on one occasion a recalcitrant pony sent him flying "like a bullfrog in a pond."

Although Will didn't drink much or play cards or smoke, he got himself into other amusements. For one thing, he liked to be in a state of constant motion, and, although he wasn't much good at it, he loved to dance. Clem built a wooden platform on the ranch, so Will could dance all night with his girlfriends, if necessary. Will sang, in a twangy tenor, in the local quartet, and showed more than a fair ability at baseball, which was becoming increasingly popular in the villages and hamlets across the country. He played on the Ooologah team, where they often used hardened old cow deposits for bases; since Clem was a mighty rich man by this time, Will even had a tiny glove when he played first base.

Any kind of party or dance suited Will just fine. At swimming parties he would often pretend he wasn't wearing anything. "Hey, girls, you can look now," he would yell. "I've got my hat on!" Despite such rash chatter, he was basically a very respectful young man when it came to girls. Somehow, he combined his innate shyness with a humor and charm that appealed to them.

But still dearest to his heart was roping. He'd go anywhere to watch someone do tricks with a rope, even if his own fast-developing reputation was such that it didn't appear that he needed to learn from anyone else. Old-timers already regarded Will as the quickest "tie man" they had ever seen. Maybe he would occasionally miss a loop but he couldn't be beaten in tying the legs.

There were times, though, when Will's expertise and skill with a horse got him into unnecessary trouble. One day he wanted to go to Claremore, but the Verdigris had swollen, so he couldn't get across it with his horse (not Comanche). That meant he had to cross over by using the railroad bridge. So he placed a rope around the horse's neck and started to move across the bridge by the foot planks, while leading the swimming horse below. But Will gave the horse too much credit for horse sense: The animal started to fight the strong tide, surged back against the rope, and, before Will could do anything to rescue the animal, it drowned.

Will appreciated that a good horse was a necessity, especially when he was entering a number of roping-and-riding contests. When he was asked by a competitor about his own Comanche—the fellow said he'd give as much as $500 for the horse—Will politely turned down the offer. "Mister, I don't know how much money you got," he said. "But there's not enough money in that whole grandstand to buy old Comanche." When he could, Will bought other roping horses, but in his eyes, Comanche surpassed all of them.

The first prize that Will ever won was recorded on July 4, 1899 in Claremore. The purse amounted to $18.50, nothing like wages in sports in the modern era—but he was just twenty years old and it gave him a good feeling, and confidence to go into other contests. Meanwhile, fresh from their public-relations triumph in the Spanish-American War, the Rough Riders staged a reunion in Oklahoma City. Cowpunchers and ranchers came from all over, as far west as Arizona and New Mexico, while Will joined a group from the Indian Territory. While he didn't win any prizes, Will contrived to meet up with his first real hero, Teddy Roosevelt, then the vice-presidential candidate running on the Republican ticket with William McKinley. Will didn't appreciate it at the time, but the self-dramatizing Roosevelt was the first in a line of American presidents that he would get to meet personally in his lifetime.

Further, Colonel Zach Mulhall, the colorful general livestock agent for the San Francisco Railroad, had been hired to stage the cowboy contests in Oklahoma City, and immediately took to young Will. Mulhall and Will became friends—an important connection in Will's blossoming show-business career. More than that, Mulhall, an expert at flummery and hyperbole, exaggerated Will's meeting with Roosevelt, always insisting that the two men became fast friends as the result of what was little more than a quick hello and handshake.

Later in 1899, the same year that Will met TR, he made a trip to St. Louis for the city's annual fair. While there, he appeared in Colonel Mulhall's roping-and-riding contest (the title "colonel" was strictly an invention, much like the Kentucky colonelcy bestowed on deserving brethren). According to Mulhall, "absolutely the best riders in the universe" were on hand for the program. Despite the hoopla, they were actually pretty good, and Will benefited doubly from his participation: He got a chance to compete with the best and also to solidify his relationship with Mulhall.

Since Mulhall intended to get out of the railroad business as soon as possible in order to enter the entertainment world, he rounded up a group of cowboy musicians, including his teenage daughter Lucille, who possessed striking skills at roping. Most of the "musicians" that Mulhall hired couldn't "ride in a wagon unless their shirttails were nailed to the floor," Will said laughingly. So Mulhall was persuaded to add Will to the assemblage, putting a trombone in his hands, even though the promoter knew Will couldn't play a note. Will's real role was to ride any outlaw horse or rope any steer in less time than anyone in the audience could, after Mulhall had made that challenge to the cash customers. Naturally, Will came through handsomely for Mulhall.

One night in San Antonio, after the band had already performed, the people in town invited Mulhall's whole crew to join them for a chili barbecue. Some prescient character thought it might be a good idea to invite Will to say a few words. The man with the talented rope must have figured, "Why me?" But as a fellow who never ducked a dare, Will rose to the occasion, cleared his throat, and proceeded to deliver one of the shortest after-dinner speeches ever made. "Well, folks, this is a mighty fine dinner—what there is of it," he drawled. This broke the audience up—music to Will's ears, the first such music he would get for talking.

When the Mulhall tour ended, Will went back to Claremore, where he could nurse his dreams. The times were changing—he knew that. The big cattle drives were now an anachronism, for the railroads were sprouting up all over the map, ending the previous isolation of the ranchers and Indian Territory. Trains from Coffeyville, Kansas, went through Oologah and into Claremore, and then could connect with the Frisco, which traveled from St. Louis to Vinita and on to Tulsa. From the moment in 1889 that Oologah had become a regular whistle-stop on the Missouri Pacific line, it became apparent to shrewd men like Clem that the Cherokee Nation, as he and his friends knew it, was destined for destruction. The area would become farm country, instead of cattle country, and settlers would come in, fence off their land, and the open range would be no more.

Already adapting to this new world, Clem became a very rich man. He was vice-president of the local bank, owned a large livery stable, and was intensely involved in the politics of the Indian Territory. He knew that it was inevitable that the Cherokees would be forced to adopt the ways and attitudes of the white man and, as a consummate realist, he worked in that direction. Certainly, as a proud and relentlessly loyal Cherokee, he had ambivalent feelings about what was happening. But he was willing to do what had to be done. As a result, he became one of the most prosperous and influential figures in the Indian Territory. Whether Will identified as strongly with the Cherokee as his father did is doubtful. After all, he had been raised in a fast-changing world and, as a young man, had already traveled farther—and learned more about the outside world—than most men of his age. He was part Cherokee, knew it, and *used* it—but he wouldn't be crushed by it.

Clem realized the end had come for cattle driving, even before a hundred thousand settlers had poured into the Cherokee Strip in the 1893 land rush, the most tumultuous in American history. This mad dash to gobble up the free land, once under the aegis of the Indians and the cattlemen, meant that the plains country would be altered forever. Clem, aggressive and tough-minded, was up to that challenge.

By 1891, Clem had built the first barbed-wire fence in the Verdigris country—it ran a distance of almost eight miles. As the first person to introduce wheat there on a large scale, he won the reputation as "Oologah's Wheat King," which is how the *Claremore Progress* anointed him in its pages. He bred hogs and poultry; he grew all kinds of vegetables, fruits, including berries and grapes, and oats, making him look like a very wise man, if not always a wise father.

Clem's overindulgence of his son should have made it easier for Will, who had now grown into an attractive twenty-year-old, with a sinewy, rugged physique, clefts denting his tanned cheeks, and merry, searching, blue eyes. But managing the ranch was not what Will chose to do; he rebelled against a future that had been carved out for him against his own wishes.

Sometimes this rebelliousness encouraged him to commit acts that enraged not only his father, but also Oologah's authorities. When a smallpox epidemic broke out in Oologah, the town was quarantined, with marshals being ordered to take up their posts at the city limits to prevent people from entering. But Will refused to heed the warnings. He rode into town with a friend, and when the marshal informed him he was breaking the law, he defiantly laughed in his face. The judge fined the two young men $19.85 each. But Will continued to take the matter lightly. He immediately wrote out a check for both fines, using his saddle as a makeshift table. To Will the incident wasn't worth thinking about, but others regarded him as a spoiled young fellow who felt that his father's prominence would excuse his imprudent behavior.

However, lurking beneath Will's sense of wilfulness was the raw ambition of a youngster fueled by boundless energy and imagination. Appreciative of the kind of money that cowboys could earn in this changing world—less than forty dollars a month—he knew that he could augment his income with prize money from roping and riding contests. Such purses could range from $200 to $1,000, if a fellow got real lucky. But managing his father's herd didn't satisfy either his desire to have more money at his disposal or his wanderlust. It didn't please him, either, that he would have to devote himself to farming, an occupation that was too limiting for his ambitions. He still dreamed of the wide-open plains, where a man could ride for days without seeing barbed wire or houses or even people. But this romantic vision of life didn't necessarily exclude the presence of women, for he liked them and they liked him.

One such young lady was nineteen-year-old Betty Blake, who entered Will's life in the fall of 1899. Betty, born two months before Will—a fact he didn't seem to be aware of—was one of seven Blake sisters, hailing from Rogers, in the northwestern part of Arkansas. She had been born in the Ozarks in a town named Monte Ne. When she was three, her father, James Wyeth Blake, a miller, died, leaving his wife to support six daughters and two sons by taking in sewing and dressmaking. After a second marriage, another daughter came along, but the union didn't last long.

Each of the Blake girls was as pretty as a picture, although an impartial observer probably would have voted Betty (whose name sometimes was spelled "Bettie") the prettiest. Blue-eyed, brown-haired, with a thoroughly Anglo-Saxon face, Betty had a lively way with words and people, an optimistic approach to life, and an air of uncorrupted innocence. According to one story, she was so unsophisticated that she'd been seen putting sugar and cream into her consommé. Unfortunately, she had recently been ill with typhoid fever and, as a result, had suffered an appreciable weight loss. She had a short haircut, which gave her the appearance of a young, athletic boy.

Under the circumstances, Betty's mother thought it advisable that she be given a change of scenery, for the sake of her spirit and her health. Cora, one of Betty's sisters, was the wife of Will Marshall, the local station agent for the Missouri Pacific Railroad. She took it upon herself to invite Betty for a visit to Oologah. Cora also issued a prior warning: that Oologah was about as lively as the waiting room to a cemetery. Betty was reminded that Oologah consisted primarily of one unpaved street, one two-story frame hotel, and a church that doubled as a schoolhouse. "There just aren't many young people around here," Cora told Betty. "But there's one boy named Will Rogers, who lives a few miles outside of town on a ranch." Despite such an inglorious preview, Betty was happy to accept the invitation.

Twice a day, a passenger train would roll into Oologah, where Will Marshall worked at the telegraph table, giving him an opportunity to see who was coming in and who was going out. One tranquil evening, Betty went to the station to lend Marshall a hand and to pass the time doing a little gossiping. It had always been necessary for Betty to work, for her family had been judged by some to be "dirt poor," though that may have been an exaggeration. She had worked in her hometown as a clerk and telegrapher and had also set type for the *Rogers Democrat*, for one dollar a day, not bad wages for a woman compositor. (Although Will made a point of kidding about his own "meager education," it was actually superior to Betty's.)

While Betty was at the station, a young man stepped off the train from Kansas City and approached the ticket window. His mission was to claim a banjo that he had purchased in Kansas City, and that had been sent ahead by express package. But mysteriously, before he could pick up the instrument, he disappeared—or so it seemed.

Betty later mused about the "disappearance."

"I looked at him and he looked at me," she explained about the chance encounter, "and before I could even ask his business, he turned on his heel and was gone, without so much as uttering a word."

Betty knew what had happened when she noticed a package, addressed to "Will Rogers," sitting in the corner. The young blade who had come by was, of course, Will. And she concluded, rightly, that he had just been too shy to request his parcel.

The next morning Betty saw this same young fellow riding past the station on his pony, under a derby hat perched precariously over a straw-colored mop of hair that came rushing over his eyes. Again, not a single word passed between them.

A few days later, Kate Ellis, a daughter of the hotelkeeper, invited Betty and Will for dinner at the hotel, which was across the street from the depot. During most of the evening, Will stayed mum, although he managed to sneak occasional peeks at Betty. When she caught him looking, he quickly looked away. However, toward the end of supper, Will announced that he had brought with him a bunch of the latest popular songs from Kansas City, known as the "big town" to Missourians. Kate at once suggested that Will sing for them. With some reluctance, Will finally sang, in a reedy tenor, without accompaniment. He had heard several of these songs in Kansas City, among them a current favorite, "Hello, My Baby, Hello, My Honey, Hello, My Rag-Time Gal." He threw in a few "coon songs," which were also the rage at the time. To finish off the evening, there was some taffy pulling and corn popping. Will also made Betty promise that if she would play the songs on Cora's piano he would come over with his banjo and sing along with her. She was pleased to take him up on the offer.

Over the next few weeks, Will and Betty spent a good deal of time together. Surely, in Betty, Will saw much of his own mother, for in many respects they were alike—their good nature, their love of music and beautiful things, their gentleness. How many times had Will stood by his mother's side, turning the pages of sheet music as she played the piano for him? As Betty spent more time with Will, his shyness lessened and he became funny and talkative. Sometimes he showed off for her, as he rode his horse, did his trick roping, or banged away on his banjo. One day, he performed for Betty on his bicycle and she was a most appreciative audience. Another time, he dressed in a garish Kemper Military Academy football sweater. Even if his days at Kemper had been scholastically undistinguished, he was proud to display the Kemper souvenir, which attested to his athletic prowess.

He constantly invited Betty out to the ranch. One day, Betty's brother-in-law drove her out there when Will wasn't around. What she saw depressed her. "We were met by the farmer's wife," she wrote about the incident. "The house was cold, ill-kept and bare of furniture. As I remember, the whole place was run down and neglected and I knew it had little resemblance to the hospitable home where the Rogers family was born and raised."

By Christmas that year, Betty had to return to Arkansas, ending, for the time being, her warm relationship with a boy from a totally different world than her own. Back home, Betty was already being subjected to some chiding about her dates with "that Indian boy." But she adamantly refused to be defensive about it. Her sister, Theda, later admitted that the Blakes were upset at the idea of Betty being courted by one of those "savages"—in Benton County, Arkansas, a mere one hundred miles from Claremore, people still spoke about Indians that way.

With Betty gone, Will couldn't forget her. On January 5, 1900, he sat down and wrote his first love letter to her. Will may not have been a grammarian or a champion speller but he had a better working vocabulary than most others in the Indian Territory. His odd and amusing contractions and subtractions of English words established a pattern for him that he employed for his entire life. In writing to Betty, he used the stationery of the U.S. Indian Service, which he'd gotten from Clem's desk.

Addressing Betty as "My Dear Friend," he said she'd probably be "madly surprised on receipt of this epistle. But never the less I could not resist the temptation and I hope if you can not do me the great favor of droping me a few lines you will at least excuse me for this I *cant* help it."

He went on to reveal some defensiveness about his racial background by remarking that "I know you are having a great time after being out among the 'Wild Tribe' so long." Then he launched into local gossip items about people they both knew in Oologah, including Kate. He boasted, strangely, of having had a good time during the holiday season, hardly a diplomatic way of informing Betty that he missed her.

This oversight was redeemed when he asked for her picture, then pleaded, mildly, for her to return to Oologah: "If you will only come back here we will endeavor to do all that we can to make you have a time, all kinds of late songs but I know they are old to you there. Skating, sleigh riding, horseback riding of which you are expert, and in fact every kind of amusement on the face of Gods footpiece."

Will ended the letter in a burst of obsequiousness: "Well I guess you have had ample sufficiency of my nonsense so I will stop. Hoping you will take pity on this poor heart broken Cowpealer and haveing him rejoiceing over these ball prairies on receipt of a few words from you I remain your True Friend and Injun Cowboy WP Rogers."

Betty's written responses to Will's letters have never been found, but it's clear from Will's own letters that she did indeed answer him, even though she allowed a suitable time to pass before doing so. By mid-March, Will put together another rambling, lovesick message, which he asked her to burn for "my sake." Obviously, she didn't. Again, as in his first letter to Betty, he expressed how much he wanted to be with her (considering that he wasn't a reluctant traveler, it's curious that Will didn't just hop over to see her), and he self-consciously suggested that he wasn't "smoothe like boys you have for sweethearts." There were other references to his being "undignified," and to his being a "broken-hearted Cherokee Cowboy" and an "ignorant Indian Cowboy."

Betty never replied to this letter. Totally smitten with this high-spirited lass, Will must have been crushed. (Years later, Will Rogers Jr., Will's son, said that from the first moment that his father had seen Betty, he knew this was the wife for him.)

In June, Will threw a big party at the ranch, with a band playing and his sister Maud serving as hostess. He hoped that Betty might attend, but she didn't. However, several months later, the two did meet in Springfield, Missouri, where Will had gone to perform for Colonel Mulhall's rodeo, which took place during the convention of the Elks Lodge. Will, beneath a small Stetson, rode Comanche. The little calf-roping pony was still his favorite, and Will let loose with cowboy yells that could be heard above all the others at the rodeo.

When Will joined Betty in the grandstand, he quieted down. Aware that her friends still regarded him as a noisy Indian, Will instinctively turned down the volume when he was surrounded by these people. He was sensitive enough to realize how Betty's associates felt about him, but he was also intimidated by them.

In the fall, Will and Betty saw each other again at a fair in Fort Smith, Arkansas. On the last night of the fair, a ball was given in honor of the girl who had been chosen as queen. Betty came, hoping that Will would also be present. All evening long, she kept searching for him. Finally, as Betty danced with another admirer, she spotted Will wandering along outside on the grassy lawn. Every now and then, Will watched the dancers, noting that Betty had a partner. But he never once came inside; nor did Betty go outside to speak to him.

Their paths would not cross again for two years. Will stopped writing letters to Betty, as his chronic wanderlust seized him again.

5

A New Century

ecurrent wisdom insists that each generation stands on the threshold of a new age. And that was true once again, as the twentieth century dawned.

By 1900, America, a land of over seventy-five million people spread out in forty-five states, was a place of promise, energy, expansion, exploitation, corruption, and large quantities of luck. With the old physical frontiers now closed, there were new frontiers dominated by men with a consuming passion for wealth and power. Monopolists and robber barons, such as the Morgans and Rockefellers, called for an abundant life for all, as long as they could plunge their own fingers deep into the rich American pie.

Henry Ford, the tunnel-visioned man from Detroit, was on the verge of developing a universal car, while Orville and Wilbur Wright gazed up at the skies and postulated that men would soon fly like birds. President McKinley had just presided over an abbreviated exercise in imperialism called the Spanish-American War, under the promotional auspices of publisher William Randolph Hearst. With an army of sixty-five thousand and only a half-dozen first-class battleships, America had become a world power.

Among the populace, a persistent clamor arose for better living conditions, more hospitals, more doctors, and homes lit by electricity. The country's telephone lines zigzagged over one million miles of land, while close to two hundred thousand miles of railroad tracks served to wipe out the insularity of the nation. Women still did not have the right to vote and there was no oppressive income tax. Beer parlors, the growing American pastime of baseball, and the synchronized singing of barbershop quartets were all the rage. Hotel rooms cost a dollar a day and less; people liked to chew gum and play poker; and still others liked picnics in the good old summertime.

Despite such a lusty, dynamic American environment, Will, the cowboy with happy feet, continued to search elsewhere for his personal paradise. He was still winning prizes in steer roping, but not enough. One time he finished far behind in a field of nineteen. He said that he had done so badly that they wanted him to tie the horse's feet, instead of the steer's. He managed to attend any number of possum hunts and dances; he went to Des Moines for a world championship contest and to St. Louis for the Pan-American Exposition.

But this roaming around didn't add up to much of a living. Will wasn't big enough or good enough, he thought correctly, to qualify as the top dog in the roping arena. In addition, handling the ranch for Clem was continuing to be anathema to him. Those itchy feet were just dying to carry him elsewhere, some place where he didn't need to open gates for cattle or farm the land.

Having already visited many places in the States, he now cast his attention on Argentina, with its wide-open pampas and ranch lands. He would read a few things about faraway Argentina, and his equally footloose friend, Dick Parris, kept whispering in his ear about this idyllic South American country, where a man wasn't fenced in by barbed wire. Will imagined this would be his own rugged heaven, a land with no barriers or restrictions.

Having made up his mind to go to Argentina, Will had to tell Clem of his quixotic plans. Whether he ever thought of revealing his adventurous program to Betty is not known. The fact that such a windy letter writer never hinted about this secret through the mail is good evidence that he didn't choose to tell her.

When Will broke the news to Clem, the old man, now in his early sixties, became angered. Most of all, he resented Will's refusal to accept responsibilities, even if he had come to terms with the fact that the boy couldn't be tamed along his own orthodox, prescribed lines. Ruffled as he was, Clem still handed over $3,000 to his son in return for the remainder of the herd that he had once given Will. Keeping his beloved Comanche for himself, Will gave the animal to an old friend for safekeeping. He sold another group of steers to another friend and, in a final grudging concession to his father, Will signed up for a twenty-year life-insurance policy, with monthly payments of some twelve dollars.

Since Will and his roping pal, Dick, had only a vague idea of the best way to reach Argentina, they chose to start the trip in 1902 by going south to New Orleans. While they were in that lively city, Will took in a play, *When Knighthood Was In Flower*, with Julia Marlowe, a well-known Shakespearean actress of that time. (Will Rogers Jr. commented years later that "it was strange that a cowboy would spend an evening at such a cultural event.")

To his chagrin, Will learned that there were no boats going from New Orleans to Argentina. So, true to his nature, he improvised another plan: head for New York.

"With the remarkable ease of roaming that poor [sic] American boys seemed to have in the days when they were restricted to a pony, a pair of bandy legs and their wits," wrote Alistair Cooke, "Will rode and bummed his way to New York."

For several days, the two young men took in the sights and sounds of turn-of-the-century New York, now the headquarters of much of America's growing café and entertainment business. Will's future mentor, Florenz Ziegfeld, who was soon to become a celebrated producer, had already beaten Will to this booming city with its plush restaurants, private ballrooms, Hell's Kitchen, Greenwich Village, Fifth Avenue, and its exciting main artery, Broadway. In 1896, Ziegfeld had produced his first show, a revival of *A Parlor Match*, featuring his petite inamorata, Anna Held, who, in the most wispy voice, sang "Won't You Come Play With Me?" Although Ziegfeld was already a name to be conjured with in Manhattan, Will probably had never heard of the colorful showman when he rambled through the town for the first time.

Informed that no ships were going to Buenos Aires from New York, Will heard that ships leaving from Liverpool, England, had regular schedules to Argentina. So off to England they would go. Will managed to sign on as a night watchman for a passel of sheep on board the S.S. *Philadelphia*, leaving on March 25. During the crossing the sheep turned out to have it a lot better than their master, for Will became deathly seasick almost from the moment the boat left the port. He was forced to spend most of the eight days of sailing time with his head between his legs. Maybe he never met a man he didn't like, but it's certain there was never an ocean voyage that he liked. In writing home about his illness-plagued trip on the S.S. *Philadelphia,* Will noted wryly, "You know I'm sick when I can't eat."

Once Will had set foot again on terra firma, he miraculously regained his composure and good humor. His letters poured forth again. In one, to his sisters, he wrote that his baggage had been searched for tobacco and spirits. "They didn't find any in mine . . . for I dont chew and my spirits had all left me on that boat," he said. "If I had any at all I contributed them to the briny deep."

When Will realized that some letters that he was writing to his family were winding up in the pages of the *Chelsea Reporter* and the *Claremore Progress,* such exposure caused him to be more effusive than usual. His notes were full of descriptions of money, and details of dress, food, and the people. He wasn't reluctant, either, to give his opinions on almost everything under the sun. He was plainly delighted to be a published writer, with plenty of dogmatic remarks on the British and deprecating references about some of their habits and customs. After twelve days in England, Will obviously had become a self-styled expert on the country. But he found British money terribly confusing and had a hard time keeping up with the language, which he felt was spoken too quickly. One day, when he asked a gentleman for directions, he pleaded with him not to speak so rapidly. "I'll be happy to pay you for overtime," Will joked.

During the time Will was in England, the preparations for the coronation of Edward VII—an event that Will referred to as "the big blowout"—were under way. He was amazed at the impact of the event on Londontown. "The whole city seems to be torn up and is being rebuilt. . . . I think they are going to stop up the Thames to make room for the people," he observed.

Will didn't seem to miss any monument or structure of note while he was in London. Dutifully, he paid visits to the London Tower, Parliament, London Bridge, Buckingham Palace, and Westminster Abbey. As far as Westminster Abbey was concerned, he confessed to a rather "creepy sensation" while gazing at all the stone tributes to Britain's most heroic and historic figures. He didn't neglect the British theatre, either, a segment of English culture that had always been highly regarded by most outsiders. "They arent up to the Americans on tragedy or comedy," said the future star of Broadway. On the whole, the high point of his time spent in London was when he caught a glimpse of "his big Nibs" (the king) from a distance.

Now it was time for Will and Dick to move on again. Even though Will had informed Dick that he'd "have to be drunk to ever set foot on another boat," there he was, in the second week of April, sailing on the *Danube,* which was chock-full with Spanish and Portuguese emigrants. Will casually referred to these people as "woolies"—a term of disparagement for those who worked with sheep and thus smelled bad. The *Danube* was a local, if ever there were one. It made stops in France, Spain, Portugal, São Vicente (one of the Cape Verde Islands), Brazil, and, finally, Sanata, Argentina. By the beginning of May, the two men reached their destination, Buenos Aires, which Will always spelled as "Buenos Ayres." They were quarantined for two days on board the *Danube* before they were permitted to set foot on Argentine soil.

Will's first impression of Argentina was that it was a "beautiful country, with a fine climate." He loved the many varieties of fruit available and thought Buenos Aires was a lovely city. But soon the dismal facts of economic life in the country became clear to him. Wages were impossibly low, around five dollars a month, and he found that "its no place to make money unless you have $10,000 to invest." Lots of men competed for every job. Since his Spanish was almost nonexistent, he was at a distinct disadvantage in pursuing work. "I'm trying to learn the language," he said. "I think I can say six words. I did know seven and forgot one."

When Will ventured five hundred miles into the interior of Argentina, the situation there was the same—few jobs, low wages. This left both Will and Dick feeling extremely downcast. Life in Argentina simply wasn't what they had dreamed it was going to be. At this stage, Dick, increasingly homesick, decided to return home. Will didn't try too hard to dissuade Dick from going back to Oologah, for he had his own misgivings about staying on in Argentina. But he ended up buying Dick a ticket back to the Indian Territory, and he loaded his friend with gifts that were to be given to his father and sisters.

The tone of Will's letters to Clem was now downbeat. He talked of the possible war with "Chili" and about the men who control Argentina—"the most corrupt, unstable government in the world." He insisted that there was no "get-up" or energy in the natives. By mid-June he was hinting strongly to Clem that he was ready to come home. While he continued to be fascinated by Argentina's "good, fat horses," he was critical of most of the techniques that were being used to round them up. "In roping and riding and any old thing," he wrote, dismissively, "they can't teach a thing to the 'punchers' in America. They all use a rawhide rope and are doing well to catch one of three." He was even more caustic in his assessment of the natives. "They are a cowardly lot," he said. "They all carry knives on their belt from a foot-and-a-half to two feet and very few have guns, if a man points a gun at a whole bunch he can put them all to flight."

With his money running out and his spirits being crushed, Will sounded like a disaffected person. Certainly he wanted little more to do with Argentina. (Amusingly, some years later, Will tried to make it up to the Argentinians by praising them as the "best ropers and riders in the world.") But at this time in life, he was unrelenting in his feelings about the country and its people.

"All the Americans I have met here are only leaving to get back to America," he grumbled. "Any part of the states is better for a man without lots of money than this place and the beauty of it is that youre among people and not a lot of 'dagoes' from all over the world and all having a different lingo. . . . You never know a country until you leave it and so stay where you are."

By now things had gotten so bad for Will that he couldn't afford the price of a hotel room. He had taken to sleeping in the park. Always in need of "loose change," Will occasionally made his meal money by living on board a U.S. battleship for a couple of weeks, teaching Negro spirituals to the sailors. Another time he picked up a few dollars singing in a concert hall.

The question now in Will's mind was whether he should tough it out and go elsewhere or simply return home, with his tail between his legs. He knew if he returned, he would risk criticism from Clem, and was reluctant to confront that possibility. But his letters to his father continued to seek approval for his peripatetic way of life. They also hinted that he was annoyed by what he construed to be the attitudes of his father's friends, who had told Clem that he was wasting his money by, in any way, subsidizing Will's catch-as-catch-can adventures. Will spoke directly to this in a letter in which he suggested that he needed financial help:

> I have spent a world of money in my time, but I am satisfied as someone else has got the good of some of it. . . . If you will only give me credit for just spending my own as I think I have I will be as happy as if I had a million. . . . You have done everything in the world for me and tried to make something more than I am out of me . . . but as to our financial dealings I think I paid you all up and everyone else. . . . I only write these things so that we may better understand each other. I cannot help it because my nature is not like other people to make money and I dont want you all to think I am no good simply because I dont keep my money. I have less than lots of you and I daresay I enjoy life better than any of you, and that is my policy. I have always delt honestly with everyone and think the world and all of you and all the folks and will be

among you all soon as happy as anyone in the world, as then I can work and show the people that I only spend what I make. . . .

Betty Blake once described Clem as a "true frontiersman, brusque in manner, a man who didn't mince words in an argument . . . but a man with the tenderest of hearts, who left a batch of worthless promissory notes at his death." But in this instance, Clem was standing his ground with his son. He refused to satisfy Will's needs by sending him money in this troubled hour.

After unburdening himself in his letters, and not reaping any satisfaction from Clem, Will had to look elsewhere. He soon learned of a job tending 300 cows, 700 sheep, 750 mules, and 50 thoroughbred horses on a boat headed for South Africa in the first week of August 1902.

Will had reservations about getting on board again, feeling that inevitably seasickness would hit him. But he felt he had little choice. So there he was, ready to ship out to a country that only recently had been embroiled in a bitter war.

Over five thousand British soldiers, along with an equal number of Dutch-speaking Boers or Afrikaners, lost their lives in the Boer War, which had come to an end in May 1902. Then in his twenties, Winston Churchill, who turned out to be a facile talker like Will, had been sent to South Africa to cover the hostilities for London's *The Morning Post* in 1899. Imprisoned by the Boers, Churchill escaped, enabling him to write dramatic accounts about this perilous episode. Within a short time after returning to England, he was elected to Parliament. In an odd coincidence of history, Will and Churchill had missed meeting in South Africa by a matter of months—but one observer has advanced the teasing proposition that Will may well have trained some of the horses that Churchill rode while he was achieving fame in South Africa.

In the twenty-five days that Will spent at sea on the *Kevinside*, going from Buenos Aires to Durban, South Africa, he barely survived his constant mal de mer. But he kept his wits about him long enough to make the acquaintance of an Englishman who had an Italian-sounding name, Piccione, and who was in the business of raising and racing thoroughbred horses. More important, he offered Will employment, enabling him to satisfy South Africa's entry requirement.

It wasn't easy working for Piccione, even though Will fed and exercised Piccione's horses in well-lit stables that were steamheated. Piccione wasn't a charitable man and, most of the time, he kept Will wondering exactly what he was earning from one day to the next. When Will wrote home about his latest experience, he described Piccione as "the richest old bloak in the country, maybe worth 35 million in America." Despite such wealth, Will complained that he was "shy of food; . . . there is no place I have been that you get the good old grub that you will get even in the poorest parts of America."

Again, just as he had done when he was in Argentina, Will advised the folks back home, and anybody else willing to listen, that they should "fight shy of this country [South Africa] because it was populated by 'wild-looking people'—kaffirs and Negroes—with rings, chains and all kinds of old scrap in their ears and nose, some with horns tied to their heads." He had reason to feel they were all "crazy as snakes." He also objected to the fact that the common labor was done by poor people, while those who were better off just stood around and watched them. Once in a while, he sat on a fence outside Piccione's house in the evening and listened to his boss's daughter—"a damsel of twenty winters or so, and they must have been a bit hard"—singing such popular songs as "Sweet Rosie O'Grady." He was never invited to come inside to hear the concert—but he scarcely minded, for he regarded the young woman as singularly unattractive.

Within several months, Will had experienced enough of Piccione's harangues. Deciding to move on again, he squired a bunch of recalcitrant mules to the town of Ladysmith, in the eastern part of South Africa. While there, he wrote to Clem, notifying him that he might be returning to the Indian Territory in the spring. Further, he tried to assure his father that he had enough money to get along.

While roaming around the country, Will put in at Capetown. There, in a rowdy saloon, he encountered an American, from Philadelphia, who was on a vaudeville tour. The man's name was William Claude Dukinfield, whose flaring nose was as memorable to Will as his misanthropic disposition. Will showed Dukinfield a few of his best roping tricks, but Dukinfield appeared more interested in drinking. He also told him he might like to be in show business, just like Dukinfield, but that left the sardonic vaudevillian equally unexcited.

The next time their paths crossed, Will caught Dukinfield's juggling act in Durban, where the Philadelphian was then a featured performer. Watching Dukinfield's "retrieved blunders," Will was in awe of the man's skills. (The lives of these two men would connect again, not too long after—back in the United States—at which time Dukinfield would be known as W. C. Fields, for strictly professional reasons.)

Misfortune still had a stranglehold on Will during these months in South

Africa. Someone walked off with his saddle, spurs, and leggings while he was in Durban, leaving him with little more than a couple of shirts and one sock. He was able to maintain his sense of humor about such vexing matters and, while in this frame of mind, he watched Texas Jack's Wild West Show, which had arrived in Ladysmith a few days earlier. Texas Jack, who actually did hail from Texas, was the real thing, Will discovered—he could rope, ride, and shoot with the best of them. Never as prominent or as publicity-conscious as Buffalo Bill, who led his own world-famous troupe, Texas Jack was a tall, handsome fellow, who wore picturesque western-style clothes under a wide-brimmed cowboy hat that could have given shade to a whole barn. Texas Jack employed his wife, a cowboy hand, a batch of roughriders, trick ropers, and a menagerie of animals, including a zebra. (Will continued to spread the story that, while in South Africa, he had roped a zebra on the veldt, but that sounded like a harmless fairy tale.)

Back home, many of Will's neighbors had joined up with Buffalo Bill's "Wild West and Congress of Rough Riders of the World." If he had been in Claremore, Will might have done the same. But now here was Texas Jack, who kept himself in the same good shape that Will did (by ignoring booze and cigarettes), and Will figured he might have the chance that he missed out on with Buffalo Bill's show. When Texas Jack asked Will if he could handle a rope, Will proceeded, then and there, to demonstrate the "crinoline," a trick in which he started with a rope that had a small loop, and he gradually let it out around his body, until the entire length of the rope formed a big circle around him. Texas Jack was duly impressed, for he had made a standing offer of fifty pounds to anyone who could perform this trick. In five years, nobody had been able to do the crinoline to his satisfaction.

As a result of Will's performance with the crinoline, Texas Jack offered him a job doing roping in a ring for twenty dollars a week. "As soon as I showed him what I could do, he took me on," wrote Will, proudly. "Of course the business is not the best business but so long as there is good money in it and its honest there is no objection to it." He added that working for Texas Jack was far better than doing day labor.

By the time Will started his job, his role had been somewhat expanded. He would not only do his tricks with ropes, but he was also commissioned to ride a bucking horse. He had always been good on horses—but bucking horses were another matter. The act was billed as "blood-curdling scenes of western life in America." Ultimately, Will was called on to do a number of parts. Sometimes he portrayed an Indian; other times, a Negro (he employed burned cork to color his face black, a technique used at that time by many song-and-dance men in minstrel shows and vaudeville). And other times, he was just plain "Cherokee Kid," a name that he truly cherished because it affirmed his Indian identity. Will had a card made up, announcing he was a "Fancy Lasso Artist and Rough Rider." The program that was distributed added a touch of hyperbole: "The Cherokee Kid—the Man Who Can Lasso the Tail off a Butterfly."

Texas Jack's troupe went all over South Africa, performing before children, old people, Negroes, Englishmen, Afrikaners, tourists, and stray dogs. There were other acts in Texas Jack's show—clowns, high-wire acrobats, equestrians, feats of strength, monkeys and dogs riding on the backs of horses, and zebras doing unzebralike things. But from the moment that Will earned two encores in his first performance, he became the headliner. The *Pretoria News* proclaimed that his feats with ropes were truly "astounding," helping him to get a raise of five dollars a week after a couple of months. That further fortified Will's belief that he possibly had at last achieved his proper rung in life. (Years later, Will's son, Jim, said that Will found his true identity in Texas Jack's show.)

Writing from Potchefstroom in December 1902, Will filled Clem in with details about the show: "There is about 40 people with Texas Jack and about 30 horses. We generally stay in a town two or three days and in the large ones longer, we have a crowded Tent every night. I like it fine and Jack himself is the finest old boy I ever saw and he seems to think a great deal of me, he is a man about 40 years old and has traveled all over the world showing he is a much finer shot than Buffalo Bill and a fine Rider and Roper, theres now about seven or eight Americans along. . . . "

By January 1903, Will was still enjoying his signal role with Texas Jack. He wrote Clem: "I dont have a thing to do all day, only my work in the ring at night. I can save a little but it takes a good deal to buy food and clothes in this country. . . . Oh I found my Saddle and brid[les and] Leggins and spurs. . . . It had been stolen and raffled off and I found it and have it now. . . . We have Tremendous crowds every night. I do the roping instead of Jack. . . . You can see how I am billed up."

Sensing Will's pleasure in what he was doing, and being impressed that his boy was now earning money, Clem wrote back, telling him how everybody missed him (generally, he referred to Will as Willie in his letters) and urging him to keep writing. Clem's letters were filled with details about people that

Will knew, money matters, and the weather. But Clem never made the fatal diplomatic error of asking Will to come home.

When Will wrote to Clem, he would usually address him as "My dear Papa." However, instead of asking for money, Will now wanted "about 100 feet of the best kind of hard twist rope and one of the boys will show you what I use, pretty small but hard twist. . . . Some nights here I rope with old ties or any old things." In time Clem did send along the requested rope.

There was increasing interest in South Africa in all types of trick roping, which caused Will to be badgered by youngsters who wanted instructions from him on how to handle ropes, so that they could win medals awarded by Texas Jack to the best lasso throwers.

In one of Clem's letters, he provided a lugubrious note about one of Will's best boyhood pals. Charley McClellan, whom Will used to play Indian with as a boy in the Indian Territory, had died of typhoid in "Tennessee, where he was going to school [Cumberland University], just before Christmas. They brought him home and buried him here at Claremore Cemetery."

In writing back to Clem, Will never commented about Charley's death at such an early age. It was not characteristic of him to fail to show concern for other people, and he certainly had an awareness of death (in one letter he talked of "the frequency of English graveyards" in areas where the Boers had battled the British), but he appeared to be preoccupied with the nuances of his own daily life.

One such complication involved his dealings with young women. Will's existence in South Africa was hardly without its romantic interludes. In his early twenties, he was a robust, virile, physically attractive man who liked women—and they seemed to like him. One female acquaintance, named Annie, who lived in the town of Graaff Reinet, saw fit to send him a letter telling him he was "breaking" her "heart." He also had something of a dalliance with a woman who was connected with Texas Jack's show: Will and Mamie (only her first name was known) must have hit it off more than passably well, for she kept writing letters to him that were designed to get him to go away with her. It wasn't clear exactly where the lovers were to go, or whether she was proposing an elopement. But what *was* clear was that she was quite taken with Will, whom she addressed as "Dear Kiddie," presumably a shortened reference to "Cherokee Kid."

"Now darling, I love you so much that it seems to me I should die if you leave me," she wrote. "So tata my darling. Think it over and let me know. Oh

I wish we had last night over." In another letter Mamie wrote: "You seem to have cut me out since last night and I heard you remark this morning about looking for a boat. Well, darling, if you wish to cut loose from me come tonight and tell me so. Even if it is a great blow to me, any thing would be better than for you to look at me as you did this morning."

Will never let on in his letters to Clem that he was enmeshed in a love affair with Mamie, for that's what was going on. She forlornly suggested to Will that "we need not be intamate [sic] We could just make out that everything is over between us. Don't you think that is a good plan?"

The affair with Mamie probably kept Will in South Africa for longer than he intended. Whether Texas Jack, who seemed like Will's surrogate father in this situation, played any role in discouraging the relationship is not certain—but Will had so much respect for the man that it's likely that he discussed the matter with him. When Will went looking for a boat, as Mamie's letter suggests, he was trying to extricate himself from her, even at the high price—for him—of sailing the high seas.

Occasionally admitting his homesickness, Will managed to stress that he was gaining invaluable experience with Texas Jack. From all appearances, it looked as if he would remain with the show a few more months to soak up more of Texas Jack's magic. "I studied him by the hour," Will said of Jack. "He could make an audience think a bum act was great. From him I learned the great secret of show business—learned when to get off."

In August, Will wrote that Texas Jack was planning to leave the show for a visit to America, where he hoped to recruit more talent. "He wants me to stay till he gets back as I take his parts in the show while he is away. . . . I will come as soon as he gets back for I am getting in a hurry to get home," Will said.

Only seven days after writing this letter, Will left South Africa. But he wasn't headed for America. He had embarked on a slight detour, by way of Australia, which meant he would be at sea for twenty-five days, a terrifying fate for Will. But he took with him a rousing letter of recommendation from Texas Jack, who was saddened to see the young man go.

Writing on stationery that proclaimed him "The World's Greatest Sharpshooter," Texas Jack's imprimatur stated: "I have the great pleasure in recommending Mr. W. P. Rogers (the Cherokee Kid) to circus proprietors. He has performed with me during my present South African tour and I consider him to be the champion trick roughrider and lasso thrower of the world. He is sober, industrious, hard working at all times and is always to be relied upon. I shall be very pleased to give him an engagement at any time should he wish to return."

A nomad with a letter like that in his pocket was unlikely to go hungry—as long as there were circuses and horse shows around. But first Will wanted to take in the sights of another mysterious new country. So after landing in Wellington, in New Zealand, a country he loved at first sight because of its magnificent scenery, great natural resources, and a government that he thought, after only minimal observation, worked extremely well, Will figured he would stay there for a week.

He wrote to his father on September 4, 1903, and told him not to get excited when he looked at the map and saw "where I am now." He added that he had had enough of South Africa and "thought I'd better be going." There was no hint of romantic difficulties, only an assurance that "I must see a bit more and then get back home."

Will spent those few days in Wellington, moved on to Auckland by boat (four-and-a-half days of torture), and then went on the Sydney, Australia. Instead of immediately looking for work, Will decided to take a closer look at Australia, for he could never subdue his boundless curiosity about new places and different people. For the first time in his life, he saw the boomerang being thrown by "woolies," and he noted, with some incredulity, that "it will shave your hat off going and scalp your head off coming back." (In South Africa he had seen Canadian soldiers playing baseball, but this was not the preferred game in Australia.)

He had never before seen that marsupial wonder, the kangaroo. Now he was seeing them almost everywhere, as frequent as rabbits. For some reason, he regarded the Australians as "the most conceited people in the world," while acknowledging that they were the greatest sheep raisers he had ever seen. Attending the Australian Derby, he watched a forty-thousand-dollar horse race, in which over forty horses stayed close together for a mile and a half—"the greatest sight I ever saw," he exclaimed.

He wrote to his sisters: "Australia is an enormously big country and very few people, only in the cities and away back in the interior is nothing but Negroes [he usually used the word "nigger"] and they are still a bit skittish. Sydney and Melbourne are greatly like American cities, more up to date than any I've seen since I left home."

In the same letter, he launched into a leisurely dissertation about America's virtues, compared to those in countries that he had been visiting. If he had ever questioned America's goodness and what it had to offer a fellow like himself, now he sounded like a boastful nationalist, perhaps preparing himself emotionally for his inevitable return to his hearth. He wrote:

> It is very amusing in all these countries, any thing new or what they havent had before will be called American. You hear electric street cars called American Tram cars. All the refreshment places are advertised in box car letters, "American cold drinks, American soda fountain." The bars will have up drinks mixed on the American plan, the barber will advertise "American barber chair". . . . I was always proud in America to own I was a Cherokee and I find on leaving there that I am equally as proud to own that I am an American for if there is any nation earning a rep abroad it is America. I have arguments of every nationality of man under the sun in regard to the merits of our people and our country, from prize fights to the greatest international questions of which I *knew* all about, for you are not an American if you dont know. All these big fish stories are traced to the Americans so you have got to uphold the *rep.*"

Many of Will's adventures during his seemingly unending travels became an integral part of his vocabulary. The problem of how many of these tales were true is hard to judge. But he relished reciting the stories and people enjoyed hearing them. One of these stories concerned Will's involvement with an elephant in the Australian town of Warrnambool. The elephant's keeper had been out on a bender, causing Will to be concerned that the unchaperoned animal might attack somebody. According to the story, Will took over, calmly leading the elephant through the streets, before a police constable arrested him for his noble civic act. Since Will was adept at handling most animals, there is no reason to believe he couldn't have massaged the feelings of the pachyderm—still, there were no witnesses to attest to the validity of the tale.

In the first days of 1904, Will promised that he wouldn't be away from home for another Christmas. "I would have given everything to be there," he wrote, wistfully. "Here [Melbourne] there are no Christmas trees, scarcely any presents given, only cards sent to your friends and to cap the climax, its hot as the 4th of July."

Will's cash reserve was fast running out. He had lost a bundle in a suspicious card game that he shouldn't have been involved in, and whatever money he had saved from Texas Jack's show had long since disappeared. Out of need, and armed with Texas Jack's gracious words of endorsement, Will put in for a job with the Wirth Brothers Circus, which operated out of Australia and was embarking on a tour of New Zealand.

Will got the job and within days, featured as the Cherokee Kid, he became one of fifteen acts on the program. According to a light-hearted report in *The Auckland Herald,* Will's roping and riding performance was "a highly original exhibition. . . . He seems able to lasso anything from the asset of a professional bankrupt to the business end of a flash of lightning." Decked out in a form-fitting, red-velvet, gold-trimmed Mexican suit, Will was an instant hit with the children. Thrilled later to receive the approval of New Zealand's audiences, he was welcome to remain with the Wirth Circus when it returned to Australia.

But he had made up his mind that, after eight months there, it was now time for him to go home. He had been on the road for two years, traveling some fifty thousand miles, absorbing knowledge, forming impressions, gaining confidence, going broke in the process, and working his way down from first class to no class at all!

In February 1904, he wrote to all the "home folks" that "I'll be there *certain* before the opening of the St. Louis Fair, honest." That meant by April 30. Now his plan could be put in motion, for he had saved just enough to buy a third-class ticket from New Zealand to San Francisco. From San Francisco, he hopped a freight train going home, most of the time bunking with a barnyard-ful of chickens. "He smelled mightily fowl," joked Homer Croy.

6

Home Again—for a Minute

There wasn't a brass band on hand to greet world-traveler Will when he got home to Oologah in the second week of April 1904. But Clem, pleased to see his boy, wasn't about to neglect the event. The main dining room of Claremore's best hotel was now the site of a big family dinner, with everybody on hand—all the sisters, cousins, relatives, and friends that Clem could assemble at quick notice. The only conspicuous absentee was Betty Blake. But, after all, Will hadn't scribbled a sentence to her since he had been away.

Questions came thick and fast to Will: What was it like "over there?" What places did he like the most and the least? Had he learned any foreign words? What did the men and women wear? How long was he going to stay in Claremore? Had he roped any zebras or kangaroos? As always, Will was accommodating and cheerful. He did explain how homesick he had been while traveling, but he also suggested that he had gotten a taste of the outside world—and a generous swallow of show business. Spi Trent, who had once engaged in so much mischief with Will, said that "he's gotten a kind of surefootedness . . . that comes to a fellow who has learned to paddle his own canoe."

Closer to home, in the Indian Territory, things hadn't remained the same, either. Autos had made their first appearance in the countryside; so had home-manufactured ice. The Cherokee senate had accepted the end of tribal government, with each Cherokee citizen receiving a homestead not to exceed 110 acres. The move to make Oklahoma a state was proceeding with all due haste, with Clem, serving his last term as a senator from the Cooweescoowee District, lending his voice and prestige to that cause. Business was booming almost everywhere, and when an oil strike occurred near Sapulpa, farms were abandoned by many overexcited locals, who thought they would get rich overnight.

A few days after Will arrived home, he demonstrated again—if anyone had doubts about it—that he was a man of action. A Claremore neighbor, Clint Lipe, was thrown off his horse. Crushed under the weight of an animal that had a reputation for bad behavior, Clint was near death. Without a moment's pause, Will mounted the unpredictable horse and rode off to get a doctor. Poor Clint died, anyway, but Will's effort won wide praise.

While he was still in Australia, Will had spoken with enthusiasm about attending the forthcoming St. Louis World's Fair. So it wasn't entirely unexpected for him to leave Claremore soon after he got there. But first he enjoyed experiencing the warmth of his family and friends after such a long hiatus. The old sights and places were terribly important to him. Yet, he also knew he was going to make a livelihood at the one thing he loved best—entertaining others. And he was eager to get on with it.

The World's Fair in 1904 was designed to celebrate the centennial of Thomas Jefferson's Louisiana Purchase of 1803 (due to various difficulties, the actual opening had been set back a year). Expectations around the country for the St. Louis spectacle had spread like an epidemic. It seemed that wherever people gathered, they chatted about the fair and many sang the lyrics of the popular songs, "Meet Me in St. Louey, Louey, Meet Me at the Fair," and "Down, Down, Down, Where the Wurtzburger Flows." Advance talk insisted that this fair would be the largest and best in history, bigger by far than the London and Chicago fairs that had preceded it.

It was not inexpensive to travel to St. Louis, but the much-anticipated foreign, science, and technological exhibits, and the touted entertainment programs, encouraged people to save for months to make the trip. (Author Richard Ketchum has noted that hot dogs, ice-cream cones, and iced tea all made their American debut that summer at the fair's midway, which was called the Pike.)

Will hadn't been back more than a week when his former boss, Colonel Mulhall, got in touch with him. The colonel asked Will if he could come to Guthrie, in the Indian Territory, to talk about joining up with his Wild West show, which was going to be on the menu in St. Louis. Word of Will's high-octane performance in New Zealand and Australia had reached Mulhall 'causing him to seek out the services of his former disciple.

It didn't need much persuasion for Will to accept Mulhall's sixty-dollars-a-month offer. Mrs. Mulhall laid out a lunch that Will devoured with great gusto, and, while at the Mulhall home, Will incidentally met up again with Mulhall's nineteen-year-old, freckle-faced daughter, Lucille, who was winning a handsome reputation as a cowgirl. When Will watched Lucille perform some of her tricks, he swore she was the only girl he had ever seen who could handle and ride a horse "just like a man." That had to be taken as a hefty compliment, for in those years, most men, including Will, certainly didn't think that Lucille was in the proper line of work. She had been breaking records for roping and tying all over the place—records that *men* had set—and though recordkeeping at the time was not an exact art, it was commonly accepted that Colonel Mulhall had himself a champion.

Will may have been more taken with Lucille than he was ever willing to let on. Several of his friends were sure that Will had a romantic interest in the lively young lady. One of Will's biographers, Ben Yagoda, has pointed out that Will's own scrapbook was crowded with pictures of Lucille as she was riding, standing still (which she didn't do much), posing with him, and, of course, doing what she did best, roping a steer.

Will may have been crazy about Lucille, but there was no evidence that he pursued her. However, she made such an impression on him that many years later, he wrote about her demeanor and dress in such loving detail—"Lucille never dressed like the cowgirl you know today, no loud colors"—that one can conclude that she never left his memory.

Before Mulhall's contingent left for St. Louis, the colonel put his ropers and riders through their rigorous paces at his ranch near Guthrie. In addition, he took people from a troupe that went by the name of the Cummins Indians. When these were added to the riders, the cast in Mulhall's show came to over six hundred—a fat payroll, to say the least.

One of those who also responded to Mulhall's call was Tom Mix, a twenty-four-year-old Pennsylvanian. Mix had done a bit of drifting around the country after deserting from the army, following his enlistment in the Spanish-American War. He wound up bartending in the Indian Territory, hitting spots like El Paso, Texas, then moving to Oklahoma City and Guthrie, where he obtained work on ranches. Mix had dark good looks, a square jaw, and the proper sun-scorched squint in his eyes that stood him in good stead by the time he graduated into leading Hollywood-movie cowboy roles. (Mix made over three hundred movies, always "clean" ones, as he carefully pointed out—and close to five million dollars. At the funeral of Wyatt Earp, the controversial gunfighter and law officer, Mix served as a pallbearer.)

One-quarter Cherokee, like Will, Mix got along well with Rogers from the start. But he never was as good with a rope as Will was, something he would gladly acknowledge. "That fellow could whisper a rope as slick as the ass on a brass monkey," said Mix, about his new pal. Perceiving that a rope literally came to life in Will's hands, Mix was grateful for any tips or lessons that Will could give him. Next to Teddy Roosevelt and Buffalo Bill, Will became one of Mix's heroes, and he remained in that niche even after the two of them evolved into screen favorites. "Will was the kind of fellow you were always happy to see," said Mix, "and always sorry to see go." Mix was one of those who suspected that Lucille "thought a great deal of Bill." In fact, he expressed surprise that "Bill" didn't "steal the colonel's daughter."

At the fair, Will generally wore baggy pants, a derby, and a prominent fake, red nose, which gave him a clown's image. But when he performed he was not a clown. Once he had thought that roping was something that folks would pay to see only in far-off foreign lands. But now he appreciated that the tricks he could pull off with ropes were appealing to many people who didn't happen to live in the Southwest and West.

His assignment at the fair—where he said it seemed to rain every day, leaving the grounds a "sight"—wasn't sufficient to satisfy his restlessness. Celebrating American ingenuity and enterprise, the fair lasted for seven months, attracting over twenty million customers. But Will didn't choose to stay there all the time. Now and then, he went home, once to sell Clem a horse and a buggy for $350 in cash ("I kinder want to buy me a horse or two up here.") On another occasion, Will farmed out his services to the Columbia Theatre, a burlesque house, where he did his rope stint with a friend, Theo McSpadden. It marked the first time that Will appeared on stage in front of gossamer-clad women—but it wouldn't be his last such performance.

The owners of the Columbia Theatre ran another theatre in Chicago, where Will was hired for a week to entertain with his on-stage rope tricks and comical patter. "I made good in Chicago," he wrote to Clem, "and may return to play two other theatres there." But he didn't go back.

Will's devotion to Colonel Mulhall and the fair was sorely tested when Mulhall got himself into a jam that almost ended the Wild West show's run. The incident occurred on a Saturday night, June 2, 1904, and involved Mulhall and his head stable man, Frank Reed, with whom he had been having serious disagreements. A man with first-rate promotional skills, Mulhall also had a temperament that could erupt unexpectedly. As Will was sauntering along with a friend on the night in question, Mulhall confronted Reed out on the Pike and, before anyone realized what was going on, pulled out a gun and opened fire on him. Reed fired back. Johnny Murray, a roper from Texas, tried to intervene by grabbing for Mulhall's gun. For his troubles, Murray got a bullet in the abdomen. Reed, on the other hand, wound up being only grazed by a bullet, while Ernest Morgan, an eighteen-year-old bystander, ended up seriously wounded.

At first, it appeared that Morgan was going to die. And on its front page, *The New York Times* actually reported he was dead, only to have to recant when it found that he was alive. If Morgan had died, Mulhall would no doubt have found himself in a heap of trouble. As it turned out, he was dragged off to jail by the local police. Released on twenty-thousand dollars bond, Mulhall was not the least bit contrite. He even waved gaily to Lucille as he left the premises.

The *Vinita Daily Chieftain* wasn't impressed with Mulhall's gunfire diplomacy. "The world knows all it needs to know about the wild and lawless spirit that was indiginous [sic] in this country a generation ago. The Wild West show has run its course, at least on this continent," the paper's editorial scolded.

Yielding to pressure, the fair's authorities barred the embattled Mulhall from the premises. Some of Mulhall's cowboys, fearful that they would be working without getting paid, packed up and went home. Will, on the other hand, remained steadfastly loyal, partisan, but uncharacteristically mean-spirited. Hours after the shooting incident, he wrote to his "Dear Papa" as follows:

> Mulhall done most of the shooting and if he had only hit the fellow and killed him it would have been all right; the other fellow was no good. I think the show will go on just the same. Cummins is the whitest man I ever saw and will keep us on just the same. I dont know how Mulhall will come out of it, he is still in

jail. He was offul good to us boys. They can all say what they please about Mulhall but he has done more for us boys than any man on earth. . . .

Some of the boys, including Will, did stay on at the fair, in a reduced version of Mulhall's original show. By this time, Mulhall had been sentenced to three years in jail and was preparing his appeal. It didn't take long for him to get back in action. He opened another Wild West show at Delmar Gardens in St. Louis, with the loyal Will immediately joining up. The Indian chief Geronimo, famous for making his Apache raids before adopting Christianity, and somewhat hostile to Mulhall as a result of the shooting fray, also went to work at Delmar Gardens. Even at his advanced age, the old warrior was still proficient with a lasso. If Will hadn't been around, Geronimo would have attracted most of the attention. As it happened, Will was fast becoming the headliner wherever he went, with his rope and wisecracks. Working assiduously on his repertoire, Will added the single ingredient that always brought appreciative roars from the audience: There was always *something* or *somebody* that he would rope during his act—it might be one of his fellow performers, it might be someone in the crowd, or it might be a dog or cat, but there was always *something* to be roped.

While the fireworks with Mulhall were a distraction for Will, Betty Blake, who had been out of his life for the past several years, suddenly returned for a brief period. Since first meeting Will, Betty had remained unmarried, despite her attractive personality and bright manner. Never lacking for earnest swains seeking her company, she was content to enjoy being with her large and loving family. She suffered little from being typecast as a spinster. The year before the St. Louis Exposition opened, Betty had spent most of the time helping her brother take care of the railroad station in Jenny Lind, Arkansas.

Will still cared deeply about Betty—but his failure to write her during his travels suggested that he feared being rejected by her. Such a fear was not without reason. Betty may not have regarded association with him as a step down on the social ladder. But he was painfully aware that her friends, perhaps even some of her family, still looked upon him as declassé, an Indian, albeit a wealthy one, who dressed and behaved strangely and belonged in a different sphere from the one occupied by Betty.

Unaware that Will had returned to the United States, Betty had come to St. Louis to visit her sister and to take in the sights at the fair, since that was just about all the folks at home were talking about. On a Sunday morning, while meandering around the exhibits in the Oklahoma State Building, with some friends, Betty overheard a girl remark about an act that she had just seen in the Wild West show, featuring "someone named Will Rogers." That was a name she hadn't heard for a while, but that didn't mean she hadn't thought about him.

Betty quickly found out Will's address and jotted down a note to him, suggesting it would be nice if they could get together while she was in town. Considering Betty's own background and the antagonistic attitudes of her companions toward Will, this gesture of aggressively reopening her relationship with such an unconventional man tells much about her independent frame of mind.

Will didn't delay for a second. Back came his reply, addressed to "Dear Old Pal," a salutation more befitting for one of his cowboy buddies. "I sho was glad to hear from you," he wrote, "and it is only a rumor that I dont want to see you right now. . . . Come to Delmar Track this eve if you can. . . . I am working there, send for me when you get to the front and I will come out and take you in. I got your letter five minutes ago Come this eve sho and we will have a time tonight." He signed it "Your Cowboy friend." (Will's speedy reaction to Betty's note indicated he couldn't wait to see her again, said Jim Rogers, Will's son, years later.) The next afternoon, Betty showed up early to catch Will's act. What her eyes also caught, was Will's unorthodox outfit. He was still performing in a gold-braided, red-velvet suit, made especially for him by the Wirth Brothers in Australia, where he had been marketed as a Mexican rope artist. Betty tried to smile in the face of Will's costume, which he had worn to impress her.

It had the opposite effect: She was embarrassed by it. But that didn't deter her from having dinner with him that night. The two then went over to the Irish Village to hear the sweet tenor of Will's friend, John McCormack, who could render a romantic Irish ballad better than anyone in the world.

During the evening, Will made an effort to tell Betty how much he had missed her, despite all evidence to the contrary. The flow of conversation also assured him that Betty had never married. They got along so well that Betty agreed to see Will again the next night.

But there was never an end to Will's bag of surprises. He suddenly cancelled the date, with an apologetic note to Betty. "The Old Man told me he had my fare home for me and I will have to go," he wrote, cryptically. He suggested further that she write to him at his home in Claremore: "Tell me where your address is please for I want to write to you, *see* I am sorry I wont get to see you."

With any other man, Betty probably would have been deeply angered by such irresponsible treatment. Surely, it was a strange way for a fellow to pursue a courtship, if that's what he was doing. When Will worked up the courage to write to her again from Chicago, in October, he was more contrite than ever. Despite everything, she remained receptive.

When Will was in Chicago, to fulfill a one-week engagement, he found out that his act had been cancelled. Unwilling to return immediately to Claremore, Will haunted the local booking offices in the hope that something would pop up. Sure enough, one agent needed a fill-in act and Will ran right over to make it in time for the afternoon performance. There he lassoed a tiny dog that had escaped from an animal act preceding his stint. He filed away the fact that audiences relished the idea of his catching something on stage. He knew now that he would have to find a small, manageable horse or pony that could be roped during his act.

One of Will's letters to Betty, in which he appeared to be searching for redemption as well as a wife, was on the lugubrious side. He told her that he didn't care for Chicago; that things were on "the Bum down home. . . . I didn't do a thing down there this trip"; and he reiterated that "I was offul sorry I could not keep my promise that day" [referring to the broken date]. He went on to give an unsubtle hint that Betty should take him seriously as a partner for life:

> I only seen you a minute and then only found out you were not married. . . .
> You know according to form we both should have matrimonied a long time ago. It wouldnt do to look at our *teeth* you know. If you are contracted for or have a steady fellow, why please put me down and out in the last round. But if not then please file my application. . . . They will tell you at home now that I am a girl hater, shows what they know about it. . . . I could just love a girl about your caliber. See you know I was always kinda headstrong about you anyway . . . but I always thought that a cowboy dident quite come up to your ideal. But I am plum Blue up here and kneed consolation and havent a soul that I can confide in. . . . Please write soon and a long letter. . . .

Betty didn't take kindly to Will's reference to her age (the fact that she should have married a "long time ago"). At the age of twenty-five, she was actually a few weeks older than Will. Like many women of her era—or any era, for that matter—she was quite sensitive about such speculations about her age. Will apologized in a later letter (the poor fellow was always apologizing to Betty for something or other) about his insensitivity.

"I am deeply grieved to think that I was so unthoughtful as to refer to something that you could in the least get offended at but it was all a joke meaning we both should of married each other or somebody by now," he wrote.

In short, things were not progressing satisfactorily in Will's campaign to win Betty as his bride. At this stage there simply wasn't any compelling reason for Betty to succumb to the clefts in Will's tanned cheeks, to his slow-motion Oklahoma drawl, or to his uncertain future. Accustomed to going with beaux who might have promising careers in law, in politics, or on the railroads, Betty had not yet fallen for Will's reassurances that he could make a good living out of vaudeville.

In another letter, Will tried to calm Betty's fears that she was dealing with a drifter or a "bad fellow." He emphasized that he wasn't taking a cent from his father and he threw in another reason for her to accept him: "I have done some good. I have spent it on other people."

During the last days of the fair, Will won a ribbon for his roping and made certain to inform Betty about it. When he returned to Claremore for Thanksgiving, he had her on his mind, though he knew there would be lots of fun and partying, even without her. His long letters to Betty beseeched her to reply in kind. Upset at how "chilly" one of her letters sounded, he kiddingly warned that when she wrote, she should take care that "it is not one that I will have to take my overcoat to read."

At the Thanksgiving party, Will dressed up as a Simple Simon or Hobo, not the most felicitous character to portray, for many in the Indian Territory had long regarded him in that light. Will was aware of how these people perceived him, but he "turned himself loose" in the part anyway. He also wanted Betty to come to Claremore for Christmas, offering her a "nice little rope" if she would come. She didn't.

If his affair of the heart wasn't panning out well, Will was still able to concentrate on his roping. There were few days when he wasn't rehearsing new routines and techniques. He experimented constantly with his lariats, to the point of monotony. It was hard, repetitious work: All the complex as well as simpler things had to be refined. Much of the time, he rehearsed with Teddy, a pony named after Theodore Roosevelt; he had bought it from Colonel Mulhall's wife.

By now Mulhall had been acquitted, after having been found guilty of assault with intent to kill; at his second trial, Will was in court for the proceedings, to lend moral support to his good friend.

In March 1905, Will was invited by the Tulsa Commercial Club to join an entourage of 100 business-promoting Tulsans on a trip through Missouri, Iowa, Illinois, and Indiana. A sixteen-piece band accompanied the troupe on its trip through the midwestern towns—and the barnstormers made sure they didn't miss many. Will's role was much like that of a triple-threat football player: He played in the band, strutted through the streets, performed his rope act, and talked up a storm, whether he was onstage or chatting with bystanders. Gaining confidence, dollars, and newspaper kudos, Will turned out to be the most solid business investment Tulsa had made in years. One local newspaper hailed him for giving an excellent exhibition of "rope-throwing that won the plaudits and admiration of the crowds."

At this stage the resilient Mulhall popped up again in Will's life. In putting together another version of his Wild West show, Mulhall wanted Will as his featured roper, at twenty dollars a week. This time, Colonel Mulhall's men (and his daughter) were not going to play St. Louis, Tulsa, or Des Moines. Rather, they were being booked into Madison Square Garden in New York City, which was becoming the unchallenged mecca of show business.

On the way to the New York cowboy carnival (which was dove-tailed with the prestigious New York Horse Show), Will and his friend, Jim Minnick, another member of Mulhall's troupe, stopped off in Washington, D.C. Mulhall had wangled an invitation to the White House for the two performers, who wanted to show off their tricks to President Roosevelt. Since the president was away on a speaking engagement, Will and Jim had to settle for President Teddy's kids. This they did, with eagerness, Will exhibiting his ropejumping to the children, while also finding time to strike up a relationship with Teddy Jr., then in his teens. Will didn't dream at that moment that someday he would return to the White House to spend a night there. But he was getting to appreciate the unlimited opportunities in America, a place where strange things often happen.

On April 27, 1905, Will, wearing his full cowboy regalia, made his first appearance at Madison Square Garden. Will had been in New York twice before, once with a stable of horses that were being auctioned off, and the other time, on a stopover before he set off for England by boat. He knew by this time that he wanted show business as a career, but there were still uncertainties in his mind about audience response to his chatty comments. Did the people laugh *at* him or with him? He also wasn't sure that what came out of his mouth was as important to his act as his horse or his rope.

Since Mulhall received one thousand dollars a day, out of which he paid salaries and expenses, there was plenty of money to go around for food and drink—and, generally, it was spent unwisely. The show's cast included Tom Mix, who often shared a hotel room with Will. They also did their share of hell-raising together, although Will was not much at raising a glass. The two also were on a Mulhall polo team playing against a group of New York locals, the first such sports experience for Will—who later developed an appetite for polo. Considering Will's roots, polo was not exactly the sport one would have expected him to adopt—but it did have to do with horses and that was enough for him. In later years, Will maintained that people were wrong if they thought "riding a horse is all there is to polo." These same people, he said, think that anybody who can walk can make a good golfer, or anybody that looks good in a bathing suit can make a good swimmer.

While they were in New York, Mulhall's crew was insistent on fulfilling the stereotypes that Manhattanites had about rough-talking, cow-punching west erners. For one thing, the cowboys proved they could handle their horses far better than they commanded their automobiles. Author Fred Gipson has related that they drove their automobiles while dead drunk, "whooping like prairie wolves at a kill."

Buffalo Bill's boys had visited the city before, but they were not as authen tic as Mulhall's men, who combined wild-horse riding with Will's expert roping and mock gun battles. "Effete" easterners gasped in amazement at such make-believe. Such events rarely happened that way in the old West, but in the entertainment field they were permissible exaggerations. The same thing applied to the show's program notes, which stated Will was a full-blooded Cherokee Indian, educated at Notre Dame!

One event that *wasn't* staged by Mulhall—or by Will—turned out to be the highlight of the carnival. Several days after the show opened, Lucille Mulhall was roping one afternoon and being softly accompanied by the Seventh Regiment Band. Suddenly an eight-hundred-pound steer—with a horn spread of five feet—that she had been trying to snare, jumped a protective fence. As the crowd of five thousand screamed and panicked, the crazed animal headed for the upstairs balcony, even as Colonel Mulhall yelled at Lucille to "follow that baby and bring it back!" This was not part of the act—but every cowboy on hand went in pursuit of the steer. One of them managed to lasso an usher.

Then, along came the conquering hero, Will himself. He chased the steer into a corner and dropped a rope around its horns. He hung on for dear life as the rampaging animal pulled him downstairs, over the seats, past any customers imprudent enough to remain on the premises. At last, a half dozen of the cowboys lassoed the steer, putting an end to the unscheduled ruckus.

Newspaper versions of the episode differed markedly, one even remarking that Will had let go of the beast. This account had Will quipping to a police officer, "What are you going to do with it when you catch it?" Another version gave several people credit, including Mix and Jim Minnick, for subduing the animal. It was natural for Will to show a preference for the story carried by the New York *Herald,* which named him as the cowboy who had played the signal role. "The Indian Will Rogers . . . headed the steer off," the paper pointed out. A subhead added that Will's "quickness had prevented any harm."

Will made sure to write home about the adventure, also sending an accompanying letter to the *Claremore Progress.* In no mood to feign humility, he gloated: "I made the biggest hit here I ever dreamed of in my Roping act and finished my good luck by catching the wild steer that went clear up in the dress circles of the garden among the people." There was no press agent in Will's life, yet he instinctively knew what a man must do to get ahead in show business.

7

Vaudeville Days

ecked out in his fringed buckskin and carefully manicured whiskers, William F. Cody, better known as Buffalo Bill, was able to cash in on his many adventures with the Pony Express, the bison herds, and the Indians, by going on the stage in 1878. Out in the open, underneath the vast western sky, he had been in total command, but indoors he was something else. By any normal theatrical standards, he was mediocre, delivering his lines much in the manner of a tongue-tied schoolboy.

The New York Times described him as being "ridiculous as an actor," while the *Chicago Tribune* wrote that nothing ever seen before on the boards was as awful as his emoting.

Yet Will Rogers owed a great deal to the old scout and Indian fighter. Without being aware of it, Buffalo Bill and other horse-happy men of the West helped to create a new style of entertainment that evolved into Will's rambling observations and calculated diffidence.

By the time that Will's participation in Mulhall's show in New York ended, he had arrived at a watershed: He would remain in town, at the Putnam House, for fifty cents a night, and pursue his career on the stage in vaudeville.

That meant trying to make it without being supported by a loud, brawling Wild West show, now becoming passé on the American scene.

American vaudeville (the origin of the term is obscure, though it is said it was derived from one Oliver Bassel, who sang songs in a French town named Vau-de-Vire, later corrupted to Vaux-de-Ville) was born in the early 1880s, with the advent of Tony Pastor's show at the Bowery Opera House in New York. At one time, Pastor booked acts into his beer hall that were conspicuously vulgar. However, he figured that if he cleaned up his act he would attract a more "decent" clientele. The soaped-up version, with a blend of coon songs, ballads, and stale jokes, was not far removed from the English variety show or the American minstrel show.

Pastor's show also borrowed from the traveling museums, with its assortment of freaks, first displayed to the public by Phineas T. Barnum, the preeminent showman of his era. When Barnum put together his *Greatest Show on Earth* under a circus tent, he was pursued by imitators. These circuses featured everything from sword swallowers to talking dogs, and drew mostly on audiences outside the big cities.

Entering into popular entertainment, Florenz Ziegfeld Jr., brought strongman Eugene Sandow from Konigsberg, Germany, to Chicago in 1893. Exhibiting his astonishing biceps, Sandow was paid over five hundred dollars a week by Ziegfeld in what was then billed as "the greatest vaudeville performance ever offered in America."

From such muscular beginnings, a higher class of people came to accept vaudeville, no longer choosing to scorn it as risqué and shoddy stuff. Properly gauging public taste, Ziegfeld worked to overcome the stigma that had previously been attached to those attending music halls.

His trademark became the lavish, expensive show that exploited big staircases and big stars. But the usual run of vaudeville was considerably less pretentious. Generally, it consisted of an olio—an eight-act mixture of specialty numbers, comics, ventriloquists, contortionists, soft-shoe dancers, acrobats, skits, songs, magic, blackface comedians, and brother-and-sister combines, all totally unrelated, with each selection being limited to about twenty minutes. Indeed a gallimaufry of entertainment, it was without any precise focus.

Earlier, an itinerant circus performer, Benjamin Franklin Keith had given vaudeville its biggest push. Tired of moving from town to town, commanding a wagonload of freaks and animals, Keith transformed a deserted candy store in Boston into the Gaiety Museum in 1883. As a chief lure for the customers, he displayed a stuffed mermaid and a one-and-a-half-pound midget named Baby Alice. When the crowds started to come, Keith expanded his program to include a tattooed sailor, a chicken with a human face, and a singer with three heads. In time, Keith added the dialect comedians Joe Weber and Lew Fields.

The defining element in Keith's successful promotion was that under no circumstances would there be any smut on his stage, a decision made in deference to Boston's bluenose hierarchy. The policy won Keith's organization the nickname—"the Sunday school circuit."

Seeking new worlds to conquer, Keith joined with Edward F. Albee in 1885 in staging Gilbert and Sullivan operettas, which had been enormously popular in Great Britain. Surprisingly, Gilbert and Sullivan caught on in America, enabling Keith and Albee to purchase a number of real-estate plots around the country. These were then turned into the largest chain of theatres in the world, with venues in Boston, Philadelphia, Providence, New York, and almost any other place where the population was over a hundred thousand.

Within a few years the Keith-Albee chain, featuring pristine entertainment, had a virtual monopoly on vaudeville in the United States. They tried to create a stranglehold on the business by also booking acts into their vaudeville houses.

Competitors soon sprang up, challenging the supremacy of Keith-Albee. One such player in the game was Alex Pantages. Another was William Hammerstein, who ran the Victoria Music Hall and Theatre in New York, at the corner of Forty-second Street and Broadway. At the Music Hall, for only a half-dollar, one could enjoy the theatrical performance and the smoking room, play a little billiards, or nurse a snack and coffee on the roof garden. Hammerstein's theatre came to be recognized as the true mecca of the world of vaudeville. Indeed, Will spoke of it often as the greatest theatre of all time—any self-respecting performer would have given his eyeteeth to play there. Many of the greats headlined at the Victoria, including Maurice Barrymore; the four Cohans, headed by George M. himself; David Warfield; Nazimova; Lenore Ulric; Harry Houdini; Ed Wynn; and Eva Tanguay. The Victoria didn't close down until 1915, a certifiably long run for a show-business operation.

This was the world in which Will now scrambled for his place in the sun. In his back pocket he carried his credentials, including his job recommendations and the newspapers' rave reviews that he had collected from his appearances in Mulhall's New York show. Day after day, while living in a tiny apartment on New York's West Side, he haunted the United Booking Office, his passage to a seductive and difficult arena. His hungry pony, Comanche, also had to be boarded and fed, and Will was never one to neglect his animal friends. Reluctantly, he sold his old pal to a buyer in New York, who, in turn, sold Comanche to Mulhall. Will turned around and bought a pony from Mulhall, one that was younger than Comanche and better adapted for work on the stage, or so Will felt.

In his letters to his family, Will remained adamant about his choice for the future. On June 3, 1905, he wrote to one of his sisters: "Here is good news for you all, it is either stage and make a good living or no show business *at all* for me, never to the Wild West show any more."

Will knew that the life that he had charted for himself would be hard and unpredictable. He was also aware of the prevailing attitudes about performers like himself. More than a few people regarded itinerant actors not only as morally suspect, but as a group that was knee-high on the ladder of social acceptance.

However, there *was* an aura of mystery and romance to the life of vaude-villians. But it was a glamorous camouflage far removed from reality. Being on the road, with its broken-down, fly-trap hotels, inferior food, lure of available women, and grueling schedules, could weaken the resolve of even the hard-iest constitution. Hard mattresses and the autocratic temperaments of em-ployers didn't help much, either. A man's discipline and character could be sorely challenged.

Will's country-bumpkin background should have kept him off the stage in the turbulent, corrupt big city. But he also had his rope and his horse and he was convinced that this would attract the normally jaundiced and mercurial audiences. After all, people were getting weary of those baggy-pants comics and jokes that were growing long whiskers.

A month of futile waiting at the United Booking Office could be enough to dim anyone's enthusiasm. But just as the composers of inspirational show-business tales would have it, Will at last got his break when a friendly face at the agency informed him that there might be a job at the "supper show" at Keith's Union Square Theatre. There was no way of knowing whether the booker was intrigued by the story of Will's heroics at Madison Square Gar-den, or, more likely, just wanted to get rid of the guy. But there it was—a job for the week of June 12. Of course, Will would be performing between six and eight in the evening, about the worst time slot in show business. He openly speculated that nobody who had a home or a place to eat would be in the theatre during those hours. But making seventy-five dollars a week, the most he had ever received, Will showed up, and so did some patrons. His act came on fifth in the pecking order and was called, in rather a demeaning reference, an "Extra Act," though his actual billing, "The World's Champion Lasso Manipulator," was more promising.

Dressed in chaps, a red shirt, a sombrero, and spurs, Will played with the lariat "as if to the manor born," glowed the *Boston Herald*. "Rogers and his bronco are typical of the plains and both do clever stunts; . . . he does some exceedingly clever lassoing with a rope of marvelous length . . . and the bronco, you expect every moment to butt through the scenery or jump into the orchestra circle, but he's really a well-behaved horse." Will agreed whole-heartedly with the newspaper critics. "My act was a hit from the start," he wrote to the "gang" at home, "and my pony is a peach."

A 5 percent commission had to be paid to the Keith combine, Will's agent received a small percentage, and the "well-behaved" Teddy had to be fed his oats and provided with housing. But none of this concerned Will, for he was on his way. A few days after playing at the Union Square Theatre, he was signed to a contract by one of Keith's fiercest competitors, Hammerstein's Paradise Roof at the Victoria. Will received $140 a week to play there— indisputably the grandest showplace in America. Will was an overnight hit among Willie Hammerstein's usual array of freaks and celebrities. Will's chief concern was getting his pony to the roof, about fifteen stories up. "I hope we dont fall off," he said, anticipating a ride with the animal in a heated elevator that Hammerstein had installed.

Will wrote home about the Victoria experience: "It is a great thing to be able to work there. They sent for me too. . . . I dident ask them for the work, if I go good there I am alright and everyone says I will be a hit there. . . . Its just a garden covered over with a sliding glass roof. Keiths was a fine indoor theatre but this has them all beat for the summer."

Will's solo stint was called a "dumb act" because it was not accompanied by any patter or off-the-cuff comments. He would make a splashy entrance, sitting astride Teddy, who was adorned with felt-bottom boots that prevented him from slipping on the stage; on Teddy's back was a saddle blanket, on which Will later embroidered his name in gold letters. Arriving at midstage, Will would jump off Teddy, and pat him on the rump affectionately, a handy signal for the horse to depart the proceedings.

Then the variety of rope tricks began, as the orchestra cranked up a medley of popular cowboy songs. Will's preparation was arduous, even though he made it look like he had been doing this since he was a babe in his crib. When Tom Mix roomed with Will, he couldn't get over the many ropes that were strewn across the floor. "It was like living with a bunch of snakes," he said.

Of course, the act didn't always run the way Will might have planned it. One evening, after a barber act had doused the stage with a slick coating of shaving lather, Teddy slipped and fell, pinning Buck McKee, also in the act, under him. The two were left dangling over the orchestra pit. Going to the rescue, Will tossed a lasso over Teddy's head, freeing Buck. Then the trembling pony was dragged back onstage, as the audience yipped in approval.

"Don't get excited, folks," Will calmly recited, "it's only part of our little act."

Will's repertoire included so many variations that it earned him the nickname "The Lariat King." He hadn't invented the lariat but he sure knew what to do with it. In *The Keith News*, which was published weekly, he won unstinting praise. "A year ago," said the paper, in the fall of 1905, "had anyone foretold that a demonstration of rope-throwing could be made sufficiently interesting and entertaining to attract big crowds, the prediction would have been greeted with smiles of derision. Today, it's an established fact and Will Rogers, who is now drawing a big salary at the leading vaudeville houses, and is admittedly the most popular novelty of the vaudeville season, is the man who has done it."

Combining amazing dexterity and timing, achieved after endless hours of concentration, Will made his ropes do everything but talk. Indeed, Will's roping in the vaudeville arena was remarkably original. He could twirl his rope, usually a ninety-footer, into small loops, or do the merry-go-round, in which he would take a constantly spinning rope, and pass it from his right hand, under his leg, to the other hand, and behind his body, where his right hand would pick it up. He could jump in and out of his spinning rope. He could jump in and out of two loops at the same time. He could perform the Texas Skip, where he would jump back and forth through a vertical loop. He could perform his ineffable Crinoline, in which the big, singing rope sailed in a huge arc over the heads of the audience. He could throw two ropes at once, catching a horse and its rider separately. (Later in his career, he actually roped a mouse with a string, which says a good deal about how he had honed his skills.)

To show his audience how long his rope was, Will assigned an usher to walk up the center aisle with the rope, while he held on to the other end onstage. The reaction to Will's act was generally positive. But he wasn't certain about how to handle it. When his performance was over, he'd usually walk off the stage without acknowledging the crowd. After one of his Victoria shows, a fellow actor pulled him aside and suggested that he take curtain calls: "You know, there's damned few of them, so take advantage of it."

Others encouraged Will to say a word or two, to break the silence of his "dumb act." But he wasn't certain that his slow-moving twang would provoke a favorable response, so he began to try talking just a bit, hesitatingly at first, then with more regularity.

One evening, Will stopped the orchestra, raised his eyes from the ground, and announced to the audience what he planned to do: "I'm gonna call your attention in this act to somethin' worth lookin' at and that's to catch both horse and rider at one and the same time." He paused nervously, then continued: "I don't have any idea that I'll get it but anyway, here goes!"

The audience reacted with laughter, throwing Will for a loop, so to speak. Instead of feeling a sense of triumph, the poor fellow was puzzled. He didn't realize that the laughter was essentially supportive. However, he had learned that integrating a few remarks into his act could prove helpful. If that's what these folks wanted, he would give them more of it, by degrees.

So on another day he tried again to entice a response. Swinging his rope, Will volunteered that "this is easier to do on a blind horse, 'cause they don't see the rope comin'." Again, he got laughs. Now the words came more easily. Could it be that he would be better off preparing comments ahead of time? Did he plan in advance to walk over to the sign bearing his name and stick a wad of gum over the letter W on his name, after he'd missed with his rope? Did he plot ahead to say, "I'm handicapped up here, 'cuz the manager won't let me swear when I miss."

In this matter of coloring up the act with talk, Will invariably underlined his mistakes. Was this an understandable strategy to explain the frequent misses that were bound to occur? Was it a carefully crafted appeal?

Suddenly, Will was in demand almost everyplace on the far-flung Keith circuit. By the end of 1905, he had taken his act to Boston, Philadelphia, Buffalo, Newark, Toledo, Detroit, Rochester, Washington, Providence, Syracuse, Worcester and Lowell (Massachusetts), Pittsburgh, Baltimore, and other way stations. Some of the stops were abbreviated, as short as two or three days, others were for a week or longer. But wherever his legs carried him and his horse, the critics were kind. In Syracuse, for example, the *Herald* wrote that Will's act was "one of the few to play a return date. . . . Last season the act created more talk than any feature of the year."

As a result of all this activity, Will hired himself a new agent, Mort Shea, who wasn't shy about booking Will in every spot that would have him—usually for sums ranging from $150 to $250 a week. Just about every town in which he played, Will was hailed for his "plainsman talk" and for his virtuosity. One critic observed, quite rightly, that Will seemed to get as much enjoyment out of his work as his audience did.

At the same time, Will's letter writing continued at its usual frenetic pace. Now he kept on sending cash sums of $100, $115, $175, and $125 to his father, supposedly so that Clem could save up enough money to bring Will home. But there was always the suspicion that Will was engaged in a little game of ego boosting. He wanted Clem to spread the word, in the Indian Territory, that his prodigal son was making a wad of money, certainly more than anyone, including Clem, thought he was ever capable of making. It would give the tough old man bragging rights. But what it *didn't* do was coax Clem to write back to tell Will how proud he was of his boy.

Even as late as September 1905, Will hinted in his letters about coming home for good. He was on the verge, he said, of getting a "bunch of cows and getting back on the farm."

His brittle, off-again, on-again relationship with Betty Blake, on hold for so long, was reignited by letters that Will sent to her and she to him. In October 1905, he wrote to her from Detroit:

My dear old pal . . . Betty I got your *plum* good letter yesterday and I dident know what to make of it. You are away past the limit, I know it is foolish of me to write to you but I just cant help it and sometime when you dont hear from old Bill it wont be because he is mad or is fascinated with some other but only because he is at least able to abide by his own judgment. You know Betty old pal I have always had about what I wanted and it breaks my heart when I think I'll never get it. I am ordinarily a good loser but I guess my nerve is fooling me at this trip. . . . I dont know how long I will stay at this, I might leave any day and go back to the ranch. I have made a success and thats all I wanted to do.

At Christmastime, Will was still on the road, despite suggestions in his letter that he was about to give up vaudeville and go back to Claremore. In touch again with Betty during the holiday period, he wrote to her that she was the "one best fellow" in his life. He followed that up by sending her a handsome lace handkerchief—"fine work done by the Paraguay Indians in South America"—as a token of his feelings for her. The old Indian lady who had sold him the handkerchief said that a man gives such a thing to the woman he is going to marry. Will claimed he had carried the handkerchief all around Africa, even when he was dead broke—but he always hoped to do as the old lady said.

"I guess theres nothing doing there for me, I will jus give it to you as I kinder prize it," wrote Will. When Betty didn't write to him, Will fretted. When she did write, usually only brief notes, he fretted even more.

Will was generous to a fault with Clem, the aggrieved patriarch, while Clem remained ungenerous and cold toward him. Clem, for instance, never sent a single receipt to Will for all the cash that was sent home to him. When Will sent Papa an expensive overcoat as a Christmas present, Clem refused to wear it, on the grounds that it didn't fit him. Clem promptly sent it back to his son. Reba Collins, the director of the Will Rogers Memorial, interpreted Clem's hostile reaction as his way of "putting Willie in his place." The next thing that Will's friends noticed was that he was wearing the coat himself.

Will constantly tinkered with his act. Sometimes there were new routines; sometimes, new comments. He added a fellow named Fred Tejan, whose mission was to sit out front and emit timely roars at Will's remarks. The audience usually followed suit.

Arriving in a new town, Will would walk down the main street in the direction of the theatre, leading his horse, who carried a sign heralding "Will Rogers, The Lariat King." Invariably, the children in the neighborhood would follow Will down the street. He had taken on the role of a Pied Piper—and didn't mind that at all.

Will continued to have mixed feelings about being a vaudeville gypsy, even though there were many aspects of the life that appealed to him. He liked traveling around; he liked staying in bed in the morning; he liked the money he was making; he liked the freedom to dress as he pleased; he liked having time to read newspapers (as soon as he read one paper, he would pick up another); and, for the most part, he enjoyed the camaraderie of his fellow vaudevillians. Despite all this, his letters continued to be larded with suggestions that he might return home and settle down at the ranch. Sometimes he would say that he really didn't love what he was doing—but that the money was too good for him to quit. Other times, he would contradict himself, saying that acting, roping, and riding onstage had the old farm and ranch "beat hollow."

In 1906, Mort Shea decided to send Will to Europe, where there was a demand for western-style performances. Will wasn't a trailblazer in this regard, for not only were more and more entertainers heading to America from

Europe (one such was Anna Held, who had come from Paris), but a good number of Americans were sailing off to Europe to perform.

But Will knew he needed a rest. So he first chose to take a detour by going from Philadelphia back to Rogers, Arkansas, where he spent a few hours with Betty. He engaged in his peculiar courting style, informing her that he was about to leave for Europe—would she come with him? But she wasn't having any part of such a flighty proposal. He promised to write to her, and she said she would be there to get his letters. From there he went to Claremore for a week, where he made the rounds with his friends. Clem still refused to regard his son as a conquering hero, but there were signs that he had given up trying to persuade Will to stay at home in the Indian Territory.

On March 17, Will set off for Paris and Berlin on the S. S. *Philadelphia*. As usual, his days at sea were full of nausea and illness. But still, he looked forward to the important bookings that Shea had arranged for him, especially in Berlin, where he would play the Winter Garden, then the most prestigious theatre in Europe. He would be there for an entire month, along with Buck and his horse, making over $250 a week.

On his arrival in Paris, Will immediately penned a long letter to Betty. He seemed pleased with himself and his surroundings, and thrilled to be in an atmosphere that was plainly remote from his usual moorings.

"Polly vue Francaise," he opened his letter. "I dont know a damned word anybodys saying. But I sho do know that I am in Paree!" What impressed him more than anything else was that Parisians appeared to have more "time to do nothing" than any other folks he had ever encountered in his travels.

"They sit at Cafes and drink at tables right on the sidewalk. . . . I have never seen such a mass of people that are out on the boulevards on a Sunday," he wrote, in amazement. Oddly, what didn't bother him was the discovery that Paris was a "wide-open place, with no laws about morality." Considering that Will hailed from an area where people were suffocated by churchly propriety, this was an unexpected reaction. But it served to point out that in most matters, Will was a profoundly tolerant human being, comfortable in receiving uncomfortable ideas.

However, Will didn't take much to the French women with their "paint and makeup, . . . oh, how they do strut!" This was somewhat balanced by his appreciation of French food, "the best cooked stuff and *Grub* that I ever eat"—with not a plate of his favorite chili in sight!

Then it was on to Berlin. If Will found Paris to be wide-open, that was nothing compared to what he saw in Berlin. "Why," he wrote, "they talk of Gay N.Y., . . . N.Y. sleeps more in one night than Berlin in a week. Honest I havent had my eyes closed while it was dark, what sleeping I have done has been in the day."

Will's persona, redolent of the Old West, was perceived kindly by most of the Germans and by the German press. They figured this strange fellow in a wild-West costume had stepped straight out of American novels about the frontier. Further, he was greeted cordially on several mornings, as he took an exercise gallop with his horse in a park near the Winter Garden. The greeter, also on horseback, was a man with a luxuriously curled mustache and a ramrod military bearing—Kaiser Wilhelm, as it turned out. Not certain at first who the gentleman was, Will learned soon enough. "He is a dandy good fellow," wrote Will, proud that he had made his acquaintance.

During the time Will had been in South Africa, he had shown a preference for the Boers over the British. In many ways the Boers were not unlike the Germans in manner and attitude. However, despite the generally good reception that Will received in Berlin, he soon became disaffected toward the Germans.

While performing his act one night, Will noted a person staring at the proceedings from the wings. The man—a civil servant—seemed to be disapproving of Will's act (Will's sensitivity to such matters had sharpened over time). On the spur of the moment, Will flung his rope over the fellow's head and dragged him to the footlights, causing the audience to boil over with anger. Failing to consider that many Germans lacked a sense of humor, Will almost got himself thrown into jail for his innocent behavior.

Another incident—at the Berlin railroad station—firmed up his hostility against the Germans. He was sternly reprimanded by a porter, who had discovered part of Will's shirt sticking out of one of his bags. The employee told him that such an infraction would prevent the bag from being checked through to Leipzig, where Will was next scheduled to perform. In the light of such episodes, Will hurriedly decided to leave Germany and move on to England, where he was booked at the Palace for a week.

In London things went swimmingly (always a bad word to use where Will was concerned). As a result, his engagement at the Palace was stretched to a full month. Playing before the "swellest London society people," Will received ecstatic reviews. Such plaudits also got him invited to the Ranelagh Club, which specialized in entertaining British royalty, including Edward VII, who, as the Prince of Wales, had earned a reputation as a womanizer.

Will's letters to Betty, addressing her as "My Dearest Girl" and "My Own Sweetheart," were full of pride in himself and his act, but still, there were continual comments about his "coming home." He talked of playing on the same bill with such favorites as Eltinge (whose repertoire featured feminine mimickry)—but the underlying note of homesickness intruded as a recurrent theme. Invariably, the letters were filled with words of endearment, but they became elegiac when he discussed Claremore and his old friends. And oddly, the warmth that radiated toward Betty in his writings was never duplicated when he was around her—in essence, his courtship worked better through the mail than in person.

By June 1906, his body and mind needed another interruption from the frenzy of his vaudeville commitments. So he planned to return to the United States by way of Rome, where he stayed at the Grand Hotel Continental; he then went on to Naples and, from there, he booked a first-class passage for New York. He had no plans to stay in New York, for he had been away from home for a year and wanted to get back to Claremore as soon as possible.

When Will arrived in Claremore, his sister, Maud, aware that Will had continued his long-distance courtship, invited Betty to be with them at Chelsea. A house party was put together, primarily for greeting Will, and Betty came in by train to join them. After all the months of impassioned letters that had zipped back and forth like Ping-Pong balls, the two were ill at ease when they finally confronted each other. One account has it that when Will took the train to Vinita to accompany Betty, on her way to Chelsea, he found her seated with "some stranger." Unable to sit next to her, Will went into a pique that caused him to retreat from her company.

When the two got to the home of Cap Lane, where the party was being held, Will spent most of the time talking, clowning, joking, and singing around the piano—but *not* with Betty. He never spent a moment alone with her. It was a curious way to win this young woman, who must have been puzzled by his remoteness. "I just could not understand him," she said.

At this point their relationship was foundering because of his shyness and seeming indifference when he was with her, and because of her own negative attitude about the life he was pursuing. In addition, Will expressed jealousy about any man that Betty was seeing—and she was never without boyfriends; this rankled him, especially her occasional relationship with Tom Harvey. Betty was equally annoyed with Will's professed interest in other women. He even volunteered that once he had gone "plum nutty" over an "actorine." Such a confession could not sit well with her.

After Will's remoteness at the Cap Lane party, Betty returned to Rogers, Arkansas, convinced that she'd never be a lifetime partner of this man. She hardly expected, only a week later, to find Will perched on her doorstep, imploring her to marry him. Once again, she informed him she could not tolerate the wandering, uncertain life that he had chosen. He reminded her of how well he was doing, while she kept telling him his life was not a stable one in which they could raise a family.

Her turndown caused Will to again make other plans for his future. He was booked solidly for the remainder of the winter, at $200 a week, sometimes more, on the Keith circuit. But as soon as he hit the road again, the letters from him poured forth. In October 1906, addressing her as "My Own Dear Betty," Will wrote that "I was as good as could be . . . and not for a minute did I forget you or never shall for you are mine and you know I am yours. . . . You will find me the most persistent lover you ever saw. . . . I just cant help it Dearie. . . . My plans are in your hands, shape them to suit yourself."

A month later, he resorted to reminding Betty of her age, a tactic that hadn't succeeded well in the past: "You wont tell me how old you are, *not even me,* why I dont care if you are a century plant. . . . You are no lemon in my estimation."

In December 1906, he wrote, on the letterhead of the Hippodrome (in New York), that he wanted to be in New York around the Christmas season, so that he could haunt the "big shops" in order to buy her a coat and muff as a "little Xmas remembrance."

By the spring of 1907, apparently forsaking his effort to nail down his marriage with Betty, Will headed off to England, remembering that he had been so well received there not long ago. This time he took Buck McKee and two other riders with him in order "to show 'em riding that was riding." But Will's last-minute plans didn't work out too well: There were entirely too many horses in the act and not enough of just plain Will. This was a lesson that he filed away for future consideration. The show was also costly to mount and Will was obliged to take his troupe on a tour outside London in order to earn enough money to bring everyone home.

8

Will Marries Betty

he British tour wasn't the only thing that went bust in 1907. Overextended credit, the issuance of valueless stock, and a run on the banks caused the American Panic of 1907, helping to widen the gap between rich and poor in the country. Indeed, the political gap between Will's White House buddy, Teddy Roosevelt, and the powerful eastern financial interests widened, too. Mr. Roosevelt denied having said that "every captain of industry should be behind bars," but few people found his denial credible.

The panic had a numbing effect on business, in general, which meant smaller crowds were turning out to watch vaudevillians like Will. It was, naturally, more difficult to get good bookings. Upon his return to the United States in June, Will found the rocky road of vaudeville more precarious than ever. Even the bidding war between the Keith combine and a new chain, run by Marc Klaw and A. L. Erlanger, failed to help Will: He still struggled to make $300 a week, even as others benefited from the heated competition in the business.

Other historic events in 1907 also had an impact on Will's life. On November 16, Oklahoma finally entered the Union as the forty-sixth state. For years

Clem had been working diligently, using his time, energy, and influence in Washington and the Indian Territory to bring about this result. While statehood brought immense satisfaction to Clem, it had never been the focus of Will's interest. His tepid relationship with Clem precluded his sharing an involvement with his father in the politics of the territory. Making a living as a vaudevillian and snaring Betty were projects that had been enough to occupy his attention.

Earlier in 1907, a more important development, as far as Will was concerned, was the staging of the first *Ziegfeld Follies* in New York, from June 8 to September 14. Ziegfeld, the Chicago theatrical producer, whose personal card read "Impresario Extraordinaire," had won a reputation for his popular vaudeville shows, in conjunction with Erlanger and Klaw, at New York's Jardin de Paris. Included in his splashy promotions were two itinerant entertainers— W. C. Fields, the juggler whose act had been caught by Will in South Africa; and Charlie Chaplin, a talented Londoner with a drunk act. However, neither Fields nor Chaplin appeared in Ziegfeld's inaugural *Follies,* which took its name from a newspaper column called "Follies of the Day." Emma Carus, the principal singer in the *Follies* of 1907, introduced, several years later, songwriter Irving Berlin's smash hit, "Alexander's Ragtime Band."

In the baseball World Series of 1907, the Chicago Cubs overwhelmed the Detroit Tigers in a four-game sweep, despite the presence in Detroit's lineup of the wretched but brilliant Ty Cobb. The Cubs, guided by their manager, Frank Chance, were led by the legendary infield of Joe Tinker-to-Johnny Evers-to-Chance, immortalized in verse by F. P. Adams.

By this time, Will had become an enthusiastic baseball fan. When he had the opportunity on lazy, sunny afternoons in cities around the big-league circuit—New York, Chicago, Pittsburgh, Philadelphia, St. Louis, Cincinnati, Boston—he took himself out to the ballpark, where he cheered for his baseball buddies. Ballplayers were not unlike the traveling minstrels of vaudeville. They shared a low-level reputation with actors and often were not welcome in the better caravansaries. Like vaudevillians, many drank to excess, slept late, and ate cheap meals. They also played their ball games around three in the afternoon, giving them a chance to visit the theatres in the evening. (Some ballplayers even shared Will's passion for lassoing—a future Hall of Fame outfielder, Harry Hooper, was a hearty practitioner of the art as a youth in California.)

Since Will was a skillful, athletic person, whose act required many of the physical credentials that ballplayers possessed, he not only followed the game closely, but he was adept at it. When he had time to work out in the big-league parks before games, he often shagged flies in the outfield or took infield grounders. Those players familiar with his roping act were delighted to have him on hand. Will probably developed his gum-chewing habits while in the company of ballplayers, to whom chewing and spitting were as natural as breathing. Will's involvement with baseball was a constant in his life and he numbered many icons of the game among his friends and acquaintances.

The only sport that didn't appeal much to him was tennis, which he may have considered an effete pastime. Later, when Helen Wills was the outstanding woman player in the world, Will was invited to watch her play at Forest Hills, then the showplace of the sport. Will begged off, sourly. "I'd rather go to my stables to look at my horses," he shrugged.

Constantly looking for work, perhaps as a means of escaping other work, Will, was still in a quandary. He was as good as any man alive with his rope; he was able to get decent employment, even in a bad economic period; he loved the restless camaraderie of the vaudeville circuit; and he was winning laudatory notices almost everywhere, including *Variety,* the show-business mouthpiece. But his life was marred by his long-running failure to make proper connections with Betty.

He told her in a letter that his never-ending travel itinerary was becoming an assault on him. Although he had a strong physical constitution, he inevitably suffered from fatigue. When he did, he'd express dissatisfaction with the life he led. "Maybe," said Betty, "he's coming around to my way of thinking." But Will's occasional mutterings on this subject were the exceptions, not the rule.

Late in the year, Will went back home for a brief visit to see how Clem was faring. There had been periods of ill health for the tough old man, and Will was concerned. While he was home, he contacted Betty and spent some time with her. But instead of pressing his case, he soon rushed off to Philadelphia, where he hoped to continue in a role that he had briefly done in Chicago. It was in a George Lederer production called *The Girl Rangers,* with three acts and five scenes. Will twirled his rope for fifteen minutes as the "Cowboy who has astonished the world with his lasso." The reviews, as usual, were kind to him, employing words like "deliciously witty" to describe his patter. Despite Will's artistry, *Rangers* folded.

Now it was back to the maddening correspondence, an integral part of

Will's daily existence. He spent almost as much time composing and scrawling his rambling, ungrammatical letters, to an often unreceptive Betty, as he did conjuring up original wrinkles for his act. His mood was interchangeably petulant, angry, contrite, and excessively candid. Always, it seemed, he operated out of the knowledge that Betty did not regard him as any sort of great catch, and that neither did her friends nor family.

But he refused to let up, even going so far as to remind Betty that he had relationships with other women. Once he admitted that he wasn't "treating her right"; at other times, he announced that they would both be bound to regret not getting married to each other. Betty, on the other hand, chose never to be forthcoming about other dates or pursuers that were involved in her life. Tom Harvey remained a bête noire to Will—but Betty did not discuss him in her letters. She just point-blank refused to discuss such intimate matters with Will, never exercising the right of equivalency, which she could have done.

Will advanced the proposition that it was only "natural" for him to go out with other women—"the other kind"—for physical reasons. But he underlined the fact that he would never care to marry one of *them*.

At the beginning of 1908, writing from Hamilton, Ontario ("it is some chilly here"), Will mildly chided Betty: "I hope you was a good girl on this trip, and did not make any new mashes and you are still heart free." Then, employing dubious judgment, Will took a letter that he had received from another girl friend, Mamie, and enclosed it in an envelope that he sent along to Betty. This letter was filled with references to Will as "my darling old Kid." It's not hard to imagine Betty's fury when she read it.

From Worcester, Massachusetts, Will wrote snidely in February about Betty "*snaring a promising* lawyer" for herself: "What all did he promise you and you him. . . . Now you better slack up on that *stuff* for it gets you in bad and I will bet getting pretty *sore* some time. . . . You know how jealous I am and what a lot you have to tell me when I see you . . . am still a bit leary on just how you stand and if you dont tell me about these things . . . well I *might find out otherwise*. . . . Now you better deal square with me."

After these warning statements, Will ended by telling Betty how he'd love to see her and, "Oh what a time we would have . . . we would never turn in we would have so much to tell each other wouldent we."

When Will got to New Haven in March, he was concerned that his caustic tactics with Betty were yielding poor results. So he wrote a length missive that tried to put his case with less irony and more dignity:

"My Dearest (and that goes)

Well Betty I received your crazy letter and honest it knocked me a *twister*. You could not of been your same old dear self when you wrote it. . . .

Now in the first place if you remember *rightly*, this coolness of which I fully admit started when you refused to tell me of that T. H. thing [a reference to Tom Harvey].

Now you know that and I have always treated you cooly since. Not because I felt like it but because I just felt that I was *getting back* at you. . . . Now *secondly* as to any other girl it is foolish to think of them ever in the same breath with you. . . . I am not ashamed of a thing I ever told you and feel *proud* of it. I thought it showed *manhood*. It only hurt me so bad because you could not trust me with a measly old *love scrape* cause I know that was all. . . . I told you I had always been a *bad boy* and I guess I will continue to be one till you are with me.

Yes I got a lot of girls not one as you say but several *on* and *off* the stage. I dont mean this as *sarcasm* or conceit its just to put you right. And I gave you credit for not being a jealous girl and take a thing that was put in a letter just for a little *sting* the same as you had put me in mine several times the last in regard to the Lawyer. Now I am the jealous one of the two. . . . Now Betty comes the thing in your letter that certainly did *hurt* and I dident think you could accuse me of such. . . . You say, I was idesreet and for that you have never thought well of me, or at least have never believed me and when I refer to other boys, you invariably grow suspiciously *sarcastic* and throw unpleasant insinuations.

Now Betty plainly that's not so and its the worst thing you could say, for all of things I admire and love you for, your being *good* and *pure* and not silly and *spooney*. . . . I know these girls in this business a *little* and I think there is a little difference between you and them. . . . Now Betty I want you to cut out all this foolish talk for when I tell you you are the only girl for me I mean it regardless of how I act sometimes. . . . Your same old boy Billy."

With Clem's health still not robust, Will went home again in late March. Despite the harshness that dominated their relationship, when Will was close enough to home and could help, he did. In his letters to Clem, Will often offered advice—"take your medicine," he said, adopting an avuncular tone— and he expressed his certainty that if his father took good care of himself, he would soon get better.

While he was at home, Will had a chance once more to be with Betty. They engaged in their usual recreations—partying, singing together, visiting friends—and all the while, there was incessant conversation about Will's future. This time, their relationship seemed in good repair. Will outlined the extensive theatrical bookings he had for the remainder of the year, primarily with the Keith people. He reiterated that the money was first-rate, considering that the times were not too good. There would be fifteen weeks at $300 a week and twenty-five weeks at $250 a week, and he told Betty proudly that he would be back at New York's Hammerstein Roof for several weeks. "That's the candy place to work for," he said.

Betty then appeared more amenable to accepting Will for what he was. However, once Will departed on his road odyssey, the old uncertainties rose again in Betty's mind. In June, when Will was in Duluth, Minnesota, he tried to reassure her that the money he was making was just too good for him to consider ever doing anything else. "Certainly, it beats the old farm ranch and store thing," he repeated, probably for the hundredth time. He did admit that it was lonely sometimes. But as for "hating the work and giving it up," that just was not going to happen.

"There's no work in the world as nice and easy as this business when things are going right," he pointed out. Obviously, Betty still objected to what he was doing and how he was doing it, and that included his relations with other women. By this time, her reservations about Will had more to do with her suspicions about his liaisons with girls on the road than with the nature of the vaudeville business.

In the ensuing summer weeks of 1908, Will wrote many long, discursive letters, full of colorful passages about people, the countryside, show business, and other quotidian happenings that less observant correspondents might have easily missed. When he wasn't describing such things, he never missed reporting on the "good money" he was making. At the same time, he never neglected to remind Betty that he wanted to make her his wife. A few times, he spoke about selling off the farm, for about $20,000. "I don't like to do it," he wrote to Clem. But he said he just might. On the other hand, he was darned if he'd accept $17,5000. This translated into a new Will, one who was taking money more seriously than he ever had in the past.

By September, the old acrimony between Will and Betty rose up again, naturally over the other women in Will's helter-skelter life. Judging from the letters Will wrote from the Far West, where he had performed in Wyoming, Idaho, and Washington and had visited places like Yellowstone Park and the Grand "Canon," Betty must have gotten the idea, mistaken or otherwise, that Will was having one helluva time with somebody. She may have distrustfully concluded that when he wrote of being "so alone" and having a "big dining room all to myself," he was protesting too much. He spoke so glowingly of the elk, bear, buffalo, and other wonderful creatures in the Pacific area that poor Betty suspected he was leaving out discussion of female companions. So dark were her suspicions that Will felt compelled to burst forth with a September letter of abject confession, written from Pittsburgh, Pennsylvania.

"Dear, dear Betty," he addressed her now. Then he went on to write a less maundering and more apologetic text than in other recent letters: "Your little note has made me feel terrible. Honest Betty I feel offul. I know you thought from the way I wrote in the last letter that I loved the woman. No you were all wrong. I wrote that way cause I did not want to appear like I was knocking her after all that had happened. . . . Still you are right when you say that I have not treated you square. No I have not Betty. It seems I have not treated any one square. I have *lived* a *lie* and now I am reaping the harvest of it, please make a little allowances for me dear. I am not now myself and seem to have no mind of my own. I am *scared* and do not know what to do Betty. This is all what comes of doing wrong. I done the greatest wrong that any one could do and I have wished and prayed a thousand times since that I had not done it. . . . No I am no man, I am the *weakest* child you ever saw. If you knew me better I am easily led and can be pulled into almost anything. I have to mind of my own. . . . I just drift and drift God knows where too. Now listen dont think of deserting me in all this. I need you and want you and I am hoping that this will soon end and I will be my own self again. . . . Im *bad* dearie all *bad* but I am trying to do better and live better. . . . Write to me girl. . . . Billy."

Betty's response to this letter of self-deprecation is not part of the record. But three weeks later, Will posted a letter from Syracuse, New York, in which he sounded confident that their longtime cross-country relationship would soon culminate in marriage. "I hope you may never regret sticking by a bum like me," he wrote.

Abruptly, Will broke off his vaudeville trek, after performing in Auburn, New York, and Wilkes-Barre, Pennsylvania, and sped home. The sudden visit took everyone by surprise, even catching Betty unaware. A passel of local gossips—some in Betty's family—had one more chance to express their shock and dismay: How could this superior young woman possibly marry such a disreputable fellow, nothing but an Injun vaudeville performer! Will was thoroughly cognizant of this disloyal opposition, writing Betty that "I sho do sympathize with you about now cause I can picture you having *trouble* and a lot of it at that."

But the mean, diminishing words had all been spoken and Betty had made up her mind. One can imagine the joy that engulfed Will when he realized that Betty had resolved at last to be his wife. (Years later, Will's son, Jim, said "that from the first moment that Dad had laid eyes on Betty Blake, he knew she was the only girl for him . . . he told me that." And wherever he went, Will used to tell the world that the day "I roped Betty I did the star performance of my life."

Now, carefully inscribed in Will's engagement book of his travels were the all-important dates: "Nov. 9—Travel Home; Nov. 16—Home; Nov. 23: GETTING MARRIED." After November 23, Will had already marked down the resumption of his career: "Nov. 30—Proctor's, in Newark, New Jersey."

Two days before the wedding date (it was actually Nov. 25, 1908), Will, ever the sentimentalist, took himself to the Oologah railroad depot, where he had first seen Betty Blake. While there, he composed a Western Union telegram, at 6:15 in the evening. It was addressed to Miss Betty Blake in Rogers, Arkansas: "Back to the scenes of our childhood wish you was at this old depot now love. . . . Billy."

Betty's close kin and most of her friends remained aghast at her selection of a mate, but Will's own family and friends breathed a sigh of relief. They liked Betty and admired here, while expressing surprise that Will hadn't brought home one of those typical show-business "bums." Will felt pleased that he had really crossed them up by landing Betty. Of course, there were some friends of Betty's who were not hostile to Will. In fact, a few of them envied her, for she was going to travel all over and get to see those romantic New York shows for free!

Will was a nervous fellow in the days preceding his wedding, more skittish than he'd ever been in standing before audiences. When wedding announcements were printed by the Blake family, Will was in a quandary about which of his friends should receive them. He ended up by resignedly junking the whole project: While waiting at the Chelsea railroad station to take the train to Rogers, for the ceremony, Will frantically sent two telegrams within twelve minutes in order to straighten out the number of the train on which he was traveling.

Wearing his dark traveling suit, Will pointedly informed others not to get "all dressed up" for the event. Whether or not he considered that Betty was obeying his edict—in her blue-and-white silk dress—he didn't say.

When the train from Chelsea arrived a little after 11:30 A.M. in Rogers, Betty's brother was on hand to pick up Will and his family in his buggy. The Blake home, where the wedding was to take place, was just a short distance from the station. Only the two families, as well as several of Betty's friends, were present for the brief ceremony, which started shortly after one o'clock.

Presiding was Reverend J. G. Bailey, a Congregationalist preacher who also doubled as town postmaster. It wasn't by any means a fancy wedding and that suited Will just fine.

The news of the wedding, duly recorded in several paragraphs in the Rogers paper, cited the fact that Betty had attractive personal qualities, as well as being "one of the best known young ladies in Northwest Arkansas." The last paragraph read: "Following the wedding Mr. Rogers and his bride left on the North-bound train for St. Louis, en route to New York City, where he is a prominent figure on the vaudeville stage."

Not long after the wedding, the New York Morning Telegraph caught up with the news: "Well, well. Will Rogers, the well-known Western Boy in Vaudeville, has gone and done it. Got married on the sly. The lucky girl proved to be none other than his sweetheart in the West."

Obviously, if he could rate the big-city press, with news of his removal from the bachelor ranks, Will had truly arrived on the social scene.

The wedding had been a private affair. But when Will and Betty arrived at the station on their way to St. Louis, they were met with stares, cheers, and rice from many of the townspeople who had come to see the newlyweds off.

Will felt good about being able to reserve a stateroom for his bride. Now he had a chance to prove to her that his universe wasn't as bad as it was cracked up to be by the naysayers. In reality, it was pleasant—and Betty soon had to admit that that was the case, as she moved away, by degrees, from her conventional background. A trip to New York or Chicago, a few years after the turn of the century, was an event for women of her ilk. Except for the very rich and those in precarious health, winter holidays were a rarity. No longer could anyone consider Betty some kind of a "bird in a gilded cage."

The couple stayed at the elegant Planters Hotel in St. Louis. But before they could celebrate in their room, Will, ever the sports fan, pulled his bride off to watch Washington University play the Carlisle Indians (of Pennsylvania), a football team that had become famous due to the exertions of its all-American player, the Sac Indian, Jim Thorpe.

In the evening they ate a five-course meal in their hotel room, capped off by a generous supply of Verve Cliquot champagne. Will was amused at how much Betty drank, for he knew that ordinarily she did not care for the liquid. "That must be an old Arkansas custom," he kidded. "Hey, just what kind of girl have I married!"

For the same night, they had orchestra tickets to see Maude Adams (who had a firm place among Broadway's elite), in What Every Woman Knows, which was then on a national tour. Betty started to feel dizzy after a few moments, so Will whisked her back to the hotel to sleep off the first drunk of her twenty-nine years.

In late November, Will was back on stage, in Newark, for the first time since his marriage. Decked out in rough leather chaps, a red cowboy shirt, and a bandanna (how people dress, Tolstoy once said, tells you more about them than nudity), Will didn't make any great impression on his wife, who hadn't seen him perform since the St. Louis Fair.

What did impress Betty was that her new life enabled her to experience many things that she'd only read or dreamed about. Since Will was playing two-a-day on the circuit, with his appearance on stage consisting of fifteen minutes or so, that left plenty of time for him to spend with Betty. In a sense, the honeymoon was prolonged. Sometimes, Betty went to the theatre to watch Will perform, and at other times she picked him up after the show.

With such a schedule, they were able to visit good restaurants, even if Will invariably stuck with his chili. They also got to attend other theatrical performances, and since Betty and Will were both curious people, they did a measure of sightseeing.

In New York, Will guided Betty around the countless idiosyncratic neighborhoods—the financial district, the Bowery, upper Broadway, Chinatown, Harlem, and Park and Madison avenues. They gaped at the French Renaissance mansions owned by the robber barons on Fifth Avenue; rode in a hansom cab through Central Park; saw the animals at the Bronx Zoo, (although Will thoughtfully refrained from lassoing any of them); took a tour to the top of the Statue of Liberty, which was less than twenty-five years old. They delighted in walking around Times Square, the hub of so many glittering theatres, and made excursions to Hilltop Park in upper Manhattan, where the Highlanders (later the Yankees) played baseball; they also took in the Polo Grounds, the oddly-shaped stadium housing the New York Giants. On Times Square their favorite restaurant was Rector's, where the "overdressed belch," Diamond Jim Brady, wearing clusters of jewels on his lapels, held forth.

When Will took his provincial wife to the Metropole Café, a hangout for the darker side of New York life, she couldn't help expressing her surprise (while her hometown friends on hearing about it, where in a state of shock).

Betty willingly went along wherever Will chose to venture. But he did pay a small price, for she dragged him to several operas, where he was forced, after a mild protest, to wear his wedding suit. She said she wanted to hear the great singer Enrico Caruso and visit Grant's Tomb on Riverside Drive. She managed to do both, although Will said he didn't really see anything funny about Caruso when he sang the role of the clown, in *I Pagliacci*.

As far as her wardrobe was concerned, Betty usually wore attire that was properly au courant. Her skirts fell to her ankle or below; her pompadour was as high as a mountaintop. She kept her hair in place with well-hidden hairpins, and it was not unusual for her headgear to be garnished with colorful stuffed birds. Her shirtwaist, with a ruffled neck, came up under her chin as a choker. Her four or five layers of clothing must have been designed by an expert in torture. Her equally uncomfortable high-top shoes (three-to-four dollars a pair) didn't encourage the kind of walking that Betty loved to do. The stockings that she wore were black cotton—silk stockings were only for the fabulously rich. In short, Betty looked like she could have stepped right out of the chorus of the *Floradora* show, dancing to the sweet lyrics of "Tell Me, Pretty Maiden, Are There Any More at Home Like You?"

Betty's energy was severely put to the test by an overnight exposure to a range of experiences that could have tried the patience of a much younger woman. "Will hated to lose a moment of his life. He wanted to do everything right now," she said. "He nearly ran me ragged." But if she had any reservations about her marriage to Will, they were not apparent. His mobility amazed and amused her, even if it was exhausting. Such un unorthodox way of life, with late-night suppers and cold sandwiches, and friendships with strange people who were exotic for her tastes—newspapermen, prizefighters, gamblers, con men, ballplayers, actors, and, if truth be told, a gangster or two; all these things fascinated her, rather than repelling her.

Will never lacked for work, at good pay, and the reviews regarded him with kindness and praise. With Betty at his side, he was more relaxed than he ever had been, and she was quickly beginning to understand a man that she had known only superficially through his letter-writing rhetoric. She was also getting used to habits that could be trying. For example, he liked to read while eating, something she might once have considered an utter discourtesy. Now she came to regard it as "just Will." When he was fatigued, he could fall asleep while talking to her. She didn't let that faze her, either.

Within months, Betty was totally devoted to Will. But if she still nursed the hope that, one day soon, he would return to Claremore to resume a more conventional life, she never let on to Will about that. Clem was now having more dizzy spells than ever, and Betty thought this in itself would persuade Will to take over the ranch, without any urging from her.

Will, in turn, was immensely proud of her. "She's a real trouper," he said.

"She can be sitting here in a kimono and hear the train whistle for the station and be on it and all packed, with the tickets bought, in two shakes of a lamb's tail."

The Rogers's itinerary for those first months of marriage took them all over the New York–New England area. In March they journeyed to the Pacific Coast, where Will was booked in San Francisco, Oakland, Spokane, Salt Lake City, Denver, Seattle, and Butte, Montana. Living was expensive, for Will was an impulsive man who loved to treat Betty to the best restaurants and hotels. It wasn't unusual for him to make purchases of jewelry for her, after seeing the gems in store windows. Although he was making $300 a week, he didn't get to save much, so Betty got into the habit of dropping one-dollar bills into a metal box, which she kept in a trunk. It was dedicated to one of those rainy days that she knew would happen along, sooner or later.

What did occur one day, when there were in Butte, was that the metal box was hacked open with an ax while they were out taking in the sights of the town. On their return, they found the door was open and the box was empty. Some $200 in cash was gone, as well as other items that had both monetary and sentimental value. Two lockets that Betty had fashioned from Will's diamond scarf pins were gone; so were a gold watch, a pair of opera glasses, and a locket with solitaire diamond settings.

Betty was angry with herself for having left the door unlocked. But she was made more furious by the attitude of the hotel managers, who told her they bore no responsibility for her loss. She had a hard time getting over the manner in which she was treated, for she had her own concept of fairness, which she thought had been seriously violated.

Betty kept on telling the story of the Butte plundering to her friends and family. The narrative included a description of how she and Will went to the hotel dining room that evening and were greeted by stares that could have burned a hole through her. "She was so upset and humiliated," Will Jr. once said, "that she dropped her plate."

With the Pacific tour at an end, Betty decided that she wanted to return to Claremore for a brief visit. After four months of an itinerant life, Betty told Will she wanted to see her family and others who missed her. Will was understanding, although he still suspected that she was trying to lure him back to the ranch, where he might stay put.

He told her that he had some profitable engagements already lined up in Louisville and Cincinnati, and that he didn't want to back out of them.

Encouraging him to go ahead with his plans, Betty said she would have complete faith in his behavior while they were apart.

This was another instance, which would repeat itself during all of Will's life, in which he managed to get his way. Jim Rogers, Will's second son, emphasized how his father was able to twist Betty around to his point of view on most things, especially when it came to his incessant need to travel.

"Dad wanted things his own way," said Jim, "to live his life as he wanted. Many of his trips, early in life and later, were not as vital as he made them out to be. I think he was inherently selfish about such matters."

Away from each other for the first time since their wedding, the couple kept up a steady drumbeat of correspondence. Before a few days went by, Will was pining for his wife in his letters, telling her how lonesome he was and how much he missed her. You'd have thought Betty had been gone for a year. He reminded her that she shouldn't let anyone at home kid her about his running off. But he neglected to add his mixed feelings about going back to Claremore. Not that he didn't have strong loyalties to his father and to the rest of his family, but he feared that once he returned home, he might be persuaded to stay there.

When an offer came from the Percy Williams chain, it was too substantial for him to turn down, so Betty went along with him for part of the time. Occasionally, she'd go back home when there was an illness in her family.

At this time, Betty happily informed Will that Clem had had a change of attitude about his son's way of life. What had caused the shift was that many people had informed Clem that Will really was doing well. "That boy is good and funny," they said to him. "He ain't actin', he's just bein' himself." Such counsel convinced the old man that vaudeville was a valid career at that. Once he had thought it was about as low an occupation as raising skunks. Now he secretly carried around in his wallet Will's more flattering press notices, and wasn't shy about forcing his friends to read them. The fact that Clem, as a hard-headed businessman, had studied attendance figures, theatre prices, and expenses, and had come to the conclusion that Will wasn't being paid half enough, also decreased his skepticism about the matter.

It didn't hurt, either, that Will was in the habit of mailing sizable checks home. This was proof positive to Clem that Will was actually making all that money for just standing around a stage and doing a few rope tricks.

For some time, Will nursed the desire to run his own show again, even though his first try overseas hadn't worked out very well. The thought kept nagging at him, so he went out and hired several champion women riders and ropers, including Goldie St. Clair and Arlene Palmer, who had starred in Buffalo Bill's troupe. However, the project turned out to be too complicated and expensive. An added threat was that Will might end up bankrupt if he continued to pursue his promotional dream. In short order, he gave up the show and folded the company.

However, the experience was worth it, for while the company ate into his bankbook, the nature of his own performance was now permanently altered. Appearing at the Mercantile Club in Philadelphia, Will was not accompanied by his horse-riding sidekick or his horse. They had failed to show up on time, so he went onstage alone, only with a lariat, gum (which was now being supplied to him free by the Beechnut Company), and a few jokes. Betty was standing in the wings, waiting for the act to end, when the theatre manager sidled over to her. He expressed the opinion that Will was far better up their on stage *without* his horses and other people surrounding him. "I think he should let 'em all go," he advised Betty, "and just do it by himself. It would save a lot of money for everybody—and it's a better act without them."

Will was a loyal man and employer. It wasn't easy for him to accept such advice, for it meant he'd have to turn his back on Buck McKee and old Teddy, who had been such an integral part of his existence for as long as he had been in vaudeville. But Betty sensed that the manager was right, and she convinced Will that that was the way to go in the future.

Going it alone, with his rope whistling through the air, and accompanied by his own extemporaneous remarks (most were off-the-cuff but a few were cannily stored up for timely usage), Will learned the value of studied self-deprecation. If he missed with his rope or got one of his feet tangled, he'd raise his head shyly (usually his head was down, focusing on the lariat) to inform the audience that he had only enough jokes for one miss. "I've either got to practice my roping some more or learn more jokes," he'd say, punctuating it with a wink.

When his quip earned laughs from a crowd, he knew he'd have to use it again; never one to squander a good act with a rope, he was willing to risk a foul-up as long as the patrons acted positively. "Laughs didn't have to happen twice for him to get the message," said Betty.

One of Will's best props continued to be his chewing gum. He'd often come on stage with a big wad of the stuff tucked in his mouth, as his teeth pounded away ferociously. At times, he'd stick the wad on some object on the side of the stage before commencing his rope twirling. If he missed on a trick, he let the gum stay there. If he completed the trick with perfection, he'd grin, shuffle over to where he had parked his gum, and stick the wad back in his mouth, in triumph. This generally brought roars of approval from the audience.

Will was an original guy in almost everything he did, but he was inspired to adopt his habit with gum by watching major-league baseball players. One of the dominant second basemen of the era, Eddie Collins of the Philadelphia Athletics, had a habit of parking his gum conspicuously on the button on his cap when he strode to the plate. Other players, before going up to hit, might rest their gum on the knob of a bat in the dugout.

A small compromise that Will was now willing to make with Betty was to try to get himself booked into theatres near New York. In that way, Betty, staying in New York, would be close to him. By now she loved almost everything about the big town and was even getting to like most of Will's show-business companions, including W. C. Fields, Blanche Ring, Marie Dressler, Louise Dresser, Chic Sale, and Fred Stone. Will did a turn with Fields at Keith and Proctor's Fifth Avenue, and he also made a friend of the comedian and bass singer, William De Wolf Hopper, who, since 1892, had been reciting Ernest Lawrence. Thayer's famous baseball poem, "Casey at the Bat," in just about every theatre, ballroom and barroom in America.

In July 1910, Will took Betty back to Arkansas for a long-overdue family reunion. In that way he had an opportunity to make peace with his father, whose health was failing. In Oklahoma, Will showed the home folks exactly what he was doing to make all that money: He appeared in several rodeos and fairs, tossing his rope around, as well as his puns. By this time, Clem had actually taken to watching his son perform from the wings, with approval being written all over his weathered features. If someone ventured by, he'd proclaim he was Will's father; then invariably the clippings were produced.

So well were the two men getting along now that Will broached to Clem the subject of a possible European trip, in which Sallie and Maud would also join. When Will went back on the road and was in Lawrence, Massachusetts, he wrote to "My Dear Dear Papa" as follows: "You are to go along for a few weeks anyway . . . this is no joke . . . we have a trip all mapped out . . . it wont cost much, we'll go over together, then you can all come back when you like, it wont cost you all over $250 or $300 apiece. . . . Now Sallie and Maud can afford that. . . . Well have a big time . . . a little ocean trip would be the finest thing in the world for you . . ."

Will no doubt feared that his father wasn't going to be around much longer. He was aware that Clem had lost most of his vigor—even his activities in the Cherokee community had dwindled. Several years before, as the oldest delegate to the convention that drew up a constitution for the proposed state of Oklahoma, Clem had sat there proudly as the delegates unanimously voted to have the Cooweescoowee District renamed Rogers. Thus properly honored, the old man had sadly gone downhill ever since. He didn't work much any more, and many of his days were spent contemplating a glorious life gone by or taking rides occasionally on a horse named Roger K.

Wherever he traveled, Will faithfully wrote to Clem, just as he always did with Betty. Any matter, such as the loss of Teddy, through robbery, or the announcement that he had offered a $100 reward for the return of the animal—without questions asked—was addressed in Will's letters. (However, there is no record of his commenting on the death of Mark Twain in 1910, a man who had had an impact on his own career.) When Clem celebrated his seventy-second birthday on January 11, 1911, Will could not be present for the party that Maud and Sallie threw, which many of Will's friends attended. Clem, too, was increasingly diligent in his letter writing to Will. The proposed European trip didn't work out—but feeling as he did, Clem didn't express any regrets. What did excite him was the news that Betty was pregnant. However, Betty informed Clem that if it were a boy, it was unlikely that they would name the child after him because there were already too many Clems in the family. The old man didn't appear offended. As a matter of fact, his own brief letters arrived at an increased pace, even when he had little to say. The subtext of his notes was that his health was not too good. "A man of my age has to be careful," he wrote, the fire in his belly diminishing.

When Will Rogers Jr. (he was given the middle name of Vann, after Clem) was born on Friday morning, October 20, 1911, at Will's apartment on Riverside Drive, on 113th Street in Manhattan, Clem promptly sent the latest member of the Rogers clan a gift package. Within a few hours, Will wrote back to thank his father: "Just a note we got your letter and the dandy little Moccasins and stockings and Betty and the baby and I were tickled to death with them . . . you have all sent some awful pretty things. . . . Sallie and Maud sent some beautiful things too. . . . We are doing fine Betty will write you . . . she sat up today."

On October 25, Clem wrote to Will again, reassuring him there was nothing to worry about insofar as "the Old Home Place" was concerned. It may not have been intended as such, but it turned out to be Clem's valedictory to Will.

The Sunday after Will Jr.'s birth, Clem Rogers died in his sleep at Maud's house in Chelsea. He never did get to see his grandson. On Tuesday afternoon, when the funeral took place in Claremore, the whole town closed its doors at three o'clock, paying final homage to the pioneer who had been so stubbornly proud of his heritage. Will was there, too, proud also that he had become reconciled to Clem in his last years.

Clem had never been a "walk-in-the-park" personality. Rich and tough, he had been monarch of all that he surveyed. If he found someone on his property who didn't belong there, he'd ride up and bang him over the head with his riding whip. He was truly a father to remember, despite his procrustean reputation.

"I suspect that Will's modesty had its origin in a tremendous respect for his father and a knowledge that, at least in early manhood, he was a disappointment to his family," Betty said, years later.

Best Pal

Will never stayed in one place long enough to make any firm friendships. He must have figured he didn't need close friends because he had Betty, as good a pal as a man could have. But aside from Betty, it was a versatile actor, Fred Stone, who became the closest pal and confidant. Trying to explain why Stone became so important to him, Will speculated that it was because Stone only got as far as the "Fourth Reader," while he only reached the "Third." "That's why I think we always hit it off so well, because neither was liable to use a word which the other wouldn't understand," he said.

Will had developed a great admiration for Stone even before they met. When Stone played the lead on Broadway in *The Red Mill,* Will took Betty to see the successful musical. It was only a matter of time before their paths would cross.

Life remained busy for Will in the months after Clem's death. He was still throwing around his spontaneous comments, off-the-cuff jokes, and stingless barbs, although his barbs weren't always so stingless. (Evidence that Will rehearsed ahead of time was found in a memorandum he wrote under the heading, "Gags for Missing the Horse's Nose: I should have sprinkled a little mucilage on his nose. This thing might hang on. . . . There's one thing I must say for the animal. He never was much for sticking his nose into things. . . .") Once, when he was sharing a bill with the Cherry Sisters, who were reputed to be as devoid of talent as a tree stump, Will kidded that their act must have been named before lemons were discovered. The sisters thought Will should be arrested for that. But he pointed out that he was a stickler for the First Amendment.

In 1911, Fred Stone, who could act the clown as well as the circus athlete, was on the road with *The Red Mill* in Louisville, Kentucky. Around the corner from his theatre, *The Cowboy and the Lady* was playing. Stone's matinee schedule, not the same as that for *The Cowboy and the Lady,* enabled him to take in the rival show with his wife. There was a rowdy saloon scene in the play, featuring a muscular Indian lad who kept twirling a rope while keeping time with the music of a piano player. Always thinking of new wrinkles to be adapted for his own plays, Stone thought he could learn a thing or two from this young fellow. So he called the boy at his hotel and told him he wanted to meet him. When they met, the youngster informed Stone that he was twenty-two years old and had been roping almost from the day he was old enough to walk. "I just wondered," said Stone, "if you could teach me to spin a rope like that."

The young man, who answered to the strange name of Black Chambers, told him had had never heard of *The Red Mill* or of Mr. Stone. He also wasn't certain, he said, that he could teach Stone anything.

However, over the next two months, Black Chambers took Stone in hand, working with him zealously almost every afternoon. He even taught him "the wedding ring," where the rope made a perfect spin around his body. By this time, however, Chambers was feeling homesick. He informed Stone he wanted to go back to Claremore and so he would have to call off the lessons. Before he went back, Chambers told Stone he knew of another guy who might be useful in teaching him things about rope twirling. "You and he will hit if off," Chambers said. "His name is Will Rogers and you'll never have a better friend in your life."

Stone returned to New York, where he was in rehearsal for *The Old Town* at the Knickerbocker Theatre. One day, Will showed up backstage to meet him. In his powder-blue suit and straw hat, without a vest, Will revealed his nervousness by continuing to hit the side of his leg with a rolled-up newspaper.

"Where's Black Chambers gone?" he asked Stone. "I'd like to borrow him for some lessons"—odd, but Will still seemed to think he had something to learn about lariat tossing.

Stone informed Will that Chambers had gone home, then died suddenly of a blood clot in his throat.

"I need lessons more than you do," Stone told Will.

"If you think it can do *you* some good, *I'll* give you lessons," said Will.

Stone was pleased to hear this. "I was just getting started with Chambers," he said. "I've got lots more to learn about dancing in and out of those ropes."

At the time, Will was playing at Proctor's Twenty-third Street. But whenever he wasn't working, he gave Stone lessons. Will also introduced Stone to a buddy who was bringing horses up from Texas to train them for polo in Red Bank, New Jersey. Stone said he'd like to try the sport, so the two of them went down to Red Bank one afternoon. Since horses were always second nature to Will, he agreed to try his hand at it, too. Before the day was over, their mallets got tangled and Will knocked Stone off his horse. It was the first time for both men on a polo field—but Will never stopped loving the game.

Initially shy about asking Fred to come see his act, Will finally summoned up the courage to ask him. Fred said he'd be delighted to take a look. Fred planted himself in the first row, daring Will to rope him and drag him up on the stage. Will took the dare and Fred enjoyed it. Will asked Stone if he'd mind if he did an imitation of Stone doing a rope dance. Of course not, answered Stone. When Will quipped that "I got a new joke for you folks today; it's all about the Ku Klux Klan, but I got better sense than to tell it," Stone laughed along with the rest of the audience.

In time, Stone told Bill (which is how Fred preferred to address Will) that he was a born showman and the best roper he had ever seen. Will was truly grateful for such an endorsement, for he knew that Stone, six years older than he was, was now one of the top performers in the legitimate theatre and someone to be respected. After his youth in Valmont, Colorado, Stone literally had been raised and nurtured on the smell of circus sawdust. He had seen it all and done it all.

Try to get out of vaudeville and into shows, advised Stone. Stay around New York, where the show-business people are, he added. But one thing, above all, Stone told Will: Stay away from circuses. "They're only for crooks, pickpockets, and floating scum," he said.

Will had no notion of doing any more circus work. But roles in shows weren't that easy to obtain. (Song-and-dance-man George M. Cohan turned

Will down for a role in *Broadway and Buttermilk* around this time, adding that he didn't think Will had enough skill.) So Will was still on the road, in Texas, when Blanche Ring, a popular singer of the day, spotted his act. She was scheduled to star on Broadway in a musical called *The Wall Street Girl* in the spring of 1912, and she thought Will would be ideal with his act during a scenery change.

Before opening night, Will was more anxious than he had ever been before—this was Broadway, not vaudeville. When he came on stage, chewing away, he owned up to the audience about his case of jangled nerves.

"I knew I could do all right at fifty cents, but I was a little afraid at two dollars," he said, in a reference to the steeper prices charged at Broadway shows.

Halfway through the performance of *The Wall Street Girl,* word came that the *Titanic,* the 42,328-ton four-city-block-long steamer, had struck a giant iceberg on its maiden voyage and had sunk in the North Atlantic, south of Newfoundland, with over two thousand people on board. Many of the passengers were prominent New Yorkers. The producer of the show asked Will if he'd go back onstage and deliver the lugubrious announcement of the disaster, a demanding assignment even for an experienced actor. In a hoarse voice, Will informed the audience. Many started to weep, while others got up and left the theatre. Those who stayed weren't in much of a mood for songs or humor.

Despite this misadventure, *The Wall Street Girl* had a decent run and Will won some enthusiastic notices. "A poet with a lariat," one critic wrote. When the show went on tour before the summer break, Betty returned home to Arkansas with Will Jr. Always eager to keep working, Will went back to vaudeville in the hot months, then returned to *The Wall Street Girl* in the fall for its national tour.

Blanche Ring, introducing "In the Good Old Summertime" in the show, maintained her top billing. But listed right under her was Will Rogers, on his way at last as a bona fide Broadway performer.

When the tour ended in April 1913, Will went back to his vaudeville routine. He was in the Rice Hotel in Houston when Betty gave birth on May 18, in Arkansas, to their second child, Mary Amelia Rogers. That night, the ebullient Will read the telegram onstage that he had just received announcing Mary's arrival; he followed that euphoric moment with a fine performance.

In 1914, even as the furies of tribalism and nationalism were again sweeping Europe, Will decided to go abroad with Betty, who had never been in that part of the world. The two children were left in the care of Betty's parents. Sensing that a true decline in vaudeville was setting in in America, and that change was a recurring phenomenon of show business, Will had anticipated the fading away of his chief source of income. The trip, on the Germany luxury liner *Vaterland,* the newest and greatest ship afloat, was supposedly an antidote to that condition. Will did manage, while in London, to win a part in a musical called *The Merry-Go-Round.* Nora Bayes, who had popularized "Shine On, Harvest Moon" for Florenz Ziegfeld in the 1908 *Follies,* and then had left his employ, was the headliner.

Again, Will received the approval of London's critics. However, he wasn't too happy with the constant noise of the hawkers during his act. He felt nobody was listening to his patter. His instinct in this case was wrong, for the Empire Theatre offered him $400 a week to continue in the show. But this time, Will opted to return to America, for the assassination of the Archduke Francis Ferdinand at Sarajevo precipitated the various moves leading to Germany's declaration of war on Russia in August.

Returning to Claremore, just as World War I broke out, Will was forced to resume his vaudeville regimen. With two kids, a third on the way, and, as Betty put it, "his haphazard way with money," Will didn't have too much choice in the matter. His strenuous tour included bookings in and around Oklahoma, where his friends continued to believe that, sooner or later, he'd quite the show-business "nonsense" and settle down on the ranch. Then he went on to Kansas City, Salt Lake City, Denver, Sacramento, Los Angeles, San Francisco, and, by the fall, back to Oklahoma. At times when no good bookings were available, he'd work at small suburban theatres, generally under another name, and for only seventy-five dollars a week.

Stone emphasized again that Will had to stay around New York if he were truly serious about pursuing a theatrical career. This advice, easy to understand, was hard to follow. However, shortly before a third child, James Blake Rogers, was born on July 25, 1915, Will rented a house in Amityville, New York, on the South Shore of Long Island, near Babylon.

Across the street was Stone's house, which made it convenient for Will to do over-the-fence visiting. By this time, Will had also purchased an Overland touring car, and he was probably the only itinerant vaudevillian in American with his own stable of horses. By now Stone was a polo enthusiast, with a polo field of his own adjoining his Amityville property. On Sundays he'd invite

Will and a bunch of his friends—including Ed Borein, a cowboy artist; Leo Carillo, the actor; and Vernon Castle, the dancer—to come over for a polo game.

"The people who watched our games," recalled Will, "soon learned that in a spill, if a falling rider hit on his feet, it was Fred. If he hit on his head, it was me. We were both equally safe." On more than one occasion Will got banged on the head with a mallet; Carillo actually knocked him out one Sunday afternoon.

"They call this a gentlemen's game for the same reason they call a tall man 'Shorty,'" laughed Will, whose populist image never quite squared with his attachment to polo.

Along with the arrival of James Blake, a small, black pony named Dopey also joined the growing Rogers ménage. Will took one look at Dopey in Connecticut, and bought him. He was convinced from the start that Dopey was "the greatest pony for children that anyone ever saw." Allowed to walk around the Rogers house at will, Dopey became as much of an institution in the Rogers family as Will's collection of ropes. When each child started to ride, it was on Dopey's back that they learned. "He helped raise the children," said Will, "and he never did a wrong thing to throw them off his back. Of course, he didn't pick 'em up, either." Of the three children, Jim loved Dopey more than the other two, for he was as partial to horses as his dad was. It helped bring him closer to Will than either Will Jr. or Mary, for he was truly a chip off the old block.

Later in July, Lee and J. J. Shubert, powerful show-business rivals of Florenz Ziegfeld, approached Will about a spot for him in their new musical, *Hands Up*. Will would come on near the finale, doing more talking than roping. On opening night, Stone was there in the orchestra with his wife, Allyn. Will was doing fine but when he continued to work his act after his allotted time, the lights were cut off abruptly, on orders from the Shuberts. Will had no idea that this was about to happen. Even after the stage went dark, he doggedly kept on with his act. Mad as hell, Stone jumped up and down in the aisle, demanding that the lights be turned on. "Don't let them do that to Will Rogers," he yelled. "It's a dirty trick! Give him a chance!"

Others picked up on Stone's plea. Responding to such welcome support, Will kept his place on the stage, at one point getting all tangled in his rope. But the patrons loved it—and him. "Shucks, I shoulda left well enough alone," said Will.

Embarrassed about the incident, J. J. Shubert went backstage after the performance to apologize to Will. "Please return for an encore," he said to him. In a few weeks *Hands Up* closed. But the noisy episode was a definitive moment for Will. If he hadn't known it before, he realized, too, what a loyal friend he had in Fred Stone.

There were regular summer guests at Stone's Chin-Chin ranch in Amityville. In addition to the usual group of polo players, Rex Beach, the author and Stone's brother-in-law, was a frequent visitor. On one idyllic day, Beach joined Stone and Will for a sail on the Great South Bay. The next morning, Will got up early to go swimming with Rex and Fred. Water, whether he was shipping out on it or swimming in it, was never Will's natural milieu. Rex, on the other hand, was an expert swimmer. Trying to imitate Rex's daredevil tactics, Will went racing ahead of his friends and dove headlong into the bay. Like so many inexperienced swimmers, he had failed to scout the area before plunging in. When his head hit a submerged rock, Will was knocked into semiconsciousness for some moments. Responding to the first aid administered by Rex and Fred, Will was asked if he hadn't noticed that the tide was out.

"Tide?" Will responded, huskily. "We didn't have no tides on the Verdigris River, where I learned to swim. We've got swimmin' holes in Oklahoma, too, but they don't try to kill you in them."

The bleeding wound on Will's head turned out to be superficial. But the next day, Will discovered that when he tried to move his right arm, it was paralyzed. He found he couldn't even manipulate his fingers. At first, Will felt a sense of panic—the future for a rope twirler could be mighty bleak without the use of his right arm. But Will wasn't ready to sit still—or switch to another profession. He started daily exercises with his left arm, trying to perform the same tricks he had always done with his right arm.

It wasn't easy at first. But he was determined to develop the use of his left arm so that he could put it to use while he gabbed away on stage. After a couple of weeks of hard work, Will found that his zeal had paid off. He had become proficient with his left arm and, meanwhile, had regained the full use of his right arm. Ironically, now that his act consisted of more talking than roping, he could get away with only limited use of either arm.

That same summer, Will experienced his first ride in an airplane. He took Betty to Atlantic City for a weekend, where one could promenade on the boardwalk or sleep late at one of the large hotels fronting on the ocean. There were "flying boats" that were available for rides and Will decided to have a go at one as a passenger. As Betty watched from the pier, Will got on the plane, waving at her right before the machine took off. Betty recalled that Will seemed slightly nervous, but pleased at his first risky confrontation with a plane.

Will's next move, now that he had made up his mind to heed Stone's advice about staying around New York, was to lease a little house in Forest Hills, Queens, not more than a half hour from Manhattan by subway. He still managed to keep his horses stabled near the public school, causing people to think that he had money. Almost every day, Will practiced his roping on a vacant lot in the neighborhood, while the children looked on in awe. When they asked Will if he could teach them some of his tricks, he obliged. Homer Croy, who lived nearby, said that "the clothesline loss was appalling."

All the money that Will earned in those days seemed to be nestled in his pockets. He'd carry his paychecks around for weeks, cashing them only when he needed money. He rarely knew how much money he had in the bank and didn't care much, either—a state of affairs that tended to drive Betty crazy. "Those were happy times in Forest Hills," she said, "but it was never easy."

A big showy review, *Town Topics*, produced by Ned Wayburn, opened that fall in the cavernous Century Theatre on Central Park West, and Will was hired for a featured role. Will got all dressed up in his top hat and fancy clothes, which befitted a master of ceremonies, and he was surrounded by more pretty young chorus girls than he had ever seen. A few of the critics thought he was the best thing in *Town Topics*, as he shyly shuffled about the revolving stage (one of the first of its kind), with a rope under his hat and a quip on his lips. He captivated the reviewers, but when the producer asked him to take a reduction in pay, he bowed out. He was able to do that because he heard from songwriter and producer Gene Buck (later to become head of ASCAP) about an opening in the *Midnight Frolic*. Buck had caught Will's act and was convinced he'd be a natural as a "cowboy comic." Most of the comics in those days belonged in one of two categories: traditional blackface or "Dutch" entertainers. (The racist relic of blackface minstrelsy in America dated back to the 1830s. At times, it also accommodated German, Yiddish, Irish, and Italian accents, even though it had originally been designed to caricature blacks.)

In recommending Will to Ziegfeld, for whom he worked, Buck had a tough case to make since Ziegfeld, a genius at judging female beauty, had absolutely no sense of humor. What's more, Ziegfeld thought that girls, not gags, were the essence of show business and the raison d'être of all of his productions, starting with the first *Ziegfeld Follies* of 1907. W. C. Fields once stated that Ziegfeld tolerated comedians (like Fields himself) only because of the public's taste.

Working Will into the *Midnight Frolic,* Buck crafted a scenario that had him doing his various rope tricks while punctuating them with tart remarks, mostly about the girls on stage. Buck encouraged Will to make kidding comments about Ziegfeld himself—always a risky proposition—and about other acts on the card. Will was warned by Buck that he shouldn't repeat any of his gags, for many of the patrons who came to the *Frolic* were repeat customers. It's unlikely, said Buck, that they'd split their sides at the same jokes night after night.

The *Midnight Frolic* (tickets were two dollars) ran as the late show on the roof of the New Amsterdam Theatre, while downstairs, Ziegfeld presented his world-famous *Follies.* When the *Follies* concluded some time after eleven o'clock, the *Frolic* would get under way. As the epitome of late-night sophistication, the *Frolic* showcased a mélange of dance and musical numbers, while the customers sat at tables close to the action, sipping champagne, eating snacks, and ogling the talent. Will described the proceedings this way: "There were the most beautiful girls of any show that Ziegfeld ever put on. . . . The loveliest ones wouldn't work at a matinee, they never got up that early . . . so they were hired for the Frolic, which was for folks with lots of money and plenty of insomnia."

He did six shows a week, receiving only $175 per week, considerably less than his usual vaudeville wages. But Buck, always the consummate salesman, pointed out to Will that he had no traveling expenses, and that because of the late hour of the Frolic, he could take on other employment during the day.

Taking no chances on Buck's unvarnished cheerleading for Will, Ziegfeld attended several of Will's performances. He remained mystified as to why anyone could laugh at his jokes. Point-blank, he announced to Buck that he didn't like Will at all. "I think that you ought to fire him," he told Buck. "He just doesn't fit in with this type of show."

Buck listened to his boss but elected not to relay the bad news to his protégé. When Ziegfeld repeated the demand a few days later, Buck went to Will with the tidings. Instead of walking out right then and there, Will counterattacked. "I want fifty dollars a week more," he said. "I need the money." Before Buck could fall over in shock at Will's gall, Will informed him, further, that he was about to add a "new idea" to his act. "Betty keeps telling me that I should talk about what I read in the papers," he said. "She says I'm always reading the papers, so why not talk about what I'm reading?" Buck reminded Will that the only reason Ziegfeld even hired comedians was to fill the time void that occurred while his chorus girls were changing costumes.

With Ziegfeld out of town, Buck relented and Will went on as usual. When Ziegfeld returned, he asked Buck how Will had reacted to being fired. In response, Buck mumbled that he hadn't yet let Will go.

"Whose show do you think this is?" Ziegfeld shouted. However, Buck asked the producer to take one more look at the cowboy. Grudgingly, Ziegfeld acquiesced and, that night, went to watch Will again, Afterward, he adamantly stuck to his opinion that Will wasn't much of an actor and that his act wasn't much of an act.

"But the people who pay seem to like him," Ziegfeld admitted, grudgingly. So Will stayed on and also got his raise, which brought him up to $225 a week.

One of the first public figures that Will poked fun at, as he implemented his "new idea," was Henry Ford, the automobile industrialist. In December 1915, Ford personally took on the responsibility of trying to halt the bloodshed of World War I. Responding to the blandishments of Madame Roska Schwimmer, an Hungarian-American antiwar activist, Ford put up close to half-million dollars to send a special "peace ship" to Europe. A Scandinavian liner, *Oskar II,* was loaded down with peace delegates, 120 or so—pacifists, feminists, and idealists—people who normally wouldn't have been found in the same room with Ford. It was Ford's notion that such a group could help to mediate an end to the madness. However, by the time the ship docked in Norway, Ford decided he had had enough of Schwimmer and her quixotic plan.

Will seized on the "peace ship" as a subject of topical ridicule. One night at the *Frolic,* while Ford's ill-fated junket was still in the news, he remarked, "If Mr. Ford had taken this bunch of girls, from this show, and let 'em wear the costumes they're wearing, and marched them down between the trenches, believe me, the boys would have been out of there by Christmas." The audience broke up over that one. Ford never quite recovered from Will's verbal marksmanship, though the two became friendly in the course of time. Later, it was hinted that Ford's ugly anti-Semitism was due, in part, to his transient relationship with Madame Schwimmer, who was Jewish.

If needling of politicians, big shots, and similarly vulnerable targets seemed the way for Will to go with his act, this put him under heavy pressure to come up with sources for his material. "I started reading about Congress in the newspapers," said Will, "and I discovered they were funnier 365 days a year than anything I ever heard of." So the gentlemen in that august body became regular subjects for Will to discuss.

But there had to be other repositories for Will—his subjects couldn't all come from the ranks of politicians. An incurable devourer of newspapers, he realized that every day the press ran stories that were excellent fodder for his "fresh-laid jokes." For instance, when the papers reported the macabre news about several people who had died leaping off the Brooklyn Bridge, Will commented that it "might be necessary to condemn the Bridge because it had been weakened by suicides usin' it as a springboard."

If anyone else had delivered such a line, the patrons probably would have swarmed the footlights and physically attacked him for his insensitivity. But Will could get away with saying such irreverent things, while others might be regarded as cruel and callous. A year later, Will used the same approach when newspapers were headlining the story of the Allied spring drive in the European war that was raging. On the day that a railroad wreck in the Midwest region of the United States killed twenty-seven people, Will commented that "I see the railroads have started their own spring drive."

Such lines, delivered in an ingenuous manner, as if he had thought them up on the spur of the moment, were marginally offensive. Yet, uttering them in his offhand, conversational style, Will was able to get away with it. He had become your across-the-table buddy, confiding the latest rib-tickling yarn. "So amazing was his native wit," wrote Jerome Beatty, one of Will's early biographers, that "he had only to open his mouth and a funny line popped out."

Yet, as quick-tongued and slyly amusing as Will could be, he wasn't able to avoid the prevailing racial superstitions of his era. On one occasion when W. C. Fields was driving Will and actor Chic Sale around on Long Island, the juggler guided the auto into a ditch. As a result, Will suffered a broken leg, while Fields and Sale were unhurt. Nursing his injury on the side of the road, Will noticed a black youngster coming down the road on his motorcycle. "Don't let that boy pass us," said Will; "it's bad luck."

Another key lesson Will was learning was never to outlive his welcome onstage. Much of the time, his act didn't last longer than ten or twelve minutes; at times, it was even as short as seven minutes. Get off while you can, while the audience still thinks you're funny, was Will's credo. He tried to follow this policy assiduously during all of his show-business life.

10

Mr. Ziegfeld

lorenz Ziegfeld's initial hostility to Will might have been expected. Aside from the showman's failure to appreciate Will's originality, the two men were extreme opposites in almost every respect—they had so little in common that one didn't expect to find them under the same theatre roof.

"Half of the great comedians that I've had in my show and to whom I paid a lot of money were not only unfunny to me, but I couldn't understand how they could be funny to anybody else," said Ziegfeld. "They may have made my patrons shriek, but they made me cringe." Will was of course included in that assessment.

It wasn't a matter of personal dislike, for, with the passage of years, Ziegfeld often volunteered that Will's qualities of character and integrity were exceptional ones. It was simply that one man was a dedicated capitalist with an uncanny instinct for knowing what people would pay to see on a stage, while the other man was a performer, an artist, with none of Ziegfeld's penchant for shocking people—and none of Ziegfeld's coarseness.

Ziegfeld came to be called "The Great Glorifier" (nobody knows who originated the name), who structured an endless line of nubile clotheshorses.

Beginning in the first year of the *Ziegfeld Follies,* the season of 1907–1908, Ziegfeld was the ultimate exploiter of flesh, although he constantly denied that his show was salacious. As a matter of fact, Ziegfeld reveled in the title of the "Great Glorifier." According to theatre critic Gilbert Seldes, he was un-touched by the mockery that often attached to Ziegfeld's cognomen. Aware of all of the vulnerable facets of Ziegfeld's productions, Seldes, nonetheless, was won over by the voyeuristic package he put together. He regarded Ziegfeld as a practical businessman, who knew exactly what he was doing. Seldes said, more as praise than criticism, that Ziegfeld had complete faith in his formula: beautiful girls and dancing.

On the other hand, another observer of the American scene, Edmund Wilson, disagreed sharply with Seldes. "The *Follies* represents the liquidation of the genteel culture," wrote Wilson. "It has something in it of Riverside Drive, the Plaza, and Scott Fitzgerald's novels and it is almost totally devoid of wit. . . . Ziegfeld's girls have Anglo-Saxon straightness but the secular frigidi-ty and purity, the frank high school girlishness which Americans like. He appeals to American idealism, then gratifies males by discreetly disrobing his goddesses."

Aside from Ziegfeld's lack of empathy for humor—Will's or anybody else's—he was generally known as a Gloomy Gus. People who knew him intimately rarely saw him break a smile from his thin lips. He was as friendly and accessible as a wild boar, as acutely uncharming as Will was warm and congenial.

Ziegfeld worshiped money, luxury, and excessiveness. He was the ultimate hedonist. Wearing the same suit of clothes for two nights in a row was heresy to him, while Will rarely carried a change of suits and would settle any day for his faded blue jeans.

Ziegfeld was an obsessive gambler and one of the more durable wom-anizers of his time. His marital commitment to the tiny Anna Held, whose career began as a singer in the streets of Paris, was tenuous. He employed his own private chef and relished exotic food. He once told Fanny Brice to "order me anything out of season." As for Will, he probably couldn't pronounce the names of most of the dishes that Ziegfeld ate, and his fidelity to Betty was unquestioned, even though he was surrounded on stage by some of the most dazzlingly beautiful females on the face of the earth. Will told countless jokes about these young women in their ostrich feathers, many of whom had married and divorced millionaires. "Every time we get to a new town, some of them marry rich guys, but in a few weeks they catch up with the show again," he chuckled.

But so interdependent and close did Will and Ziegfeld become that Will chose to work for Mr. Ziegfeld (which is how he always addressed him) without a written contract. The story goes that when Ziegfeld decided to put Will in the *Follies,* and in the *Frolic,* he went to Will's dressing room to talk the matter over. He suggested that Will come to his office the next afternoon to discuss the terms of the contract and then to sign it. Will shook his head. "Mr. Ziegfeld," he said, "I don't like contracts. You can trust me and I know I can trust you." Ziegfeld didn't ordinarily conduct his business in such a casual fashion, especially in the predatory world in which he functioned. But he must have felt sure of Will, for he called in Charles Dillingham, the producer, who happened to be backstage at the time, and asked him to stand by as a witness to the verbal agreement ($600 a week the first year, $750 the second year).

When Will finally left Ziegfeld to make movies in Hollywood, Ziegfeld presented him with a platinum watch, marked by an engraving: "To Will Rogers, in appreciation of a real fellow, whose word is his bond."

For many months, Will was the unquestioned hit of the *Frolic,* whether he was roping chorus girls or delivering one-liners. He even overshadowed a new entry into the *Frolic* lineup, Eddie Cantor, whose blackface performance and amusing songs caused Ziegfeld to consider him for advancement to the *Follies.* Will had even been used as a foil in an act where a group of gorgeous models came onstage wearing progressively less lingerie. As the audience waited expectantly for further disrobing, Will suddenly appeared as the "masked marvel," to the utter disappointment of many male hearts. However, Will drew laughter, always music to Ziegfeld's ears.

Buck no long had to make the argument for retaining Will in the *Frolic.* By this time, Ziegfeld had agreed that Will would be a fine addition to his 1916 *Follies.* The producer was convinced that Will would have no objection to joining up after his successful apprenticeship on the roof. Getting Will into the *Follies'* entourage had now become important to Ziegfeld, for he understood the need to add a so-called wholesome element to the show. Shrewdly, Ziegfeld sought this balance, since many accused him of producing an extravaganza that was only a step removed from girlie shows or gritty burlesques.

But Ziegfeld was in for a surprise, for Betty had adverse feelings about Will going on the road with the show. She felt that they had now established something close to a normal home life for their family, and she was reluctant to have Will away for months on end. She also believed he wasn't being paid enough for his idiosyncratic services—not enough, anyway, to remove him from his wife and children for such long periods.

The *Follies* in the past had adhered to a strict schedule: In the spring and summer, it played in New York; for Thanksgiving it went to Pittsburgh; and by Christmas it was in Chicago. It was this kind of rigorous itinerary that Betty was anxious to avoid. Thus, she urged Will to say no to Ziegfeld unless more money were forthcoming.

On the opening night of the *Follies*, like criminals returning to the scene of their crime, Will and Betty went to the show, along with Betty's pal, Tom Harvey, and his wife. (They paid for their own tickets, refusing to turn to Ziegfeld for complimentaries.) The *Follies* that year fielded such already prominent performers as Fannie Brice, W. C. Fields, Bert Williams, Ina Claire, and Marion Davies (who would later become William Randolph Hearst's mistress). As usual, Ziegfeld had not stinted with his money on the production. Between the scenery and the opulent costumes, his bill had come to over $50,000. But as Will and company sat through the long evening, Will expressed his irritation, not only at what he considered to be a boring show, but at his own decision not to participate in it.

"This could have been my big chance," he said, turning to Betty. "I should-da been up there on that stage!"

All hands agreed that Will's act would have enlivened the dull proceedings. Betty felt guilty about the matter, now agreeing with Will's belief that he should have accepted Ziegfeld's invitation to join the *Follies*.

However, all was not lost. Ziegfeld's instinct told him that the show was not as entertaining as it might have been. Never shy about rectifying things, he approached Will. "I'd like you to be in the show by tomorrow night," he said, practically commanding that Will change his mind. But it wasn't necessary for him to do any further pushing, for Will had already decided that he wanted to be part of the *Follies*. Betty, too, wasn't inclined to keep a leash on him any more.

The verbal contract that had been agreed to in the presence of Dillingham set the terms for Will's pay. He felt anxiety about being in the *Follies*—the essence of theatrical glamor—but he knew this was what it was all about, if you were going to be in show business. Without any notice to the public, and with no mention even in the playbill, Will just took the stage one night after consenting to Ziegfeld's offer. Out front, quivering in anticipation, was Betty.

Later she said that "it was the most important and proudest moment of our lives when Will went on and when the audience broke into applause. Never had Will gone so well before." He was called back for an encore. Then, as soon as the curtain went down, he hopped upstairs to the *Frolic*, where, Betty insisted, "his magic" stayed with him. Never had Will and Betty known such excitement as they had that night. They stayed up late to grab the early editions of New York's morning papers. In those days the restless town had over fifteen dailies and not one of them gave Will a bad notice.

The immediate result of Will's overnight success was that Betty became a "newspaper widow," as each day, he spent a lot of time looking for his sources of jokes in each paper, much like Javert on the trail of Jean Valjean. When he arrived onstage, for both the *Follies* and the *Frolic*, he'd lead off with a self-abnegating pronouncement: "Well, folks, all I know is what I read in the papers." One of the more cynical members of the *Follies* suggested that Will's preoccupation with the content of the daily papers was the main reason he never laid a paw on any of the beauties assembled by Ziegfeld: He simply didn't have the time!

Two of the stars associated with Will's first *Follies* were most unlikely friends. One of them, Eddie Cantor, born Isadore Iskowitz, into an Orthodox Jewish family on New York's Lower East Side, said about Will that "he was the first guy that I ever met from west of the Bronx." The other friend, Fanny Brice, who shared top billing in several editions of the *Follies* with both Eddie and Will, was a Yiddish dialect comedienne. Eddie, as thin as a celery stick in his youth, was mothered by Fanny from the start. Will got no such treatment from her, for he seemed less vulnerable.

The relationship between Cantor and Will began in 1912, when both of them were playing at the Orpheum Theatre in Winnipeg, Canada. Eddie didn't get good reviews in Winnipeg, so in later years, when Eddie was winning raves all over the world, Will would wire him: "Those critics are a little bit late. I knew that back in Winnipeg."

Cantor thought Will was the best roper he had ever seen, although he had to admit he had never seen a cowboy or a roper on the Lower East Side. He came to respect and admire Will, even though Will kidded him about eating kosher foods. Since Eddie's dietary habits precluded his eating food like pork, oysters, lobsters, or crabs, he rarely joined Will for supper. But Will asked Eddie to take him to one of those "places that you're kosherin' up for me." The first Jewish delicatessen that Eddie ever took Will to was on Euclid Avenue in Cleveland, where Will gobbled three large portions of chopped liver. "It's too late for me to turn Jewish." Will told Eddie. Years later, when Will had to undergo a gall-bladder operation, he put the blame on Cantor. "That's what I get for goin' to all those kosher restaurants with you," he said.

The two men once decided to exchange hometown visits, with Will taking the subway to Cantor's Bronx apartment, and Eddie going out to Oklahoma. Will, however, complained that "Eddie's apartment was just 'like a jail.'" Cantor responded that Oklahoma left him cold. "It's like a big, empty, lonesome place," he said.

After a while, Eddie went with Will to Will's favorite little chili parlor off Forty-seventh Street, near Times Square. Not more than five or six people could fit into the place at one time—but to Will it was chili heaven; it was about as small and unpretentious as Will's dressing room at the *Follies*. The monastic room had one window, a couple of beat-up old chairs, and no carpet. But Will didn't care to have it "fancied up," even when Betty threatened to send a decorator in to make it more livable. "I've been in far worse than this," Will explained.

In his memoir, *Take My Life,* Cantor says he knew that Will felt embarrassment while watching all those scantily clad chorines prancing around backstage or leaving their dressing-room doors wide open. But Will was never puritanical about it, although there were times when he offered some protest to what he considered "going too far."

Will's lines remained as fresh and topical as ever. He always worked with the house lights on, giving him an opportunity to see who was out there in the audience. He'd often spot well-known people and friends and before they knew it, he'd be throwing his rope over their heads and wrestling them up to the stage. Before each show, Ziegfeld also might tip Will off about some celebrated personality who was in the theatre. Generally, those who were roped took it with good humor. One night, he even captured Fred Stone, who protested mildly at being lassoed and dragged up to the stage. But Stone knew it was all good, clean fun.

In the 1917 *Follies,* after Cantor had stopped the show with his rendition of "That's the Kind of a Baby For Me," Will went to Eddie's dressing room to congratulate him. It was typical of Will; he did this many times with others in the show. He found Eddie bawling like a three-year-old. "What are ya cryin' about, Eddie?" asked Will. "They're still clapping for you downstairs." Eddie reminded Will that his dear grandmother had died recently and that his tears were for her.

"What makes you think she didn't see you—and from a very good seat," Will answered.

Cantor was not above playing practical jokes on his associates in the *Follies*. Figuring that Will was such an expert at kidding people, Eddie decided, in alliance with W. C. Fields, to kid Will back a little. There was an old Rogers pal from Oklahoma named Clay McGonigle, who occasionally dropped in on the *Follies*. So one time, Eddie and Fields prepared a fake note, "signed" by McGonigle, that read: "I'm in town and I'll be out there in front watching the show." Before Will went on that night, they had the note delivered to Will in his dressing room. Pleased that his pal from his ranching days was on hand to see him, Will's act that night consisted wholly of a ten-minute monologue addressed to McGonigle, reliving many adventures they had shared together—and probably some they hadn't. As he spoke, Will's eyes searched the audience for any sign of McGonigle. But he failed to locate him. Nor was there a single cowboy "yup" from anyone who might have been Clay. The audience, of course, was mystified: What was Will prattling about? Who was McGonigle?

After the show, Will visited Eddie in his dressing room. "I wonder whatever happened to Clay," he said to Cantor. Eddie confessed nothing. Then Will went out to see if he could find Clay, visiting the usual haunts—bars, restaurants, and hotel lobbies. But there was no Clay. It wasn't until many years later that Cantor confided to Will that the whole affair had been concocted by Fields and him. Will's response was laughter: He appreciated a good joke, even when the joke was on him.

As World War I became increasingly savage, with America's doughboys traveling overseas, under the presidential aegis of Woodrow Wilson, Will often made allusions to the fighting. However, it was never an easy task to make light of killing and dying, especially now that American youngsters were involved. But Will demonstrated how artful he could be. "Those Germans don't know that our training manual only teaches the boys to go one way; there's nothin' about retreating. In that way you can train 'em in half the time," he said at the *Frolic* one night. During another show, he said, "Our soldiers can win wars faster than our diplomats can talk us into them." When President Wilson sat down at the Big Four's talks in Europe, to try to negotiate terms with the enemy, Will said: "We finally handed the Germans our peace terms in eighty thousand words. It took that many to tell them what we thought of them."

Although he was a sternly religious man, Mr. Wilson still found time to visit the theatre. The first time that Will played in front of the president, he was seized with a kingsize case of stage fright. Since he wasn't convinced that "joking" the president was permissible, especially during such sober times, Will had some reservations about what he was about to do.

However, he was also convinced that presidents, as well as other important public figures, should be treated just like ordinary human beings. When Mr. Wilson and his new wife attended a benefit performance in Baltimore, marking the first time he had left Washington for such a purpose, Will resolved to "tell it to the president." With butterflies in his stomach, as he stood on center stage, Will finally blurted out: "Folks, I'm kinder nervous here tonight." This opening remark was hardly humorous, but polite laughter from the audience assured Will that an auto-da-fé was not in the cards for him.

"This is really my second presidential appearance," Will continued. "The first time was when Mr. William Jennings Bryan spoke in our town and I was scheduled to follow his speech and do my little roping act. As I say, I was to follow him, but he spoke so long that when I finished it was so dark nobody could see may act. . . . By the way, I wonder whatever became of Mr. Bryan."

With one glance at the president's box, Will knew he had reached Mr. Wilson: The president had thrown back his head and was laughing heartily. Having broken the ice so successfully, Will went on to talk of other government difficulties, including the touchy subject of the country's lack of military preparedness.

"There's some talk of gettin' a machine gun if we can borrow one," said Will, now warming to his role as a gadfly. "The one we've got now, they're usin' it to train our army at Plattsburg. If we go to war, we'll have to go to the trouble of gettin' another gun." Again, the president laughed, along with everybody else. On the theme of diplomacy, Will remarked that "Wilson is gettin' along fine, compared to what he was a few months ago. You gotta realize that a few months back, in our negotiations with Germany, that he was five notes behind." This time, Mr. Wilson laughed even harder. (The president would say later that this joke was just about the best one ever told about him while he was in the White House.)

It was widely reported at the time that Germany's submarines were having some trouble operating in the Gulf Stream. That led to Will's joke: "If we can learn to heat the ocean, we've got 'em licked. I ain't worked the thing out yet."

One of Mr. Wilson's most persistent tormentors during this period was the notorious Mexican revolutionary, Francisco "Pancho" Villa. Reduced to a prerevolutionary status of bandit, Villa struck at Columbus, New Mexico, a town on the Mexican border. The daring move prompted some in the United States to call for American intervention against Villa. Wilson obliged by sending General John J. "Blackjack" Pershing to chase after Villa and his men. Weeks of trailing after Villa ended in total frustration for Blackjack. The Mexican insurgent continued to elude the Yankees, producing a series of sensational newspaper stories

"I see by the headlines that Villa escapes 'Net' and 'Flees,'" commented Will. "We'll never catch him then, 'cuz any Mexican that can escape fleas is beyond catching. . . . I also see where the morning editions of the papers capture Villa, then in the afternoon editions they let him get away."

Will won as hearty a laugh from the crowd, including Mr. Wilson, as he had for all of this other jokes. After the show, Mr. Wilson and his wife came backstage to shake Will's hand, ending a sublime evening for Will. By chiding the president and being rewarded with approbation not only by Mr. Wilson himself, but by the general public, Will overnight became the accepted tribune of the people. His jokes were greeted as common sense, uttered by a man who appeared to have his finger squarely on the public pulse. Will himself said that folks were "more capable of laughing during the war than at any other time—and the more serious the situation became, the better they laughed if you happened to hit the right spot."

In addition to his double duties in Ziegfeld's *Follies* and the *Midnight Frolic,* Will, who (at thirty-eight) was too old for the draft, and who had a large family to provide for, played fund-raisers to help the war effort. At one time, he pledged to give 10 percent of his yearly income to the American Red Cross. That was quite generous, for, with an income (at that time) of less than $7,000 a year, Will was not wealthy, by any means.

Whether he appeared in the *Follies,* the *Frolic,* or at benefits as an after-dinner speaker, Will continued to display a level of topicality and audacity that kept the laughter going. One night he was introduced by Will Hays, a Republican politician who, as a speaker, had a tendency toward flatulence. "There he is," said Hays, pointing to Will, "the cowboy who has roped Broadway and has something, besides hair, underneath his ten-gallon hat." Getting to his feet, the humorist Irvin S. Cobb, a friend and admirer of Will's, riposted: "It's about time that somebody said a good word about dandruff." The remark broke Will up—but he knew he couldn't have said it any better than Cobb had.

Ziegfeld was a taskmaster who rehearsed everybody until they were on the verge of dropping. Homer Croy said members of the cast were as "limp as dandelions" after the impresario got through with them every day. But such treatment never disturbed Will, a man who never had a lazy hour.

Spring rehearsals of the *Follies* invariably found Will sprawled in a dark corner of the theatre. Betty joined him much of the time, for she was always curious about how the *Follies* evolved from its often crude beginnings into the ultimate of all Broadway spectacles. Will's eyes seemed to be half closed, much like a dog in repose (but he was always ready to spring into action). Nobody ever accused him of missing anything, whether it was the latest wrinkle that Ziegfeld introduced, or the cue for his entrance onto the stage.

Many of the *Follies* shows of the late teens were choreographed by a Pittsburgher, Ned Wayburn, who was credited with inventing tap dancing. Wayburn was said to have compiled a master list of ten thousand show girls, with particular emphasis on their home addresses, hair color, and chest measurements.

Ziegfeld, from his command position in the center of the dimly lit theatre, followed every nuance and movement of his girls. The list of beauties who sparkled under Ziegfeld's aegis included names that were instantly recognizable to New York's newspaper readers, more for their romantic entanglements than for their achievements on the stage. One of these was the charismatic and unfortunate small-town Ohioan, Marilyn Miller, with blue eyes and blond hair, and with whom Ziegfeld had fallen in love when she was only in her teens. While Ziegfeld's marriage to Anna Held was declining—Held died in 1918, at the age of forty-five—he tried to maintain his connection with Marilyn, even after she was married to another man and had developed serious problems with alcohol.

Others that Wayburn helped bring into the Ziegfeld fold were Ruth Etting; Gladys Glad; Helen Morgan, the sultry-voiced ex-manicurist who won fame for her role as Julie in *Show Boat;* Hazel Forbes; Ann Pennington, the tiny, dimple-kneed popularizer of the "Black Bottom" dance; Marion Davies, a chorine from Brooklyn; Ina Claire; Billie Dove; Olive Brady; Peggy Shannon; Martha Mansfield; Mae Murray, graceful and tempestuous; Doris Eaton; and Katherine Burke.

Even with Wayburn's expertise at his disposal, Ziegfeld was unrelenting in his scrutiny of every phase of the productions. Nothing escaped his attention, whether something was amiss with a hairdo, or the color of a flower clashed with a girl's rompers. However, Ziegfeld never tried to tamper with Will's words; he had the good sense to refrain from making suggestions or alterations.

In recalling Ziegfeld's behavior, Betty said that "he was an artist, rather than a businessman. . . . Once he threw out an entire set of costumes for a finale, costing him at least $15,000." Rehearsals often ran until dawn, with a call being scheduled for eleven the same morning. At these rehearsals, Will would amble onto the stage when his name was called out. Once there, he'd mumble a few words, with his rope in his hand. At such times he did not reveal the material that he'd employ in the show, for he insisted on preserving the freshness of his act, not only for the paying public, but also for members of the cast. In that way, when his act emerged in the *Follies*, his working companions, gathering in the wings, were as eager to hear his latest musings as the people in the theatre were. At rehearsals, his remarks were usually confined to innocuous, kidding comments about either Ziegfeld or the girls in the chorus. Scarcely the most tolerant employer in the world, Ziegfeld took such joshing well, for by this time he had become fond of Will. Will returned the feeling by presenting Patricia, Ziegfeld's daughter, with a pony as a birthday gift.

Will never stopped throwing verbal buckshot at celebrated names in the audience—it had now become standard procedure in his act. "We've got Diamond Jim Brady here tonight," Will might say, with a wink, "and if anybody tries to steal one of his diamonds and starts to run away with 'em, I'll rope him." Needless to say, most of those anointed by Will enjoyed being singled out, even if they usually put up a mild protest.

The *Follies of 1918*, Will's third, was jam-packed with all of the headliners that Ziegfeld could corral, including Cantor (for the first time he was not in blackface), Fields, Pennington, and Marilyn Miller. An armistice had been declared, ending the Great War, and Will found that he could play off of that event for a while. "It reads like a second mortgage," he said, about the terms of the peace. Regarding all those Yankee doughboys who were not returning to the United States fast enough to satisfy their families and friends, Will insisted they should be released soon so that "they can get the mail sent to them during the war." He was especially scornful of all of those noisy parades that had been staged for "the boys over there." If they had taken all the money spent on parades and divided it among the boys, the soldiers wouldn't have to be looking for jobs, he said. His remarks about war were consistently antagonistic to the sordid business of mass killing. Sometimes it made him look like a pacifist, not the most popular ideological bent in those fervently nationalistic days. Yet, such derisive comments never cost Will any of his growing popularity, because his humor remained relatively tame. He rarely went for the jugular, and wasn't vicious. Fred Stone always said, about his friend, that he was "unconfused in a world of confusion."

While Will worked at his postwar jokes, Ziegfeld couldn't go wrong encouraging his cadre of songwriters to come up with unabashedly patriotic selections (George Gershwin, not yet a legend, had been hired as the rehearsal pianist). But if all appeared to be going well for Will's future, and Ziegfeld's, that was not in fact the case. Ziegfeld now had stiff competition from others, such as George White and his *Scandals,* and Actors Equity was raising a ruckus over money matters and unpaid rehearsal time. The fact that Cantor and Ed Wynn, a Ziegfeld comedian with a famous lisp, were both active in Equity, added to Ziegfeld's displeasure. In addition, a burgeoning silent-movie industry had begun to lure performers away from Broadway, and was creating its own captivating personalities, including Charlie Chaplin, Mary Pickford and Douglas Fairbanks, Sr. By the start of World War I, over twenty thousand movie theatres, known generally as nickelodeons, had sprung up all over the country, and there was no telling what impact that would have on people like Ziegfeld, who laid out vast sums of money for his many enterprises.

For the most part, Ziegfeld was a generous man to work for. Will didn't have any complaints about his own working conditions, nor did most of the others who toiled for the producer's "family." Ziegfeld had even given some thought to staging a one-man show, built around Will, much as he had previously done with Anna Held. When Will got wind of Ziegfeld's notion, he batted out, on his old L. C. Smith typewriter, a summary of what he might do. Oddly, despite all of his inspired roping skills, Will was a hesitant hunt-and-peck guy, whose brain moved faster than his fingers on a typewriter. However, nothing ever came of Ziegfeld's "plan."

Under no circumstances did Will regard his daily effusions as an easy way to make a living. "It's a terribly hard job," he insisted. "The guys that tell you that they can be funny at any minute, without any effort, are guys that aren't funny to anybody but themselves. I depend on newspapers for most of my inspirations. Some days this materials is good for several good lines. Then there may be a week when there's not a little worth mentioning. Maybe once a month I turn out a gag that I get a big kick out of myself."

Will reaped some reassurance about his humor when a publisher decided to put out two books of his sayings. The books, which hit the stores in 1919, were titled *Rogerisms: The Cowboy Philosopher on the Peace Conference,* and

Rogerisms: The Cowboy Philosopher on Prohibition. On the dust jacket of the latter tome, Will wrote despairingly: "You won't find the country any drier than this book."

For some time, Will's jokes about Prohibition and the Volstead Act of 1920 (which caused Ziegfeld to drop the *Frolic* for a season) became standard fare in his act. He predicted that the only good thing that would emerge from Prohibition was that it could stop men from trying to repeat stories they had heard. As for sales of his books, they weren't nearly enough to retire him from the *Follies;* but the books were, as Will realized, another means of cashing in on his agile wit.

Despite his busy schedule, Will found time to have fun. When there was an influx of deer on Shelter Island, not far from his Long Island home, he was recruited by game wardens and local farmers to help out in an organized deer hunt. Operating out of a power boat, Will lassoed one of the creatures, after the animal had panicked and run into the water. The deer was crated and shipped back to the Adirondacks. A Pathé newsreel man happened to be on the premises to record this moment for history. It marked Will's first appearance on a movie screen, although he expressed concern about how his big right ear might look to the world.

11

The Celluloid Coast

amuel Goldwyn didn't invent motion pictures but he did manage to invent himself. He as born Schmuel Gelbfisz in 1882 in Warsaw's ghetto. And Gelbfisz translated into Goldfish. By the time he was fourteen, he had walked all the way to Hamburg, Germany—his destination was America. By 1896 he got there.

After his arrival, he worked for three dollars a day as a glove cutter in a small upstate New York town. But he had made up his mind that gloves would not be his future. In 1913, in an almost incomprehensible metamorphosis, he allied himself with his brother-in-law, Jesse L. Lasky, and with a former actor, Cecil B. DeMille, to form a motion-picture company. The three men set up shop in an abandoned barn in Hollywood, California, where the sun never failed to shine. Their first project was to turn *The Squaw Man,* a successful stage play, into a motion picture.

Within a few years, Goldfish cut himself loose from the DeMille-Lasky tandem and joined with Edgar Selwyn—a playwright with an appreciation for good writing—to form Goldwyn Pictures. Part of Selwyn's last name was affixed to part of Goldwyn's—Sam Goldfish had officially become Sam Gold-wyn.

Goldwyn handled the English language in much the same way as a one-armed utility shortstop might pursue ground balls. But he boasted an enor-mous capacity for hard work, an unerring instinct about the place of motion pictures in America's future, and a dedication to his adopted land that knew no bounds. In time, Goldwyn's malaprops—one suspects that some were artfully crafted—became part of American folklore.

In 1918, Will knew little about motion pictures. In fact, his connection to the flourishing new industry, aside from his friendship with Tom Mix—already a cowboy idol of the silent screen—was limited to a visit he had made with his sisters, Maud and Sallie, to see *The Birth of a Nation,* at a New York theatre in 1915. The David W. Griffith opus, with its Ku Klux Klansmen emerging as little short of sainted figures, was a sensation throughout the country. There is no recorded evidence of what Will thought of such a portrayal, although not long afterward, he made the KKK the butt of many of his jokes. However, Sallie wrote home after seeing the picture, saying it was the finest movie show she had ever seen.

Away from the Broadway scene, in his perch on Sunset Boulevard, Gold-wyn relied on one of his writers, Rex Beach, to keep him informed about promising acting talent. Beach kept churning out he-man yarns set on the rugged frontier. (His wife was Fred Stone's sister-in-law.) Goldwyn once asked Beach if he could get Washington Irving to write the script of "The Legend of Sleepy Hollow." But Beach informed him that Irving had been dead for more than 60 years.

Beach had written a book, *Laughing Bill Hyde,* and had concluded, with Stone's urging, that Will would be a natural to play the lead in a film version of this adventure story of the Klondike goldfields. With this in mind, he went to Goldwyn and suggested that he go to see Will perform in the *Follies* or in the *Frolic.*

"Every man brings his wife to see my act," Will was fond of saying. But Goldwyn went by himself. On the night that Goldwyn was in the audience, Will wasn't even aware of his presence. If he had been, he might have thrown his rope over Sam's head.

After the show, Goldwyn, convinced more by Beach's endorsement than by his own observations, asked Will if he'd like to be in *Bill Hyde.* In a burst of unaccustomed braggadocio, Will told Goldwyn that he couldn't understand why it had taken so long for somebody to hire him for motion pictures.

"Heck, out in Hollywood these days," he said, "they're signing up everything from trained seals and cats and grand opera singers. Everybody in the world but me." Shortly after, he said, "When Goldwyn decided to make fewer and worse pictures, he immediately sent for me."

Before signing on with Goldwyn, Will reminded him that he had never done this kind of acting before. "I don't know anything about those blamed cameras," he said. "I thought pictures were only made by people like Chaplin and Fairbanks." Beach tried to put him at ease. "You can learn," he assured Will. Will then said he'd take a crack at it, which was consistent with his adventurous spirit.

Late in the summer of 1918, *Laughing Bill Hyde* went into production at Goldwyn's Fort Lee, New Jersey, studio. After each day's takes, Will would leave the studio in time to make the nightly curtain of the *Follies* at the New Amsterdam Theatre. He kept thinking he could have the best of both worlds, the *Follies* and Goldwyn. But Ziegfeld wasn't happy with Will's association with Goldwyn. He wanted to hold onto Will for the *Follies,* even though he was enticing a number of new faces into the performing cast—people like Eddie Dowling, Moran and Mack, Charles Winninger, Hazel Washburn, and Walter Catlett. At the same time Irving Berlin had crafted "A Pretty Girl Is Like A Melody," the most enduring song that was ever featured in the show.

Ziegfeld thought he had sole rights to Will's services, overlooking the fact that Will's agreement had been sealed only by Will's word. Will fully intended to stick to his word. But in his own mind, that meant he was also free to work for others. Indeed, he had never granted Ziegfeld *exclusive* rights to his talents, even if he openly credited the producer for giving him his first opportunity.

Moviemaking with Goldwyn turned out to be arduous. Commuting back and forth to Fort Lee, or to nearby Boonton, where some of the Klondike scenes were shot, put heavy pressure on Will's normally rugged constitution. Not yet forty years old, he faced up to the schedule, using Hudson River ferries to get him back and forth in order to fulfill all of his commitments on time. But he had more trouble with the way scenes were created than with his feelings of occasional fatigue.

He never could accommodate himself to the fact that movies were not always shot in a structured way—the chronology of the story oftentimes was overlooked. In one scene of *Bill Hyde,* in which Will broke out of jail to rush to the aid of a pal who was dying in a doctor's office, the director, Hobart

Henley, asked Will to cry on cue. "But I haven't broken out of jail yet," Will complained. He also expressed displeasure at having his face smeared with "paint," a tactic that he tried to avoid in the later years of his movie career. "That makeup stuff," he said, "just can't disguise this old, homely pan of mine."

Goldwyn quickly mastered the art of shooting his silent movies with dispatch. By late September, *Bill Hyde,* a bit more than one hour long, opened at the Rivoli Theatre in New York. People didn't queue up for it, and yet it was a modest success. Will's reviews were generally good. The *Motion Picture News* put its critical finger right on Will's pulse. "You'd never know he's acting," the publication said, in praise of his natural style. *The New York Times* was equally as enthusiastic, using phrases such as "magnetic personality" to describe Will. "Whether he can do anything before the camera except be himself is not the question," the *Times* concluded.

In truth, the silent screen did not show Will off to best advantage: The essential Rogers touch—a warm personality and charm that were strongly underlined by his own spoken words—did not project favorably. Spoken titles, written by platoons of writers, didn't reflect the nuances and wryness of Will's humor. Will did not specialize in those long gazes and frozen looks that so characterized the silent screen.

Yet, *Bill Hyde,* yielded enough dividends to encourage Goldwyn to stay on Will's trail. When he caught up with him in Cleveland, where the *Follies* was playing, Goldwyn offered Will $2,000 a week for the first year, with an option for a second year at $3,000 a week. At the time, Will was being paid $1,000 a week by Ziegfeld. Chaplin and Fairbanks were Hollywood millionaires at this point but Will and Betty were overwhelmed by Goldwyn's offer.

As far as Betty was concerned, going to California to live and to make silent movies sounded like heaven. After all, they would have a real, honest-to-goodness home for the first time, in an area of the country that was more like Oklahoma than the hard, paved streets of New York. A fourth child, Freddie (named for Fred Stone), had just been born, also making it necessary for the Rogerses to procure more living space for the family, which included a number of horses, goats, dogs, and other household pets.

When he got wind of Will's desire to accept Goldwyn's proposal, Ziegfeld at first became enraged—he didn't like being thwarted. But not even his pleasing words could keep Will from making the journey to California: In a few days, Will signed on the dotted line for Goldwyn. In spite of his anger toward Will for his decision to leave the *Follies* for several years (he didn't return until 1922), Ziegfeld wrote a wonderfully forgiving note to him, leaving the door open if Will ever cared to return, which he did: "My dear Will: It is with sincere regret that the time has come where you are leaving the *Ziegfeld Follies.* I have never had anyone appear in one of my attractions that was a greater joy to be associated with than you. Give my love to your family and it is with regret that I must say 'au revoir' to my friend, a real man. Very sincerely yours, Ziegfeld."

In the spring of 1919 Will journeyed to the coast alone to scout for a new house for Betty and the kids. When he got there he was troubled by the fact that he couldn't find sufficient stable space for the animals. However, Goldwyn, ever the enterprising capitalist, offered Will an old building and a fenced area on his Santa Monica lot, where the children—especially Jim—could ride to their hearts' content. In addition, Will located a comfortable house on Van Ness Avenue. It was now time to summon Betty and the kids. When Betty arrived on the coast, she was met at the station by a big, black Cadillac sedan, driven "by my first chauffeur." It was her introduction to a world unlike any she had ever seen or experienced.

In the early 1920s, Hollywood was "far out there." It was a place where nobody seemed to worry about money; where the rising breed of millionaire silent-movie luminaries entertained royalty; and where producers were constantly on the prowl for faces that could project pantomimed agony or delight on the screen. It was equally important, in the scheme of things, to have a reliable bootlegger available at all times. "It's a great place if you're an orange," said writer Herman Mankiewicz, about Hollywood. This was a world that was not in accord with Will's basic personal ethic. But he had long since learned to accommodate himself to all manner of idiosyncratic working conditions.

Somewhat disparagingly, he referred to the silents as "bucking pictures." Immediately, he coined the phrase "Celluloid coast," his snappy nickname for Hollywood. He joked that porters going on the trains to California actually weren't black. "They're only made up for the part," he said. He imagined that there was a Corona typewriter in every train berth, where would-be screenwriters were busy pounding out movie scenarios.

Notwithstanding his personal feelings about lavish parties, Will soon became a regular guest at many of Sam Goldwyn's soirees. One evening it was Doug Fairbanks and Mary Pickford, king and queen of Hollywood, who would be at his side. On another, it would be Rudolph Valentino, who overnight had become the slick-haired idol of *The Four Horsemen of the Apocalypse* and *The Sheik*. In time, he also met John Gilbert, Chaplin, Harold Lloyd, Rod LaRoque, Vilma Banky, Marion Davies, the Talmadge sisters—Norma and Constance—and he had a reunion with his old buddy, Tom Mix, now riding high atop his horse, Tony.

"Out in Hollywood they say you're not a success unless you owe fifty thousand dollars to somebody, have five cars, can develop temperament without notice or reason and have been mixed up in four divorce cases and two breach-of-promise suits," Will said, a few years after he started to make movies for Goldwyn. "I guess I'm a rank failure. I hold two distinctions in the movie business—I'm the ugliest fella in 'em and I still have the same wife I started with."

As a member, in good standing, of Hollywood's elite group, Will also managed to retain his reputation as the community's certified populist. In that role he found an unlikely friend, Anzia Yezierska, an immigrant from the Polish village of Plotsk, who had emerged from New York's sweatshops to write two unheralded books, *Salome of the Tenements* and *Hungry Hearts*. In some way, her work came to the attention of Goldwyn, who paid ten thousand dollars for the properties and immediately whisked her out to Hollywood—where she was expected to excel as a young sob sister.

At the first party she attended there, Anzia, without makeup and fancy clothes, felt totally out of place. In this mecca of unheard-of salaries, eternally blue skies, and ubiquitous palm trees, and surrounded by celebrated writing talent such as Elinor Glyn, Alice Duer Miller, and Gertrude Atherton, Anzia needed a friend. She found one in Will. As the women, in their low-cut dresses, and the men, in their custom-made tails, were departing, Will approached Anzia. "See here, gal," he said. "Can I give you a lift home?" Shocked that anyone bothered to talk to her, Anzia said she'd be pleased if he would. "I looked at the farmer's sunburned face, with the funny flop of hair hanging over his forehead, the laughing eyes, the blue flannel suit," she later wrote of the incident, "and asked him if this was Hollywood's four hundred, and how did he ever crash into this society without evening clothes."

"I can't say your name, sister," said Will. "But come on." With that, he led her to his car; and not long afterward, invited her to his home. A loner and hothead who promoted many forgotten social causes, she had an instant rapport with Will. The writer Louise Levitas Henriksen, in analyzing

Yezierska's relationship with Will, concluded that he recognized a fellow peasant in Anzia. Having seen how desperately lost she was in Hollywood, he took her to his bosom.

Anzia asked Will if he thought he could get along with the denizens of a crowded tenement on Hester Street. "Well, I never lived there," he told her, "but folks are pretty much the same on Hester Street as they are in Kalamazoo. When I was a kid on the farm, the cowhands used to talk about mean horses and stubborn yearlings. But I never met a calf or a critter I didn't understand and that didn't understand me. I saw mighty little difference between 'em. Some was ornery and some less, but I got along with 'em all."

This odd couple were close for a while. She even encouraged Will to speak before a Jewish Actors Guild affair that raised money for vacations for needy boys. "He made a crowd of Jews laugh away their heritage of sorrow," she said.

Ultimately, Will's friendship with Anzia fell apart, for he couldn't help regarding her as a yammering yenta. He objected to her constant stream of criticism about the venality and greed of the Hollywood community. "Stop fiddling the same sad tune," he told her. "Lap up the cream while you can." He granted that her hard work and talent had played a part in her rise and in his own—but so had luck. "Don't be like a punch-drunk fighter who's striking an opponent who's no longer there. You've won your fight and don't know it," he said.

Will was now part of Hollywood's highly burnished movie colony—and yet he wasn't. He never rejected Sam Goldwyn's star-studded, opulent parties and he rarely missed the hoedowns that Mary and Doug presided over at Pickfair. Neither did he turn his back on outlanders like Anzia Yezierska. But his true link was to those in the community who honored the cowboy culture, just as he did.

Men like Charlie Russell and Ed Borein, artists who had migrated to Southern California around the same time as Will had, were his more intimate pals. Both Russell (born in St. Louis in 1864), and Borein had contributed handsomely to bolstering the mythology of the old western cattle country, just as the prolific artist Frederic Remington (born in 1861) had done before them. Remington saw the West for the first time in 1881, an exposure that began for him a lifelong romance with it and included two winters in Butler County, Kansas, as a sheeprancher. He then spent his years as an illustrator for national magazines, mainly as a black-and-white artist. Charles Lummis, a transplanted easterner (curiously, Remington, too, had come from

Canton, New York, and the Yale School of Fine Arts), who was a journalist and publisher, also was close to Will—or about as close as anyone could have been to him, considering that he was essentially a loner.

Will was greatly enthusiastic about Russell's art work, which was full of action scenes featuring horses, cowboys, range animals, soldiers, and Indians. Russell possessed sincere, honest feelings about the Southwest and his work was assiduously collected and displayed by Will at his ranch.

Will was attached to Russell and Borein primarily because they were glorifiers of the cowboy mystique. His association with them enabled him to bond with those who shared his visceral reactions about the frontier. He may have escaped the frontier culture; yet he had helped to re-create it in Southern California.

Most of the silent movies Will acted in for Goldwyn were unmemorable, beginning with *Almost a Husband,* which was notable only because Peggy Wood was his costar. In this film, while Will worked as conscientiously as usual in the part of the schoolteacher in a small southern town, he realized, as did Goldwyn, that the silent screen was hardly the milieu in which he would flourish. It was Will's high-pitched, sincere voice, uttering words of wisdom and perception, that was his stock-in-trade. What was Will *without* the benefit of that voice? Then, too, the majority of the women who attended movies preferred tall, dark, and handsome leading men. Will simply didn't qualify in those respects.

While Will was away on location, filming *Almost a Husband,* three of his children simultaneously became ill with the dreaded diphtheria; only Mary escaped it. The sickest was Freddie, then less than two years old. Will was alerted to the fact that Freddie was dying. No antitoxin was available in Hollywood, causing Will to drive all night for some that he had located elsewhere. But the trip turned out to be futile, for by the time that Will arrived back home, little Freddie had died.

The tragedy hit the Rogers family hard. For a while, Will stopped working—the sap had been kicked out of him. The period of mourning for the family ended at last with a decision to abandon their house, which simply carried too many melancholy memories for them. Their new home, perched on a several-acre plot on Beverly Drive, wasn't far from Pickfair, where everyone from the Sultan of Swat (Babe Ruth) to the King of Siam came to pay homage to Fairbanks and Pickford. The Rogers place featured every kind of creature comfort that one could imagine, including a stable, a swimming pool, a tanbark riding ring, two log cabins (one with an open fireplace and five bunks along the walls), a playroom with a little stage for the children in the basement, and an eight-foot-high brick wall that enclosed the grounds.

In time, Will became sheepish about the wall, for it made the premises look like a prison or a reformatory, rather than a merry place for children to roam. He decided, therefore, to cover the walls with ivy. He got in touch with a landscape man, who told him it would take some time to grow the ivy. But Will, always an impatient man, wasn't buying that notion. "When I want ivy," he told the landscaper, "I want ivy that I can see." The man obliged him, hurriedly putting in the long creepers that had already grown out. The bill that Will received was a considerable one. But he never paid attention to such matters.

For Will's next movie, Goldwyn suggested that "Jubilo," a short story that had appeared originally in the *Saturday Evening Post,* and was written by the prolific Ben Ames Williams, would make an ideal vehicle to exploit Will's talents. The plot centered on a happy-go-lucky tramp who had been framed for a train robbery, but who finally triumphed over all adversity. A great one for tinkering with plots and titles, Goldwyn came up with a different title for the movie—*"A Poor But Honest Tramp."*

Will reacted caustically to this Goldwyn effort at bowdlerizing. In New York at the time, he sent a wordy telegram to Goldwyn, asking him what he would have called *The Birth Of A Nation.* "I thought I was supposed to be a comedian," ran the wire, "but when you suggest changing the title of *Jubilo,* you are funnier than I ever was. . . . I suppose if you had produced *The Miracle Man,* you would have called it *A Queer Old Guy!*" Finishing off his message, Will listed a number of other possible titles for *Jubilo,* all of which were obviously not meant to be taken seriously. The worst was *The Vagabond With a Heart as Big as His Appetite.*

As far as the script was concerned, Will also was appalled at what a batch of uninspired writers had done with it. He told Goldwyn that if he didn't go back to the lines used in the magazine story, he would wash his hands of the whole project. In an effort to placate Will, Goldwyn finally consented to use *Jubilo* as the title. What's more, *Jubilo* was "filmed as it was written," Will proclaimed, with a touch of pride.

Jubilo turned out to be one of the more successful early Goldwyn films. The fact that the original story had been quite popular certainly helped the movie. *Jubilo* was directed by Clarence Badger, who wisely exploited an old Negro spiritual, "In the Days of Jubilo," which evolved into a signature song for Will. Commenting on why Goldwyn had selected him to play in *Jubilo,*

Will had a ready answer: "They put me in it because they saw me one day in street clothes and figured, 'That's the guy to get—he's already dressed for the part!'"

Will continued to act in two-reelers for Goldwyn—a dozen in all over the next few years. In 1920 he was especially active, making six silents in short order, "epics" including such titles as *Jes' Call Me Jim; The Strange Boarder; Water, Water Everywhere; Honest Hutch; Cupid and the Cowpuncher* (in which Will tried to marry off all of his friends); *An Unwilling Hero; A Poor Relation; Guile of Women; One Glorious Day;* and *Uncensored Movies.*

In *Uncensored Movies,* Will tried to come to the rescue of a young woman who was being preyed upon by a lustful villain. While she was trying to fight off the evil-intentioned man, Will rallied a group of listless farmers, exhorting them to "stop shootin' craps while an American woman is carried off." Breaking down the door of the villain's cabin, Will peered searchingly into the woman's eyes. "Thank heaven, I'm in time!" he said to her. End of two-reeler.

Lila Lee, a popular female player of the 1920s, appeared opposite Will in *One Glorious Day.* Will's role called for him to debunk fake spiritualism and politics. Originally, the popular Fatty Arbuckle had been scheduled to play the part; but a major scandal involving the death of a young beauty in a sordid manner not only deprived Arbuckle of the role, but also disrupted his career.

Doubling for Romeo, the brainchild of a gifted young New Yorker named Elmer Rice, was one of the first silent-screen send-ups of the Western genre. It was the type of part that suited Will to perfection, for it appealed to his sense of the ridiculous. As a bashful cowboy, Will had a girlfriend who preferred to dream of screen heroes as her lovers—old Will took second place to them. Will saw the fun of it; so did the critics. *The New York Times* placed the film at the "top of anything Will had done." While making the movie, Will met another actor under contract to Goldwyn—Lon Chaney, the master of make-up and ghoulish portrayals. Chaney was enlisted to apply makeup to Will's face for one scene—but he had difficulty because Will made him laugh.

In another silent, directed by James Cruze (the director of *The Covered Wagon*), the script called for Will to puff on a cigar. When Will informed Cruze that cigars invariably made him as sick as the devil, he was excused from the movie.

Most of the parts that Will played under Goldwyn's aegis were much the same: He was an amiable, good-natured southwestern cowpoke who usually managed to win the girl despite his faintheartedness and chronic awkwardness. He was aided in his bashful approach on several occasions by Irene Rich, an actress friend of Betty's. Rich later achieved some prominence as the ubiquitous shill for Welch's Grape Juice.

Will's own assessment of himself underlined the image that he always tried to project on the silent screen. "I'm just an old country boy in a big town trying to get along," he'd say. "I've been eating pretty regular and the reason I have been is because I've stayed an old country boy." About the cultural merit of his movies, Will was reduced to this: "If people think my pictures are no good, I'll put on a beard and say each movie was made in Germany. Then folks will call it art!"

On-screen, his clothes looked like he had slept in them and his hair seemed not to have confronted a barber's scissors in months. But he wasn't much different offscreen, even though he already was making a bundle of money. That he never appeared to care much about the wads of cash that were coming his way served only to reinforce his profile as a generous soul who didn't have a greedy bone in his body.

For the most part, Will's films for Goldwyn made money. But when Will's contract with Goldwyn came to an end, Goldwyn left the studio. With the industry in another of its periods of ferment, Will had to make up his mind about what he planned to do with his future. Betty didn't have any doubts: She wanted to stay in California, which she thought was a wonderful place for her children. But Will had to think about where the money was going to come from. (At this time, Will had already made a down payment on a 155-acre tract of land west of Beverly Hills. The purchase price was $2,000 an acre, an outrageously steep sum of money for a site that was remote, wild, and hard to reach. Eventually, this acreage became Will's Santa Monica ranch.)

Apparently forgiving the man who had left him for the vagaries of moviemaking, Ziegfeld had not forgotten his protégé. He kept Will's phone ringing, in a ceaseless effort to lure him back to the boards in New York. But this only caused Will to glance over at his Hollywood pals, Chaplin, Fairbanks, and Pickford, and to note that they had formed their own corporation, United Artists, which was destined to make them more powerful and even richer than they already were. This helped him decide that there didn't seem to be any reason why he and Betty couldn't do the same thing. In short order, Betty and Will were producing, writing, and directing their own movies, with Will, of course, starring in each production.

They worked diligently at the new project, reading a mass of material—

manuscripts, books, plays—anything that came their way. They even mortgaged their house to raise the necessary money. A distribution deal was made with Pathé, the company for whom he had made a series of shorts (called *The Illiterate Digest*) while he had been working for Goldwyn. Presumably, Pathé was going to pay Will royalties, when and if Will's movies made any money.

Three movies were produced by the Rogers tandem: *Fruits of Faith, The Ropin' Fool,* and *One Day in 365.* Artistically, they were as good as, maybe better than, anything Will had done for Goldwyn. But the fact that Will practically invested everything he owned in this business was a dreadful tactical mistake. None of the pictures made any money and Will stared bankruptcy in the face. He lost his shirt—and was down to his cowboy hat and stock of gum. "When a loan is made for a moving picture," he remarked, "the president of the bank wants to write the story for you. The directors want to know who the leading lady is, and if they could, they want to keep her as collateral."

Of the three pictures that Will made, *The Ropin' Fool* was the best, although *One Day in 365,* a documentary of sorts, which detailed how Will and his family spent one period of twenty-four hours, was the forerunner of similar treatments presented on television a half century later.

From the start to finish, *The Ropin' Fool* was written by Will himself. In it he showcased almost every rope trick he had ever created or imitated. He used a white rope and a black pony to increase the visibility of both, and most of the tricks were shown in slow motion. (In the outtakes Will was seen missing his mouse, dog, horse, and goat targets plenty of times.) Will played the roping fool; Irene Rich, his reliable screen companion, was again his girl. The foreman in the movie, Guinn "Big Boy" Williams, became one of Will's closest pals offscreen. In the picture, Big Boy was dragged to death by a rope, with the Roping fool being blamed for his extinction. A vigilante group then pursued Will, in order to lynch him. But everything turned out to be a joke.

What wasn't a joke was Will's artistry as a roper. In the film his detractors said of him that "he oughtta be a dogcatcher." In reality, he demonstrated forcefully that he was capable of roping anything—man or beast. He could make "pretzels" with his rope, do running skips with it, or switch hands on horseback. "There's thirty years of hard practice that's gone into it," Will explained.

Despite his impecunious state, Will still had some dependable resources: his boundless energy plus his compulsive work habits. Ziegfeld again urged him to return to the *Follies,* and any number of admirers, who went around quoting his latest humorous remarks on war, peace, politics, national affairs, and other random things, encouraged him to put his pen, as well as his mouth, to work.

In 1922, Will went back East to give the *Follies* another go, at $2,500 a week. He shared honors with Gilda Gray, a shimmy artist, and with Ed Gallagher and Al Shean. The latter duo performed their hit song, "Oh, Mister Gallagher and Mister Shean," the most popular act in the show.

Not to be totally outdone, Will appeared in a funny baseball scene called "The Bull Pen," which he wrote in conjunction with Ring Lardner. By this time, Ring's enchantment with the national pastime had been sorely dimmed by the revelations concerning the 1919 Black Sox scandal.

"It was the only time, I think, until his movie career began in the thirties, that Rogers used another writer's material," wrote Ring Lardner Jr. "But the relationship between my father and him continued to be an uneasy one." This was due to Ring senior's feeling that Will always reached for the first cliché that came along.

In the sketch, Will lounged easily into the role of a veteran pitcher exchanging quips with a rookie hurler, played by Andrew Tombes. At one point, the bush leaguer says he'd like to pitch against "this fella Cobb." Will asks if he means Irvin Cobb. "That one went good," Lardner later commented, "and was thought up by Rogers." Such critics as Heywood Broun and Robert Benchley were particularly impressed with the baseball scene.

Pleased to be on Broadway again, Will missed Betty and the kids. She made several trips to New York to be with him. But that meant leaving the children at home, which was more than Will was able to tolerate. When Betty left California, the children were placed in the care of her reliable sister, Theda. However, Betty and Will remained in close touch.

About this period in Will's career, Betty wrote: "He worked as hard as he ever did in his life. There were no breaks or vacations and he hated to be away from the children and the ponies. But when he came home the following summer, to accept a new movie contract, much of his indebtedness had been paid."

By signing with Hal Roach to do a series of two-reel comedies at $3,000 a week, Will was forced to abandon the *Follies* for a year. Ziegfeld suffered from this arrangement, for the show was considerably weaker without Will. Fields joined Will on the sidelines, while Cantor delayed his *Follies* appearance until November. The critics remarked that the book for the *Follies* was poor, lacking spark and comedy. That only served to underline how important it was for Ziegfeld to keep Will around.

Doing his shooting in Culver City, Roach liked to render takeoffs on Westerns, so he cast Will in *Two Wagons, Both Covered,* a thinly veiled joshing of the original *Covered Wagon.* Not only did Will star in the film, but he also wrote a good deal of it. In the process of proving to himself that he was adept at the typewriter, Will did not tarnish the reputation of *Covered Wagon.* More important, as far as Roach was concerned, the picture made money.

One disconcerting note during Will's employment with Roach was when he ran in to trouble one day on the highway. A traffic judge fined him $100 for going forty miles an hour in a twenty-five-mile-per-hour zone—since he was en route to a speaking date at a veterans' conclave, when he was stopped by an officer, Will got sore as hell. When the story of Will's transgression hit the newspapers, he insisted it was worth paying the fine in order to appear before such a patriotic group. "No matter how much I may exaggerate," he said, "there's a certain amount of truth."

Will appeared again in the *Follies* in 1924, and for a final time in 1925, making it six appearances in all. His salary was now up to $3,000 a week, topping Fields and Ann Pennington by over $1,500 a week. In the 1924 *Follies,* Will wrote some of the dialogue, helped along by William Anthony McGuire. The orchestra played several of Victor Herbert's hummable melodies, marking the tenth time that the Dublin-born composer had worked for Ziegfeld. The four Tiller Girls, using luminous ropes, inspired by Will's routines, skipped rope on a totally darkened stage. Will's monologue was greeted enthusiastically, especially when he noted that the difference between a good *Follies* and a bad *Follies* showed up in the gross receipts at the end. "There was about a $1.80 difference," he laughed.

One might have expected that, by the time the 1925 edition of the *Follies* came along, Will would have been immunized against any personal reaction to nudity on Ziegfeld's stage. However, in always reaching for new ways to transform the musical theatre, Ziegfeld encouraged Julian Mitchell, who did his staging, to undress his beauties to a greater extent than usual: On this occasion, the girls would be in the nude under chiffon coverings, something that Will deemed unconscionable. "Fix it or I quit!" he warned Ziegfeld. The producer caved in to Will's streak of puritanism. The act was "cleaned up" and Will appeared in both the spring and summer versions of the *Follies.* It's hard to believe that anyone other than Will could have successfully threatened

Ziegfeld in such a way. However, Ziegfeld's attempt at striptease failed to alter Will's positive feelings about the man. After he left the *Follies,* following the 1925 version, Will wrote that there was never a musical show produced "that wasn't a weak imitation of Ziegfield." And Will misspelled Flo's name, just as he always did.

Will's encounter with Louise Brooks, "the girl in the black helmet," in the 1925 *Follies,* dramatically illustrated that he had his troubles with some women. Brooks had left a Kansas farm to become a symbol of the Jazz Age—a negative one, moralists huffed. Before she joined the *Follies* in 1925, she had danced with Martha Graham and Denis Shawn and shared a bed with the notorious womanizer. Chaplin,

Ziegfeld found a spot for her with Will in a specialty number that put her atop a fifteen-foot tower in the middle of the stage. Starting with a tiny noose on his lasso, Will twirled faster and faster, bigger and bigger, until his rope hissed around Louise and her fellow chorines. One evening, while ascending a staircase chock-full of glorified girls, Will's lasso wrapped around Brooks, his young flapper associate. When he reached Brooksie, as she was called, Will, in a moment of nasty inspiration, stuck his cud of chewing gum smack on the end of her "haughty nose." For his delicious insolence, the audience rewarded Will with a mighty roar.

But when the curtain came down and the two performers went backstage to take off their makeup, Brooks flew at her tormentor, as only she could. "You son of a bitch, I'll kill you!" she shrieked. Will thoughtfully backed away before she could blacken his eyes. He never tried such a stunt again with her. She disliked him intensely, judging him to be nothing more than a "hayseed with a gimmick." She was aware that Will was the darling of the public, but to her, Fields was the real artist, while Will was simply a cowboy without talent.

Will Rogers, as a lively but not-very-good student at Kemper Military Academy. *AP/Wide World Photos.*

Betty (right, chin in hand) and Will (left) were still far apart in this 1900 photo.
AP/Wide World Photos.

In the 1917 Ziegfeld *Follies* Will was surrounded by chorus line beauties.
UPI/Bettmann.

An unlikely Follies star.
UPI/Bettmann.

The merry cast of *Three Cheers,* with Will at left, entertains Fred Stone, Will's best pal (right), who was recovering from plane crash injuries. *UPI/Bettmann.*

TOP: Preparing to lay the cornerstone of a New York theater in 1926, Will, dressed better than usual, joined impresario Flo Ziegfeld (right). *UPI/Bettmann.*

BOTTOM LEFT: Cowboy actor Tom Mix (right) was a favorite of Will's. *Culver.*

BOTTOM RIGHT: After Charles Lindbergh (left) flew alone across the Atlantic in 1927, he became Will's hero. *Brown Brothers.*

Top: Irene Rich appeared in a number of Will's movies. This one was *So This Is London*. *UPI/Bettmann.*

Left: Will Jr. learns the ropes from his proud Dad. *AP/Wide World Photos.*

At Children's Hospital in Boston, Will and baseball idol Babe Ruth got together to cheer up the kids. *AP/Wide World Photos.*

Only Blue Boy in *State Fair* could dare to upstage Will. *Brown Brothers.*

Eddie Cantor (second from right) co-starred with Will in the *Follies.* Comic Joe
E. Brown is on the left. *Culver Pictures.*

Will didn't last long as honorary mayor of Beverly Hills. *AP/Wide World Photos.*

Opposite Will in *A Connecticut Yankee,* seductive Myrna Loy thought he was something of a prude. *Brown Brothers.*

Will's wisecrack at 1932 political rally gets a reaction from (left to right) FDR, his son James, William G. McAdoo, and Jim Farley. *Culver Pictures.*

At work on a precariously
balanced typewriter.
Culver Pictures.

In *Judge Priest*, Will exchanged comments with Stepin Fetchit. *UPI/Bettmann.*

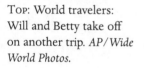

Top: World travelers: Will and Betty take off on another trip. *AP/Wide World Photos.*

Right: British actress Madeleine Carroll chats with Will in Paris. *UPI/Bettmann.*

Top: Will was usually a winner at polo. Actors Leslie Howard, Carole Lombard, Spencer Tracy, and Johnny Mack Brown (left to right) shared his love of the sport. *UPI/Bettmann.*

Right: Charlie Chaplin mimicked Will, so Will returned the favor. *UPI/Bettmann.*

LEFT: By the mid-thirties only Shirley Temple rivaled Will in popularity. Actress Janet Gaynor also was an admirer. *UPI/Bettmann.*

BELOW: Breakfast with Gashouse Gang pitcher Dizzy Dean (left), joined by columnist Damon Runyon and Dizzy's wife, was a highlight of Will's coverage of the 1934 World Series in Detroit. *UPI/Bettmann.*

TOP: Rival riverboat captains Will and writer Irvin S. Cobb in *Steamboat Round the Bend*, Rogers's final film. *AP/Wide World Photos.*

RIGHT: Less than two weeks before his death, Will made out his will. *AP/Wide World Photos.*

I, WILL ROGERS, hereby publish and declare my Will:

My wife's name is Betty Rogers; I have only three children now living, namely: Will Rogers, Jr., James Rogers and Mary Rogers.

I give, devise and bequeath all of my property, both community and otherwise, unto my said wife, Betty Rogers.

In the event my wife shall not survive me, I give, devise and bequeath all of my estate unto my said children who shall survive me, share and share alike; provided, however, that should any of my said children predecease me, leaving issue, the share to which such deceased child would have been entitled if living, I give, devise and bequeath to his or her issue.

I hereby appoint my wife, Betty Rogers, O. N. Beasley, of Beverly Hills, Oscar Lawler and James K. Blake, as Executors hereof; should my wife not survive me, I appoint my said son, Will Rogers, Jr., in her place as such executor, and direct that no bond be required of my said wife or son as such executor.

Dated August 3rd, 1935.

Will Rogers

The foregoing instrument, consisting of one (1) page only, was, at the date thereof, by the said Will Rogers, signed, sealed and published as, and declared to be, his last will and testament, in the presence of us, who at his request, and in his presence, and in the presence of each other, have subscribed our names as witnesses thereto.

Residing at _____

Residing at *Jalama Ranch Ca*

Preparing for his last adventure, Will looked over Wiley Post's ill-fated plane.
AP/Wide World Photos.

Sad news for Claremont's citizens. *AP/Wide World.*

Death in Alaska: August 15, 1935.

12

Kidding the Famous

ach generation of Americans has suffered from its share of cockeyed beliefs, absurdities, and humbuggeries, many of which have become fair game for critics tempted to ridicule them. Will was one of those who had joined the voluble club of critics and persistent conversationalists, which included people like Heywood Broun, Herbert Bayard Swope, politician Al Smith, Irvin S. Cobb, Alexander Woollcott, and theatre analyst George Jean Nathan. These gentlemen were an all-American talking team, and Will was one of them.

As he approached his task, Will's penchant for being relatively noncombative, even when he delivered messages that were scornful, accounted for much of his rising popularity. He challenged clichés, truisms, and stereotypes (even though he went along with some), poking away merrily at supposedly sacrosanct institutions. He specialized in the polite but sly insult, which became his chief weapon in dealing with the high and mighty.

By the early 1920s, Will had already achieved considerable renown as a kidder and needler of the famous. Although he acknowledged that he was always anxious stepping up to the dais to perform his verbal chastising of

143

others, he took on a grueling schedule of after-dinner speeches. "I never saw an audience that I ever faced with any confidence," he insisted. But for fees as high as $1,000 per engagement, he was willing to undergo stage fright. He appeared constantly before groups at the Lambs and Friars clubs. He worked charity functions and corporation banquets, and spoke before bankers and automobile manufacturers. He even appeared before an audience at New York's Sing Sing Prison.

Many of Will's after-dinner speeches were bluntly aimed at the very people who invited him as a paid speaker. In fact, it became his stock-in-trade to rough up the hosts. One night he called a group of car dealers "old-time horse-trading gyps with white collars on." An audience of advertising men was greeted as "the robbing hoods of America." Shoemen at a convention were dubbed "brigands and pasteboard highbinders." Retail milliners held a high-fashion show at the Astor Hotel ballroom, where Will was even more of an attraction than five hundred assorted hats. "Some of those hats are as funny looking as I am," said Will, with his usual dose of self-deprecation.

Speaking at an elegant banquet at the Waldorf, under the auspices of the association of corset manufacturers, Will said, "This shows you what a degrading thing this after-dinner speaking is. I want to get out of it in a few weeks and get back to the movies." (This was clearly a disingenuous remark, for at the rate he was being paid, Will had no such notion of abandoning the banquet circuit.) "These corset builders might not do a lot to help civilization but they are a tremendous aid to the eyesight," he continued. "The same problem confronts them that does the people that run the subways of New York City. They both have to get so many pounds of human flesh into a given radius."

If he wasn't berating his cash customers, Will could always fall back on Congress, and he did: "I defy every congressional investigating committee— and you certainly can't pick any more useless body of men than they are—to say that a bathing suit on a beautiful girl don't come under the heading of legitimate advertising."

He once told a hall filled with bankers that, next to after-dinner speaking, they belonged to the most nonessential industry in the land. He was equally firm in putting down the Chamber of Commerce of the United States, which he characterized as "elite ladies' sewing circles." When a fellow gets into the chamber of commerce, Will added, "he quits mowing his lawn." Before a lawyers' group, he jokingly added up the number of their profession in the country—approximately 90 percent of America's population of 110 million—

and he deduced that you couldn't find two of them who hadn't worked for an oil company at some time. He put in a deprecating word or two about men who served as Secretary of the Navy. "Sometime this country," he said, "is going to get some man as secretary of the navy who has at least received a picture postcard of Annapolis. Josephus Daniels had never been in anything bigger than a rowboat up to the time he was made secretary."

His earliest targets had been men like Woodrow Wilson and Henry Ford. Ford's peace ship had been subjected to Will's needling in the late teens. Now after Ford engaged in a virulent campaign of anti-Semitism through his personal newspaper, *The Dearborn Independent,* Will had another opportunity to chastise the industrialist. The paper hinted that there was a worldwide Jewish conspiracy under way, which was revealed through exposure of the "Protocols of the Learned Elders of Zion," a document purportedly drawn up at an 1897 Zionist Congress in Switzerland. Taking note of a Jewish boycott of Ford cars, in retaliation for the spread of such lying propaganda, Will quipped that the "boycott may not be a complete success yet—but it will be as soon as someone learns how to make a cheaper car." This was a typical example of Will's benign sarcasm—how badly did he *really* rough up Ford through such a remark?

Faced with broadening his net of "victims," Will did not lack other convenient targets. Taking note of the fact that a federal judge named Kenesaw Mountain Landis seemed to spend more time watching baseball games than he did in his own courtroom, Will remarked that the Judge "is in Comiskey Park (Chicago) almost every day, anyway, so they might as well name him baseball commissioner." Shortly after, Landis, indeed, was named to the job, at a moment when the infamous Black Sox Scandal had just broken.

President Warren G. Harding had been an especially juicy butt for Will's jibes. He possessed few obvious credentials for being chief executive of the United States, following an election in which he campaigned against Democrat James M. Cox on a platform that heralded the fact that he would restore the country to "normalcy." (In commenting on the defeated Cox, Will said, quite accurately, that he didn't know of a quicker way to be forgotten in this country than to be defeated for president. "A man can leave the country and people will always remember that he went someplace. But if he is defeated for president, they can't remember that he ever did anything!")

Harding's version of normalcy consisted of his playing golf and poker with his cronies and entertaining his girlfriend in the White House clothing closet.

A particularly poor speechmaker, Harding was derided by others besides Will. Mencken described Harding's words as sounding like a "string of wet sponges." It was clear that Harding's suntanned, classically handsome looks had helped win him the election when Americans were war weary and fed up with trying to solve the world's problems.

When Will was in Washington, on a tour with the Ziegfeld *Frolic,* he performed in a skit (written by him) in which Harding talked incessantly about his golf game during an important cabinet meeting. Shortly after this broadside attack, Will found himself actually paying a call on the president in the White House. Because he hadn't yet seen Will's skit at the theatre, Harding acted congenially toward Will. But Will knew something was amiss when the president, who enjoyed inviting fellow sportsmen to join him for a game of golf, later excluded Will from a group including Ring Lardner and sportswriter Grantland Rice, both friends of his.

Will soon learned what was wrong when one of Harding's emissaries dropped in at the theatre and asked him to cease from making any further ad hominem remarks about the president's golfing habits. Surprised at such a request, Will nevertheless omitted any comments on the subject in future performances. Despite the alterations in Will's monologue, the president failed to put in an appearance at the *Frolic.* During one of his curtain calls, while seeking to make amends for the rift with the president, Will offered this comment: "I have cracked quite a few jokes on public men here, both Republicans and Democrats. I hope I have not given offense. In fact, I don't believe any *big* man will take offense." He added that both Teddy Roosevelt and Woodrow Wilson had laughed along with everybody else at his barbs directed against them.

Much was made in the newspapers about the "vendetta" between Will and the president. But it wasn't clear whether Will appreciated the publicity or resented it. However, one night at the *Follies,* after Will learned that Harding had chosen not to attend any of his performances, he concluded out loud that "the humorous relations between the White House and myself are rather strained." In the following months, Will made other mildly negative remarks about Harding. In an open letter to the president, Will put himself up for appointment as ambassador to the court of St. James, promising he would accept the job for "pin money" and take a chance "at what else I can get." He advised the Democrats that in the upcoming 1924 election, "there is only one way to get even with Harding now and that is to leave him in there for another term." Will added: "It must be getting near election time. He has commenced taking up all the babies and kissing them. Mothers, when you see your baby picked up by someone these days, it is either one of two men—a kidnapper or a politician."

Will, of course, did not know that Harding was about to be faced with scandals, of a personal and political nature, that would wreck his administration and his health. In desperation, Harding left for a trip to Alaska, in an attempt to free his troubled mind from the rising stench of his regime.

When Harding, an unwitting prisoner of his own ineptitude and corrupt friends, collapsed and died in mid-August 1923, while on his escape journey, Will wrote a tribute to the dead president. Feeling guilt over the jabs he had taken at Harding, Will said: "He had a great sense of humor and could stand all the jokes ever told about him and his policies. The first time I ever met him, Will Hays [the movie industry's "czar"] introduced him to me in the White House and he repeated to me a lot of the jokes that I had told a way before. . . . I like President Harding. You see I had met him and didn't believe any man could meet him and talk to him and not like him. I was scared when they took me to meet him but he made me feel just like I was talkin' to some good old prosperous Ranchman out home." If Harding had a weakness, Will continued, it was in trusting his friends and "the man that don't do that, then there is something the matter with him. Betrayed by friendship is not a bad memorial to leave."

Will wound up by anointing Harding as a "REAL HONEST-TO-GOD MAN." Such an appraisal surely reflected Will's obsequious side. Better yet, he didn't care to say anything mean about a dead man.

Politicians continued to be red meat for Will, even though he sometimes backed away from things he uttered. If his targets protested, Will's rebuttal was rarely malicious. Once, after a minor tiff with New York's playboy mayor, Jimmy Walker, a better songwriter than politician, Will countered: "There ain't nobody but Jimmy and me should be slower to get mad at each other. We both make our living by kidding the public."

After Franklin Delano Roosevelt's losing race as the Democratic vice presidential candidate in 1920, his wife, Eleanor, became increasingly active in various social causes. In 1923 she was named a key member of a group participating in the judging of the Bok Award, a one-hundred-thousand-dollar prize given to a person who could devise a workable plan for world peace. As thousands of plans poured in, isolationist senators derided Eleanor for her quixotic rule. Some even called her "subversive." Will made several joking remarks about Eleanor's activism. But he carefully avoided joining the bitter naysayers.

However, at the next year's Democratic convention in New York's Madison Square Garden, he seized an opportunity to needle Eleanor. Having supported Governor Al Smith of New York for the presidential nomination, Eleanor sat knitting furiously, in the 100-degree heat, as John W. Davis, the colorless corporation lawyer, won the party's designation. Observing Eleanor's grim-faced behavior from the gallery, Will asked her if "she was doing the names of future victims of the guillotine." It was hardly complimentary for her to be considered a latter-day version of Madame DeFarge.

Al Smith was a popular politician whom Will had gotten to know as a result of an after-dinner speaking gig. He was a down-to-earth operative with an enormous appeal to the citizens of New York. Called on to introduce Smith at the Newspaper Women's Club in 1922, Will provided the listeners with a swatch of history about the governor.

"When Al grew up as a barefoot boy on the Lower East Side of New York," Will drawled, "there were only two professions open to the youth of New York City. One was newsboy. The other was bootblack. Al chose being a newsboy because there was no work attached to it. Newsboys all turned out to be politicians and the bootblacks all turned out to be bankers."

Smith was cagey enough to accept Will for what he was, an ingratiating entertainer with a good line. Even when Will advised Smith not to run for president against the Republican Herbert Hoover in 1928, because "you got no issue . . . you can't lick this prosperity thing," Smith refused to become angry with him. But with the approach of the 1928 campaign against Hoover, Smith, now the nominee, was confronted with an estimate of his chances that didn't bring a smile to his face.

"There's darn little difference between Smith and Hoover," began Will, already anticipating that radio, for the first time, would play a significant role in the election. "I've been studying up on them and here's the difference: Hoover wants all the drys and as many wets as possible [a reference to the heated struggle over the issue of Prohibition]. Smith wants all the wets and as many drys as possible. Hoover says he'll relieve the farmer even if he has to appoint a commission. Hoover says that the tariff will be kept up, Smith says the tariff will not be lowered. Hoover is in favor of prosperity. So is Smith. Hoover wants no votes solely on religious grounds, Smith wants no votes on religious grounds [Smith's Catholicism was a heated issue in the campaign]. . . . If a man can tell the difference between them, he could make a sucker out of Solomon. The only difference I can see is Al uses 'woids' like 'foist,' 'poisonal,' 'raddio,' 'dese,' 'dem,' 'dose,' and 'horspital.'"

Although Smith may have sought an endorsement from Will, he was forced to settle for Will's ambiguity. In addition, after Smith and Hoover were nominated, Will announced that he would run for the presidency himself. "I want it understood," he declared, "that my platform is made out of planks carried in by voters. Anybody with ten votes can have a plank and that policy is already getting us a lot of support. . . . We are also leaving room between planks for any wisecracks that we think should be inserted. . . . Whatever Hoover or Smith promises, we'll raise 'em twenty percent. We will not only give the farmers relief, we'll cure 'em of being farmers."

Curiously, a half-dozen years earlier, Will had actually gone out on a limb for a politician he didn't even know. Asked to speak in behalf of a patrician bluenose named Ogden Livingston Mills, a candidate for reelection to Congress on the Republican ticket, Will unleashed one of the most peculiar supporting speeches in history (Teddy Roosevelt Jr. had urged him to make the speech, and Will said he couldn't possibly refuse a Roosevelt). Showing up at a rally at New York's Town Hall in October 1922, he began by informing the audience that he didn't really want his speech to go over, for that might draw him into politics, which would be disastrous. "I've always tried to live honestly," he averred. Then Will acknowledged that he didn't even know the name of Mills's opponent. What's more, he didn't know Mr. Mills and hadn't even met him. "Maybe that's why I might say something good about him, more than anyone else."

As if the crowd of Mills partisans weren't already in a state of shock, Will didn't stop there. Mills, he said, had taken up politics even though he was wealthy *before* he went into politics. Will then wound up his reverse paean by reminding everybody that Mills was the only politician other than Henry Cabot Lodge, who could get past the front door of an exalted Fifth Avenue residence without delivering a package. "His platform is a living wage for bootleggers and free medical examinations for those who drink the stuff they sold."

Throughout the speech, Mills sat frozen and unsmiling. Will later said that Mills could never figure out whether Will was "for him or against him." Miraculously, Mills won the election, but it was not recalled if he ever sent a thank-you card to Will for his idiosyncratic endorsement. (The crowning moment of Mills's life arrived in the middle of the depression when President Hoover named him to the thankless job of secretary of the treasury.)

The New York Times, on hand to hear Will's words, reported on the event. In fact, the newspaper's editorialists clucked about "humorists as campaigners," praising Will's alertness, while questioning whether Mills could possibly benefit from such odd support.

This publicity won Will innumerable after-dinner engagements, further testing his endurance. The Mills story also came to the attention of V. V. McNitt, the founder of the McNaught Newspaper Syndicate. McNitt admitted getting a chuckle out of Will's role, and he contacted him to make him an offer to write a weekly humor piece. Will responded by saying that he was flattered, but they he had already promised the New York *Evening Herald* that he'd do such an assignment for them.

However, a sample piece Will produced for the *Herald* turned out to be flatter than a turd on Will's ranch (as Homer Croy delicately put it), so McNitt felt free again to approach Will on the subject. After some prodding by the ingenious cartoonist, Rube Goldberg, who presciently saw the makings of a budding genius in his friend Will, McNitt joined his partner, Charles V. McAdam, at a bargaining session with Rogers at the New Amsterdam Theatre. Will was still appearing there in the *Follies,* which had had a successful summer run that was extended into the winter season.

McNitt encouraged Will to write material that would be much in the mold of his topical nightly humor at the *Follies.* The syndicate offered him $500 a week. The clincher for the deal, a handshake agreement—true to Will's tradition—came when Carr Van Anda, the managing editor of *The New York Times,* also expressed an interest in picking up Will's output, for $150 a week. Will knew the *Times* was not noted for its irreverence. On the contrary, it had a reputation for a journalistic hauteur that annoyed many people. Yet, an opportunity to appear in the *Times*'s august pages intrigued Will. After all, it wasn't as if he had never written before for money. He had done it years ago when he was traipsing around South Africa and South America. At that time, he had written reports for the Claremore newspaper. In 1920 he had covered the political conventions for the *Los Angeles Record,* even though he was miles away, making the silent movie *Cupid, the Cowpuncher.*

With the help of Charlie Driscoll, an editor at McNaught, Will embarked on his role as thumb-sucking commentator about whatever came into his mind. (By signing with the McNaught Syndicate, Will joined a stable of distinguished contributors, including his pal, Irvin S. Cobb; Dale Carnegie; gossip columnist Walter Winchell; O. O. McIntyre; and the troubadour of the sports pages, Paul Gallico.) Almost anything was fair game for Will's pen, whether it was presidential inertia; economic conferences; labor agitation; the Red scare and Attorney General A. Mitchell Palmer's raids on the unpatriotic; rich men's greed; big-league baseball; the bigots of the Ku Klux Klan; Prohibition; military parades; oil scandals; or Mr. Ford's automobiles. Driscoll was put in charge of laundering the spelling and punctuation in Will's column, which rolled blithely and ungrammatically off his typewriter. But it wasn't Driscoll's role to touch either the substance or the dominating theme of each column.

The inaugural column appeared in the *Times* on Sunday, December 24, 1922, and within a short time the column was being widely syndicated in places like Chicago, Boston, Sharon (Connecticut), Galveston, Washington, D.C., and Lexington (Kentucky). The fees paid by the papers ranged from a low of $3 in Sharon to the *Times's* own $150. For a while, as he developed his routine, Will wrote rather short pieces. But as he got going with his punchy, pointed observations about congressmen, sports icons, scoundrels, and poor Mr. Harding, Will was able to knock out as many as fifteen hundred words per column, pleasing his sponsors no end. (One piece entitled, "Batting for Lloyd George," referring to his "blossoming out as a weekly infliction"— Driscoll let the misspelling of "affliction" go by in order to capture Will's flavor. Will went on to explain that the *Times* had originally signed up Lloyd George, Britain's prime minister, for a "pack of his memoirs," but after the last election, Lloyd George couldn't remember anything "so they sent for me to fill in the space where he would have had his junk.")

A rival syndicate approached Will, offering $800 a week and causing him to mention it to McAdam. When McAdam quickly raised Will to $1,000 a week, Will told McAdam he thought McAdam was "nuts" to make such a concession. But, naturally, Will took the money. McAdam, of course, knew what he was doing, for Will had caught on around the country like a prairie fire. Within a couple of years, over one hundred newspapers subscribed to Will's weekly prose, and eight years later, nearly four hundred papers were in his camp.

Betty was a tempering influence on Will, whether it related to his behavior on the stage or to his words in the column. She didn't always agree with what he said and felt free to tell him so. She was a stern critic of some of his off-the-cuff barbs—for example, she complained that she thought Will had been tactless in his after-dinner gig on behalf of Ogden Mills—and if she saw a sentence or two that bordered on gratuitous meanness, she was quick to hold up the red light.

Will didn't have much patience with censors. But Betty came as close as anyone to filling that difficult role for him. After he typed out his musings, in that painful hunt-and-peck manner, she'd often scan the remarks, not paying attention to butchered syntax or misuse of language (which were Driscoll's domain), but only to make certain that he hadn't unfairly attacked anybody. Once he had completed the column, Will would look it over with dispatch, with a pencil in his hand in order to make minor corrections.

Rarely did Will work on second takes. Over the years, he learned to become less of a rambler, sticking to one theme or personality in a column, rather than proceeding in a stream-of-consciousness mode, which was often the case in his earlier columns. It got so that Will's readers expected him to address almost every important or unimportant issue that faced the country. He generally didn't disappoint them. His approach was seldom arrogant and he managed to hit the nail on the head most of the time. Like most writers, he usually cleared his throat at the beginning of his column, with such words and phrases as, "It seems to me"; or, "Well"; or, "Let's say." But inevitably he'd get rolling with the same line that characterized his *Follies* opening: "Well, all I know is just what I read in the papers."

Will never changed his habit of emphasizing certain thoughts by employing capital letters. He had always done that in his endless stream of love letters to Betty and in his correspondence with his late father. While he worked at his pieces, he invariably chewed on something—whether it was gum, paper, pencils, string, rubber bands, or food, it didn't seem to matter much. The chewing process may have facilitated his thinking, but it didn't help his syntax. Letter writers constantly excoriated him for his ignorance about such matters. In a rebuttal, he said: "I'm not sure what a syntax means. But it must be bad because it's got 'sin' and 'tax' in it."

He confessed that his grammar wasn't very good, simply because he didn't know any better. But when critics lashed out at him, he showed some sensitivity to such attacks. His response was that the policy of *The New York Times* was in "direct contrast with mine. . . . I'm in no way responsible for *their* policy." By implication, that meant the *Times* wasn't responsible for his beliefs, either.

In a biography of Rogers, Ben Yagoda suggests that Will's fractured style—

full of irony and flat-out sincerity—"has led some to surmise that he was a direct descendant of nineteenth century 'Phunny Phellows' like Charles Farrar Browne (creator of Artemus Ward), Henry Wheeler Shaw (Josh Billings), David Ross Locke (Petroleum Nasby) and their follower Finley Peter Dunne (Mr. Dooley). Yet those humorists were all ventriloquists, fashioning untutored characters through whose broken grammar . . . comic truth could be spoken. Will was speaking for himself, more or less."

Will's early columns often dealt with peace and economic conferences, which seemed to occupy much of the attention of American presidents and their representatives. And by 1923, Will had gone from one-liners into more detailed, cogent explorations of these conferences, always managing to express the average citizen's frustration and contempt in regard to such pompous events.

The following are typical excerpts and analyses from his columns:

> Every time there is a big conference there is always a war to go with it.
>
> There is a mess of conferences going on. But they are just like the poor and the Democrats, they will always be with us.
>
> As I go to press there is just about to be wound up in Paris what is called an Economic Conference which at this early day and date looks like it will be awful lucky if it don't wind up in an awful nice war.
>
> Germany made some sort of proposal that there would be no more war for a century. But it was turned down by England and France. You see, they been fighting for over forty years and it's awful hard to go against custom in those countries.
>
> A conference is just an admission that you want someone to join you in your troubles. The world can't improve till it gets so poor that it can't send delegates to a conference. Then it will begin to improve by depending on itself.
>
> The big news of the week was President Harding ordering our boys back from Germany. Senator Jim Reed reminded the President and Congress that they were still over there. I tell you it's lucky some time to have a fellow around that keeps his eyes open for little things like that.
>
> You can't gain ground at a conference. You only try to remedy the damage done at the last one. . . . Generally our delegates arrive at a conference with a band and leave incognito.
>
> The best omen of international good will is that conferences are getting shorter. Now if they will do away with 'em entirely there will be no war.

These weekly columns, as well as a series of essays that Will wrote in support of Bull Durham smoking tobacco, attracted considerable favorable comment. He drew some criticism for connecting his material with these tobacco ads, but he saw nothing wrong with it. After all, very little research in those years proclaimed the deleterious impact of tobacco on a person's health. In one of his Bull Durham commercials, Will noted that "they are trying to pass an amendment to keep children from working. Now children didn't want to work, but they got tired of waiting for somebody else to do it. If they would just put through an amendment to *make* grown people all work, there would be no need to have this children one."

The Readers' League of America, working in conjunction with publishers Albert and Charles Boni, asked Will if he'd like to assemble a choice selection of his pithy thoughts for a book that would be titled *The Illiterate Digest*, a takeoff of the weekly magazine, *The Literary Digest*. The publishers of *The Literary Digest* felt that Will's use of such a title would diminish their prestige. (This was long before *The Literary Digest* helped to do itself in with a misfiring poll in 1936 that predicted that Alfred M. Landon would overwhelm Franklin D. Roosevelt in the presidential election that year.)

However, despite the protestations of *The Literary Digest*, Will went ahead, insisting that his only problem was finding an appropriate person to write an introduction for the book. The first person Will had in mind was William Allen White, the publisher and editor of the Emporia (Kansas) *Gazette*. Will kind of liked White because of his middle name, "which sounds so literary." When White went home to Kansas after announcing his candidacy for governor, Will figured that that disqualified him. "It would make the book a laughing stock," Will said.

Then he thought about Arthur Brisbane, William Randolph Hearst's distinguished editorial writer. But when the stuffy Brisbane told Will that everything he wrote about must point up a moral—"There must be a lesson in every paragraph," he said—Will dismissed his candidacy out of hand. Next he considered his pal, Irvin S. Cobb, who punched out a column called "My Favorite Story." But Cobb informed Will that he was going duck shooting in Louisiana and wouldn't care to miss out on a single duck, even for the pleasure of writing an introduction to the *Encyclopaedia Britannica*. Ring Lardner might add a little touch of comedy to his book, Will thought. But when Will invited Ring to write the intro for free, Lardner responded that there wasn't a reason in the world that he should cough up a joke for nothing.

Elinor Glyn, the Hollywood writer, was another possibility. Will had a notion that she might drape her first few lines in tiger skins. Finally, he thought of the Spanish writer, Vincente Blasco Ibáñez, author of *The Four*

KIDDING THE FAMOUS ❖ 155

Horsemen of the Apocalypse. The funny thing, said Will, was that Blasco Ibáñez "is the only author I ever read." But he was afraid that Blasco Ibáñez would write the introduction in Spanish and that nobody could read it.

So it all boiled down to Will having to write the introduction himself. "Why monkey with those writers?" he asked. In addition, Will reminded everyone that his full name was William Penn Adair Rogers. "Let some literary guy top that," he crowed.

In *The Illiterate Digest,* Will covered everything, including Fred Stone ("he was brought up to do right and never knew anything else"); secondhand gum; the state of the state of California; a presidential boomlet for himself; the Teapot Dome Scandal; and the fact that Henry Ford had announced that 90 percent of the people in the United States were "satisfied." He even turned one chapter over to the thirteen-year-old Will Jr., who described how he filled in for his dad at the 1924 Democratic convention and found himself talking to an "old man" named Jackie Coogan, who was only a few years removed from being a silent-screen child star. "Papa," wrote Will Jr., "told us that we didn't have to be very good at reporting . . . the only thing necessary was *endurance.*"

When the book was published, it was generally well received. Even normally acerbic book critics raved about it. "His droll comments on men and events have become so popular," said *The Nation,* "that he finds himself— probably to his surprise—a national figure. It is just as well for Mr. Rogers that his caustic observations are wrapped in humor. If they were delivered without the funny tags, his audience would set the dogs on him."

The *Saturday Review of Literature* was equally ecstatic: "Somebody once gave him the license of free speech—or perhaps he took it without asking. But at any rate, in the past few years he has probably turned over more heavy stones and thrown hot sunlight underneath than any man in the United States."

The Illiterate Digest appeared before Will had a chance to talk about the personality and character of the dour Calvin Coolidge, who succeeded to the presidency after Harding's death in 1923. But by 1928, when Coolidge uttered his famous statement in which he declined the nomination, "I do not choose to run" (which Will insisted was the best-worded refusal of a nomination ever uttered by a candidate: "He spent a long time in the dictionary looking for that word 'choose,' instead of 'will not'"), Will managed to have enormous fun at Coolidge's expense.

To Will, Coolidge was "Old Stoneface," a person who made a specialty out of professional taciturnity. "If a man will just stay hushed, he is hard to find out," explained Will. "Coolidge either does one of two things. He does what nobody thinks he'll do or he won't do anything. Generally, the latter."

From the days when Coolidge had risen from New England politics, he had developed a well-deserved reputation as a man without a spark of humor. When Will paid a call on him at the White House (Will seemed to meet every well-known person of his time), Alice Roosevelt Longworth, the sharp-tongued daughter of Teddy Roosevelt, bet Will a box of bonbons, against a new hat, that he couldn't force a laugh out of the president. Upon being officially introduced to Coolidge, Will leaned over and asked: "What was the name again, please?" Every witness to the event agreed that the president broke out in a smile. Will won the bet.

Once, when Will asked Coolidge how he kept fit for his job, Coolidge responded that he did it "by avoiding the big problems." It was difficult to tell whether the president was being sarcastic or just plain truthful. Will was inclined to give the president the benefit of the doubt and assume that Coolidge was just being candid.

Economist and historian John Kenneth Galbraith has described Coolidge as a man of "singular aridity." Many other critics of the period also scorned him as a second-rater, a "sphinx," a man as narrow as a tape measure, "a study in inertia." Will never went that far. He nursed a certain fondness for the man from Vermont, because he was partial to Coolidge's directness and economy of expression. But he always regarded him as a convenient target.

In appraising the Republican convention in 1924 that nominated Coolidge, Will said the delegates could have saved themselves a good deal of trouble. "He could have been nominated by post card," quipped Will. Going on to predict that Silent Cal, as he came to be known by supporters and detractors alike, would have as much trouble getting elected as a fish would have swimming underwater, Will proved his political savvy. The Democratic de-signee, John W. Davis, was drubbed by almost two to one, as Will told everyone that Coolidge's landslide election was "about as big a surprise as the announcement that Xmas was coming in December."

The first message to Congress that Coolidge delivered—or mumbled, which would be more precise—was summed up by Will as follows: "When you figure that the gentleman hasn't used his voice in months, why, any defects in delivery can easily be overlooked." Will considered himself lucky to have Coolidge in the White House, for he provided him with unmatched fodder for his column. In another of his wise-cracking columns on Silent Cal,

Will enumerated all of the problems that Coolidge had failed to solve in his first months in office. He pointed to the fact that Coolidge hadn't gotten France to pay off its war debts to the United States and, more important, he'd never "taken a stand on what size baseball bat Babe Ruth should use." Also, admonished Will, Silent Cal hadn't come out against boll weevils or produced rain for the beleaguered farmers. Will's tongue-in-cheek remarks were seemingly permanent when it came to politicians like Harding and Coolidge. Yet, when he discussed the impact of Coolidge's election, there was an undertone of seriousness that couldn't be mistaken.

"Wall Street never had such a two weeks," began Will, about the start of Coolidge's run. "People would wire in: 'Buy me some stocks.' The brokers would answer, 'What kind?' The buyers would wire back, 'Any kind, the Republicans are in, ain't they all supposed to go up?'. . . . What makes these things worth so much more on November fifth than they were on November third? You mean to tell me that in a country that was really run on the level, 200 of their National Commodities could jump their value to millions of dollars in two days? Where is this sudden demand coming from all at once? I am supposed to be a Comedian, but I don't have to use any of my humor to get a laugh out of that."

Only a few years later, the country was plunged into an economic disaster that had no precedent in American history. When the Great Depression cast a shroud over the country's spirit, Will learned to deal with that, too.

Will continued to have fun picking on any number of trivial matters concerning Silent Cal. He remarked that Coolidge didn't look as if he were born to wear an Indian headdress. For some inexplicable reason, the president had encouraged the Sioux to adorn his high forehead with Indian feathers, and Will couldn't resist the opportunity to comment about it. "I never like him in that yachting cap, either," said Will.

But during a nationwide radio broadcast with the biggest audience in history, on January 4, 1928, in which Will appeared from his Beverly Hills home as master of ceremonies, he managed to get into real hot water with Coolidge. What made it especially embarrassing was that only a few months before, when Will was engaged in a painful bout with gallstones, the president had sent him a "Get Well" telegram.

During the radio show, Fred Stone and Dorothy Stone were tied in from Chicago; Al Jolson came on from New Orleans; and Paul Whiteman's orchestra, with its portly (three hundred-pound) conductor at the peak of his popularity, broke in from New York—all in the name of Dodge automobiles.

Shortly after the program got under way, Will informed his audience that he had a pleasant surprise for them—they were going to hear a few words from the president of the United States. "He's a friend of mine and he wishes to speak to you," Will announced.

But then, instead of Mr. Coolidge coming on to talk for a few minutes, in his nasal, twangy Vermont accent, it was Will who came on, giving a precise imitation of the president. The mimicry was indeed so authentic that many listeners were convinced it was Silent Cal himself, who was not being silent for a change.

"Ladies and gentlemen," Will began, "I am supposed to deliver a message every year on the condition of the country. I find the country as a whole prosperous. I don't mean by that, the whole country is prosperous. But as a whole it's prosperous. That is, it's prosperous as a whole. A whole is not supposed to be prosperous. There is not a whole lot of doubt about that." After that opener, which should have suggested to anyone that this was not really Mr. Coolidge offering a state-of-the-union summation, Will talked about Andrew Mellon (the secretary of the treasury) saving up enough money for the country, "with a little set aside for himself."

"Mellon is the only treasurer that has saved faster than Congress can divide it up," Will said. "Congress is here now to split up the swag. The cheapest way would have been to have taken each senator's and congressman's address and just mail him his pro rata share. That would have eliminated any cause for holding this session at all and been cheaper in the long run on the people."

He went on to discuss some of the men around Coolidge: "They are doing well: Hoover, Dawes, Lowden, McAdoo, Smith. . . . 'Course none of them are doing as well as they hope to be doing this time next year. . . . I sent Dwight Morrow to Mexico. He is doing good work. Smart boy Dwight. One of the smartest boys in our class at Amherst. . . . Lindbergh is down in Central America. We seem to get in wrong faster than that boy can get us out. Wish he was twins. . . . I still don't choose to run. . . . Prohibition is going down about as well as usual. . . ."

Many believed that Coolidge had actually delivered the speech. Thinking he might have overstepped his bounds, and hearing that Coolidge was offended by the imitation, Will shot off a letter of abject apology to the president. Including the actual text of his controversial broadcast, Will's letter to Coolidge said that "how can anyone be so devoid of humor that they would picture you uttering such nonsense . . . how could it ever be mistaken for you?"

The tone of Will's letter was obsequious: "Due to my utter stupidity, my lack of good taste . . . why you and your wife have been nicer to me than anyone high in public life in America. . . . I was never invited to the White House by any other president [he seems to have overlooked trips to visit Teddy Roosevelt and Woodrow Wilson]. . . . I would cut off my right arm rather than have people think I have been in any way rude to you. . . . It does hurt me to think that I have to resort to bad taste to make my living from men who have befriended me. . . . I did the little talk in a moment of jest. . . . I just misjudged the intelligence of the people listening . . . it was not the proper thing to do under the circumstances . . . if ever there was a sad comedian, I am one and I do ask all the forgiveness that it's in your and Mrs. Coolidge's power to give . . ."

Not long after sending his letter, Will received a response from the president, in which Coolidge insisted that he "thought the matter of rather small consequence, though the office was informed from several sources that I had been on the air. . . . I am sure that anything you did was in good-natured amusement." Coolidge appeared publicly to be dismissing the whole brouhaha. However, in private he was rumored to be considerably annoyed with Will. Indeed, Will was never again invited to darken Coolidge's White House doorstep. However, breathing a sigh of relief, Will averred that the incident merely proved that "you can always joke good-naturedly about a big man but be sure he is a big man before you joke about him."

Will never believed that Coolidge actually meant what he said about not choosing to run for the presidency again in 1928. He accused Coolidge of using ambiguous language to describe his intentions, going so far as to bet $5,000—with publisher William Randolph Hearst—that Coolidge would again be the Republican nominee in 1928. It might even be by draft at the convention, concluded Will. (He was partial to this procedure, for he was getting used to people, both in Oklahoma and on the national level, casting votes for him for governor and president. It may have been one of the best ways for some folks to express their protest without voting for a Socialist.)

However, the Republican who won the nomination was Herbert Clark Hoover, the World War I relief administrator in Europe, and Coolidge's secretary of commerce. Hoover's ascendancy caused Will more than a little distress, aside from the loss of the bet, for the colorless Hoover, from West Branch, Iowa, never had much appeal for him. "He layed down on me," wrote Will, about Coolidge. "I think he should pay half of my bet with Mr. Hearst." (In just a few years, Will's gut reaction to Hoover became the consensus reaction to the depression president. He was "an evil spirit dragged up for political condemnation," wrote author Gene Smith.)

In the general election, Hoover beat the Democratic candidate, Al Smith, handily. Will was fond of Smith. He had commended him for being a Catholic, at a time when that religion was enough to get a man licked. "What do we care about a man's Religion," he wrote. "We dont want to be saved spiritually we want to be dragged out of the hole financially. He has been three times Governor of New York. The Jews elected him. Now if they can trust him to run the biggest state in the world where they own 90 percent of it and trust a Catholic over a Protestant why we shouldn't mind. . . . What do we care about a Presidents religion. They dont do any business on Sunday anyway. Its weekdays we want to use him. Its one relief to find somebody mentioned for President who we do know what their religion is before they get in. There is not 2 out of 10 that can tell me what religion Coolidge is."

The only thing that pleased Will about Hoover's victory was that Hoover's running mate for vice president was Charles Curtis, a Kaw Indian from Kansas and a onetime resident of an Indian reservation. "It's the first time we Indians have gotten a break," said Will. "Charlie's mother was a half-breed Indian. She's a Kaw Indian. It really means 'Kansas Indian,' but they couldn't spell Kansas, I guess, so they called it Kaw." When some Democrats had suggested it might be good to counter one Indian with another—by putting Will on the ticket somewhere—Will howled with delight. "Vote for Rogers and scalp the Kaws," he said. Will didn't want to run for anything, while sticking to the premise that he was "a member of no organized political party—I am a Democrat!"

13

Travelin' Man

Everywhere one looked in the 1920s, Will Rogers was a presence. He slouched amiably on the silent screen. He joked through the *Ziegfeld Follies*. He pounded out his weekly column and other articles. His book sold over sixty thousand copies. He chatted on the radio, a medium that he didn't particularly favor, since he doted on audience response. He put his imprimatur on advertisements. His voice, whining like a lake wind, crackled on recordings. His words and deeds constantly flashed over the wire services.

This was a time of instantaneous, overnight celebrity. If one threw a punch harder than any other man (Jack Dempsey); if one threw a fastball faster than any other pitcher (Walter Johnson); if one lugged a football for more yards than any other halfback (Red Grange); if one could hit a golf ball with unequaled finesse (Bobby Jones); if one played tennis like a ballet dancer (Bill Tilden); if one could exhort a college football team to new heights (Knute Rockne); if one could crunch more home runs than any other slugger (Babe Ruth)—if one did any of these things, one could promptly win second-coming-of-Christ headlines.

When Charles A. Lindbergh completed his daring lone-eagle mission across the Atlantic Ocean to Paris in 1927, he at once joined this iconic herd, surging to the top of the list. Lindbergh's feat was hailed as "the climactic stunt of a time of marvelous stunts," as writer John Lardner put it. "The farther the hero went"—and Lindy was the ultimate hero, with his photogenic looks, his cool efficiency, and his apparent modesty—"whether he went upward, downward, sideways, through the air, land or water or hand over hand on a flagpole, the better, provided he went alone."

However, Will's heroism was possibly more unique than that of the others, since he was able to attain his niche through his flow of phrases and nonstop talking. He did for talk what Clarence DeMar did for marathon racing, what Gertrude Ederle did for the English Channel, and what Lou Gehrig did for baseball endurance.

Florenz Ziegfeld, himself a celebrity of the first magnitude in this era of wonderful nonsense, loved to hear Will talk, as long as he did his talking in the *Follies*. So he lured the "poet lariat" back to the stage for the 1924 *Follies*, after Will had remained out in 1923. The version of the *Follies* (in 1924) was already jammed with talent (Ann Pennington, George Olsen's band, the Tiller Girls, Vivienne Segal, Al Ochs, Victor Herbert's music), but Ziegfeld wanted Will and his dialogue on hand, anyway.

"It's time you were back," Ziegfeld wired his old friend. "Please let me know after talking to your boss, Mrs. Rogers, of your decision. I would endeavor to get two great scenes for you, practically making you the star of the organization. I hope you realize your pictures should come second to your public appearances. I want you to come without fail, Bill. Answer quick."

Such entreaties were supplemented by expensive gifts that Ziegfeld sent to Will's children. There was a magnificent mah-jongg set for Mary; a motorized scooter for Will Jr.; and the pièce de résistance, an enormous sailboat for Jimmy. Will must have realized, when he returned to the *Follies*, that he was being bought off by Ziegfeld's grandiosity. But he lived to regret it, for despite his own expanded role and Ziegfeld's promise, there was scant humor in the 1924 edition. The accent remained on the glittering staging and the beautiful bodies of Ziegfeld's overpublicized chorines.

With Will's final *Follies* under his belt, one more mountain remained for him to conquer: the profitable lecture circuit. He had already broken into it in the first years of the Roaring Twenties, but not to the extent now envisioned by a gentleman named Charles L. Wagner, one of the most enterprising lecture managers in America. Wagner kept telling Will that he could emerge as the true star of this prolix business, if only he would come under his wing.

Will didn't need that much coaxing. He always had energy to burn, and he wasn't a charity case—he had an income in 1924 of close to $160,000 (with half coming from *Follies* work)—but he relished the chance to turn his never-ending flow of words and sidewalk wisdom into more cash.

He may have felt some trepidation about his ability to fill fifty minutes (thirty five minutes more than he was responsible for in the *Follies*) with gems of humor. But Wagner, having put money into the pockets of such diverse personalities as the singer John McCormack (on concert tours), author Jack London, and the evangelical politician William Jennings Bryan (on lecture tours), tried to instill into Will the idea that he had the makings of another Mark Twain.

Wagner's basic proposal involved a countrywide tour from October 1 to November 30, in which Will would reap $1,000 from each lecture, plus travel expenses. After December 1, Wagner upped his fee to $1,500 a lecture, which meant that in a relatively short period, Will could earn more money than he was getting for his silent-movie appearances.

In a year, if he followed through on Wagner's plan, Will could almost double his income of 1924. A male singing group—the de Reszkes—would accompany him wherever he was booked, (presumably to employ their own voices when he became hoarse). He was mighty pleased with Wagner's plan, for he felt that he was going out into America to visit with those folks that New Yorkers generally deprecated as rubes. "These are the same people," said Will, "that just look at New Yorkers and laugh."

He was trying to have it both ways: He had made his name and reputation mainly through the *Follies,* among these haughty, naughty New Yorkers; but now he was slapping their hands, mildly, of course, in favor of the rubes, who by implication, were possessed of virtues sorely missing among the big-city people.

If he needed further rationalizations before embarking on such a grueling duty, he could point to his need to breathe once again the pure air of middle America. Hanging around his headquarters in Los Angeles and New York, he had supposedly been missing such life-enhancing fuel.

The opener of the tour took place in the upstate New York city of Elmira. Mark Twain had once lived there and was buried there, far from his roots in Missouri. Since Wagner was trying to sell the notion that Will was a reincarnation of the melancholy humorist, Elmira was not chosen haphazardly.

In a twenty-five-cent program that accompanied Will's lecture, he was billed as "America's Greatest Humorist" and the rightful successor to Twain.

Unfortunately, the citizens of Elmira weren't buying such salesmanship: The house didn't sell out, and every time Will tried to crack a joke, the audience clammed up. Also, the site chosen for Will's appearance was a local church, not an ideal venue for puns about the "riffraff going down to Florida" or the goings-on at the *Follies*.

Will was used to friendly audiences; never in the past had he failed to win over his fans. Now he was faced with listless, if not hostile, crowds. Wagner realized that Will had to find a way to get the folks to warm up to him, or else the ambitious project could go down the drain, carrying a dejected Will along with it. When audiences in the next few towns reacted just as they had in Elmira, Will informed Wagner that he was tempted to pack up and go home to Betty.

But Wagner held out. He insisted that part of the problem was that there had been poor advance work to advertise Will's coming to each town. Indeed, few knew that Will was coming—and they didn't know what he was coming for. Wagner hired a young, energetic advance man—Will's loyal nephew— and that quickly helped matters. Soon Wagner couldn't find theatres, auditoriums, or meeting halls large enough to hold the crowds that started to come out.

However, more than advance work was needed to hold Will's audiences. Wagner told Will about a letter he had received from a woman advising him that Will should start talking about meatier topics: How about the same things that Will handled so felicitously in his weekly column? Accepting Wagner's suggestion, Will changed his tactics. In his engagements over the next half-year—151 lectures in all—Will invariably brought down the house. (Even at New York's prestigious Carnegie Hall, when Will got cold feet and offered Wagner $1,000 if he'd cancel the appearance, he was a hit.)

Traveling the length and breadth of the country by a hired car, by train, or by his beloved airplanes, Will tried not to miss a town or hamlet that wanted him. There were occasions when he booked himself a date without informing Wagner ahead of time. That made him hard to find sometimes, causing his manager to judge rashly that Will was truly money-mad. "He's temperamental and hard to work with," added Wagner, "and he's not all sunshine and jolliness . . . but I can't help thinking that he's a great man."

Some supportive evidence of Wagner's charge appeared when Will addressed a full house at the Chicago Athletic Club, only to have a large number of people unable to get in to hear him: There had been a traffic jam in the neighborhood, and they couldn't arrive on time. The president of the club asked Will if he'd consent to do his half-hour monologue again. "Sure," he responded, "I'll be happy to do it for the same price." Since the club didn't have the money to give Will, many never got in to hear his performance.

Gratifying to Will, as he rushed around the land ("If a smart man was going around the country doing this, it would be a lecture. If a politician was doing it, it would be a message"), was the fact that he got to return to his old stamping grounds in Oklahoma, Texas, and Kansas. Many of his friends of earlier years got to see him again, and he felt a sense of pride in what he had accomplished.

Taking a tip from Lewis Carroll's *Alice in Wonderland,* his agenda on the lecture circuit included "talk of many things—of shoes and ships and sealing wax, of cabbages and kings." Nothing that was in the news or on the minds of his listeners seemed to escape his notice. His subject matter ranged from local items to state, national, and international themes. One day he'd muse about Cal Coolidge or Al Smith; the next day, about that perennial ole devil, Congress ("Every time they make a law it's a joke and every time they make a joke it's a law"). He might talk about dirigibles or airplanes or battleships or ballplayers, including his pitching hero, Walter Johnson. Taxes were bound to draw his attention. New York's subways and the strange people who crowded into them could be the subject of a brief discussion. He liked to talk about the mayor of whatever town he was in (having briefed himself thoroughly by visiting the local newspaper office where he would make carefully penciled notes on hotel letterheads, which he never referred to while he was onstage). He provided clever insights about silent movies or about the latest Washington controversy on war and peace. Treaties with foreign countries could always get a laugh, as did the mere mention of Prohibition. When he talked about the recrudescence of the race-baiting Ku Klux Klan, he never came down too hard on this organization, leading one to believe that he preferred to play it safe when it came to really sticky issues.

He told about his meetings with famous people, such as Great Britain's dapper Prince of Wales (who later became Edward VIII, before abdicating his throne in 1936). "The Prince went to see a ball game at the Polo Grounds one afternoon," said Will, "and got hit on the back of the head by a foul ball. 'Good heavens,' the Prince exclaimed, 'I thought it was a mule!' "

Everything and everybody was a target for his incessant chatter. In his tireless way, he tackled as many topics as there were people who had paid their way in (usually at three dollars a head) to listen to him.

Despite Wagner's crack about Will being money-hungry, it wasn't unusual for Will to donate some of his lecture earnings to charitable organizations—on occasion, the Red Cross was the beneficiary. This set a lifelong precedent for Will, who enjoyed playing the role of an eleemosynary institution. One time, when he heard that members of a small-town baseball team were ashamed to take the field because they had no respectable uniforms, he gave up a week's salary, to buy the team the best suits, gloves, bats, and balls; he had never even been in the town before and was just passing through on a one-week engagement. As he distributed large chunks of money to help all manner of beleaguered people, from down-at-the-heels actors to alcoholic chorus girls, Will kept no reliable records about such giveaways. Neither did he ask to see Wagner's books. The epitome of responsibility, as far as his shows were concerned, he never missed one of these and was always on time. When he feared he might be late for a performance in Wichita, Kansas, he rented a private train—at a cost of over one thousand dollars—in order to arrive on time.

Children never failed to melt Will's heart. While driving through Arkansas, on his way to a benefit performance, he spied a clutch of kids on a street corner, displaying signs that read, "Welcome, Will Rogers." He ordered his driver to stop so that he could hop out and demonstrate a few tricks with his lasso.

He had his own favorite towns, such as Ann Arbor, Michigan, where he believed the people were smart enough to catch on to all of his jokes. But he considered Waxahatchie, Texas, about as bad a place as you could get to.

Critics sometimes flayed him. But he managed to take it with grace. In Boston, one such expert admonished him for daring to appear at Symphony Hall, a local cultural shrine. "Give me credit for one thing," said Will: "Wasn't that English of mine the worst ever spoken in that hall?" Such self-deprecation was the surest way to deflect his detractors.

Will's stage manner rarely changed from one engagement to another. What did sometimes vary was the duration of his act. Although his lectures were scheduled to run ten minutes short of a full hour, he often violated this rule. If his audiences were just "eatin' him up," he would be happy to ramble on and on. It wasn't unusual for him to drawl, cackle, and tell jokes for as long as two hours. Sometimes he'd go for three. He probably uttered more words than any filibustering congressman that ever lived—but he made more sense.

Only in the largest halls did Will work with a microphone. Marvelously, he rarely suffered from seizures of laryngitis. He was so casual, so loose in his manner and delivery, that he gave the impression that everything that came out of his mouth was extemporaneous, which, of course, it wasn't. It was just that he never looked at those scraps of paper he addressed to himself, which he'd hurriedly scribbled on his arrival in every town. He might take a last look at his memos *before* he got onstage. But once there, his memory took over—and he seemed to be infallible, a man with total recall.

While he strolled and talked, from one corner of the stage to the other—occasionally settling precariously on the edge of a stool in one corner—he rarely peered straight at the crowd. He'd gaze down at his feet, sort of sheepishly, or at the wings, where you might have suspected that someone was ready to haul him offstage with a butterfly net. When the audiences roared appreciatively, he'd tell them that they'd "get out early tonight, . . . it takes twice as long to get out when you have to explain the jokes." This would be the catalyst for more laughter, so Will would warn them that he was getting tired. "Now you folks go on out of here and go home," he'd say, "if you've got a home."

It was all such good fun, and if he wasn't thoroughly enjoying what he was doing, he was doing an artful imitation of it. From his point of view, what made it even more enjoyable was that the money kept rolling in. Wagner cut in for only 5 percent on each performance, with Will winding up with about three-quarters of the gross. For each show, 1,000–2,000 people plunked down two-to-three dollars for a ticket. Considering what a hard-headed businessman Wagner was reputed to be, Will outmaneuevered him all the way.

"He is as shrewd, satirical and clever as they make 'em," *Vanity Fair* reported in 1924, about Will. The magazine could have been referring to his talent for making money, or to his artistry on the stage and in the lecture hall.

Will's constant belittling of many politicians who cluttered the American landscape provided him with much material for his lectures. But one cause that he adopted—aviation—came to him as naturally as spinning his lasso. Having overcome his original fear of flying, Will emerged in the 1920s as one of the most fervent advocates of aeroplanes in the world. He had concluded that aviation was going to be an integral part of the nation's future—or, at least, it *should* be—and he appointed himself as the unofficial Ambassador of Flying. As the number-one aviation buff in America, even at a time when flying was costing the lives of a number of people, he often spoke out on the lecture tour, and in his written statements, about his favorite means of transportation.

"If flying is dangerous, pass a law and stop it," Will said. "But don't divide your nation between a class that should fly and one that shouldn't. Aviation is not bad, it's a necessity and will be our mode of travel long after all the people who are too valuable to fly have met their desired deaths by the roadsides on Sunday afternoons. . . . If there is a safer mode of transportation, I have yet to find it."

There was often a caustic note in Will's lobbying for airplanes: "It looks like the only way you can get any publicity on your death is to be killed in a plane. It's no novelty to be killed in an auto any more." He added that America had invented airplanes, but that after it had invented them, was that all you were supposed to do with them?

Owing to this infatuation with air travel, Will was one of the first to come to the defense of the embattled French-born Brigadier General Billy Mitchell in 1925. To Will, Billy Mitchell was "the flying Napoleon." But to many aggrieved members of the army, navy, and Congress, Mitchell was just a loud-mouthed pain in the neck, whose almost-daily rhetoric scorched the brass hats and do-nothings in Washington.

Mitchell had long called for the creation of an independent air force, with an accent on long-range bombers. He also believed strongly that the government should subsidize commercial aviation. Citing America's lack of air-transportation development, Mitchell predicted that this fact would inevitably make the United States a second-rate power in the event of a large war. He espoused these positions in national magazines, using language brimming with denunciations of "fossilized admirals." The secretary of the navy threatened to resign if Mitchell weren't demoted. Thus, for his pains, Mitchell was reduced to captain and set off to lick his wounds in Texas.

Just when the brouhaha over Mitchell seemed to cool down, the navy's dirigible, *Shenandoah,* was struck by a lightning bolt as it cruised over Ohio on a "goodwill" flight. Fifteen of the crew members were killed and their remains were scattered gruesomely all over the countryside, making for a week of stomach-churning newspaper coverage. Mitchell promptly seized on this tragic accident to accuse the navy's top officers of embarking on the flight merely as a public-relations gesture. President Coolidge, having previously avoided taking any position relative to Mitchell, now was forced to conclude that Mitchell's attacks on the army's and the navy's incompetence and criminal negligence, as well as his diatribes about "their pointless commitment to dirigibles," had earned himself a court-martial.

The day before the court-martial board convened in Washington, Mitchell picked up Will at the New Willard Hotel and drove the two of them out to Bolling Field. Before taking off in his plane, Mitchell handed Will cotton to stuff in his ears. "I only use cotton in my ears," Will informed Billy, "when I sit down in the Senate gallery."

Nonetheless, Will was captivated by the aerial view of the nation's capital, with Mitchell acting as pilot and tourist guide. Acknowledging that he still suffered from some anxiety while flying, Will said he loved it, despite his fears. "If it's any honor to you," Will said to Mitchell, "you've taken me on my last flight!" Of course, that was balderdash—and Will knew it. He was just trying to lighten matters for Mitchell on the eve of Billy's trial.

Mitchell was found guilty by the court-martial board. His rank was reduced and he was suspended for five years, without pay or allowances. However, Will remained a loyal Mitchell supporter, frequently making references to the truths that Mitchell had uttered. Two years later, when Lindbergh made it across the ocean to become "the brave Lochinvar out of the West," Will had himself another air hero. This one also became as controversial as Billy Mitchell—but not during Will's lifetime.

The next year, as Will was concluding his lecture tour in Philadelphia, he was invited to have lunch with George Horace Lorimer, the veteran editor and writer of *The Saturday Evening Post*. The *Post* was then the primary buyer of first-person, bylined articles by famous Americans. In line with this policy, Lorimer proposed to Will that he go to Europe for the magazine and write a series of pieces called "Letters of a Self-Made Diplomat to the President."

Will was no stranger to the *Post*'s pages, for he had previously written some ruminations for them on his beloved Democrats, always handy whipping boys for his comments. But now, for $2,000, for each article he wrote Will, restless and proud of his journeys, would be traveling again and visiting Europe for the first time in many years.

He hadn't spent too much time with Will Jr. in recent months, so Will decided to bring the young man along with him on his journalistic mission. However, even as the self-styled ambassador to Mr. Coolidge, Will ran into some difficulty obtaining his passport, since he claimed he had no birth certificate. When Will got this little matter cleared up, he sailed on the *Leviathan* at midnight on April 30, 1926, became seasick within moments after the ship pulled out of the harbor, and stayed that way for most of the voyage. (It's no wonder that Will preferred air travel to sea voyages, although how he avoided airsickness remains a mystery.)

Will pretended that his trip had the endorsement of the Coolidge White House, although in truth it never had any official sanction. He did drop in informally on Vice President Charles Dawes, at which time he informed him that he didn't think Coolidge did too much fretting about his job. His other purpose for the visit was to get Dawes to provide him with letters of introduction. The vice president responded readily with a stamp of approval: "He is a friend of mine." That opened enough Dawes for *The Saturday Evening Post*'s roving reporter.

William E. Borah of Idaho, a blunderbuss as an orator in the Senate, a promoter of Prohibition, and a hater of foreign entanglements, also issued a letter for Will. And a letter was even coaxed out of illustrator Charles Dana Gibson, in order to ease the way to a chitchat with Gibson's relative, Lady Nancy Astor, the first female member of Parliament and an unreconstructed elitist. Will had no letter of introduction to Benito Mussolini, the Fascist dictator of Italy, but he still eagerly looked forward to meeting the man. Congressman Sol Bloom of New York gave Will a letter, too, although it wasn't clear what kind of influence he had with any of the people on Will's long list of potential interviewees.

The intrepid "big-name hunter" (as Homer Croy had labeled Will) had his heart set on meeting almost everyone in Europe he had ever heard of, including several who could have been his opposite number, had they made a living in the United States. This group included the wickedly amusing George Bernard Shaw and *Peter Pan*'s author, Sir James M. Barrie. "Mr. Shaw and me know the world's wrong," said Will. "But we don't know what's the matter with that."

Will also made it his daily business to stop in the street and talk with any number of ordinary citizens—people who owned little stores, those who rode the buses, and some who were out for a promenade. He believed this was the best way to find out what people were thinking and what they cared about, always relevant matters to be included in his written observations.

During his whirlwind half-year tour, Will stopped at historic sites, such as Parliament and Westminster Abbey. He was as thrilled as any tourist viewing Big Ben and to take side excursions to Shakespeare country. It turned out that Lady Astor didn't know who he was, but she ended up liking him enough to invite him to have dinner with her inside the houses of Parliament. "Sure have come a long way from Oklahoma," said Will. When the Virginia-born Lady Astor remarked that Will sounded "just like a nigger," he was unsure about how to respond—so he didn't, which marked one of the few times he was lacking in a clever riposte.

When he got to meet the thirty two-year-old Prince of Wales at York House, he referred to the encounter as a renewal of an old acquaintanceship.

The prince swapped stories with Will, causing Will to come away convinced that this heir apparent to the British crown wanted little to do with the role of king. "He cares as much about that," said Will, addressing himself later to Mr. Coolidge, "as you care about going back to being vice president again!" The later tumultuous events in the prince's life—when he gave up the throne— would eerily bear out exactly what Will had suggested.

Despite the long summer of travel and interviews, Will didn't overlook the rest of his family. He summoned Betty, Mary, and Jim to join him in London. They would stay there and in Switzerland, while Will Jr., excited about flying, accompanied his father to Paris by air. While in France, Will made a trip to Nice, which he said was pronounced "neece" because "there's no word for nice in French." In Monaco he noted that gambling could readily support the economic structure of that little country, so Americans should take a look at it. "People don't mind spending their money as long as they know it's not going for taxes," he observed.

Occasionally experiencing anxiety about the sudden "ups and downs" of flying, Will went on to Spain, where he met the Duke of Alba and King Alfonso XIII. He also took in a bullfight while he was there—but he was no Ernest Hemingway. As he watched an enraged bull attack a blindfolded horse, Will cringed. "I'm a pretty tough egg," Will said, "but I couldn't go for that horse business."

In Germany, Will could see that people were still smarting over World War I. He talked to the American ambassador there but didn't stay long because he was eager to have his cherished audience with Mussolini in Italy.

At the time of Will's meeting with Mussolini, the dictator had been in charge of Italy's affairs for over three years. Curiously, the Socialist newspaperman-turned-authoritarian had already won plaudits from respected people all over the world; many chose to regard him as a benevolent technocrat, and he was adored by the Hearst press. Winston Churchill had spoken glowingly of him, as did Albert Einstein, André Gide, Stefan Zweig, Ezra Pound, and Jean Cocteau. They praised him for damping down the Mafia influence in Sicily, for making the railroad trains run on time, and gave him credit for building the first automobile superhighways, long before America did it and even before the German autobahn. They were willing, too, to give him credit for draining the marshlands around Rome.

Thus, Will's hearty endorsement of Mussolini, extended before he had a chance to meet him face-to-face, wasn't exactly sui generis. He chose to look upon the humorless Il Duce as a "Napoleon" (a descriptive word that he'd previously used for Billy Mitchell)—"but with peace, a man who's done more for one race of people in a few years than any living man ever did." Will believed that Mussolini had raised Italy's esprit de corps more than a notch or two and he was, therefore, willing to forget that the dictator had been forcing castor oil down the mouths of his political foes, a habit that might ordinarily have alerted him to Mussolini's potential for cruelty.

Will's actual interview with Mussolini, if it could be called that, lasted slightly more than an hour, according to Will's own computations. It was preceded by Mussolini thrusting a vigorous Fascist salute in Will's surprised face. In retaliation, Will threw up his hands in mock surrender. "Don't shoot," he shouted. Mussolini, not amused by Will's response, finally managed to break out in a smile, as he went into a long, broken-English statement about his high regard for Italian-Americans. "I am a regular guy. . . . I like a good time, to be gay and laugh, as well as anybody else," Mussolini rambled on. "Tell that to the Italian-Americans back in the United States."

That Mussolini was seeking to deflate the stern-visaged image of him that had been projected, mostly through the American newsreels, appeared obvious. But that objective appeared lost on Will, who came away from the meeting with a good opinion of "this greatest man in Europe." He also wound up with an autographed picture of Mussolini, a close-up of the heavy-set dictator astride a horse–"Compliments, Mussolini" was the inscription.

"He's an idealist who has made the system work," Will noted in his postmortem on his visit. Such assurances from the cowboy sage probably encouraged some uncertain tourists to go to sunny Italy for a visit.

Armed with a brief letter of introduction ("Please help me out if he gets in too bad") from *The New York Times*'s managing editor to the Moscow correspondent of the *Times*, Walter Duranty, Will arrived in the Soviet Union on the last lap of his trip. It took three changes of planes to get him into the brooding center of world Communism, thus fortifying his feelings about the uses of aviation. "It's the best way to get anyplace," Will continued to claim.

He was intent on meeting Leon Trotsky, the Russian who was perhaps best known to the American public for his role in building the Soviet military. But Trotsky already had fallen on hard times in the eyes of his Communist superiors. In short, he had lost esteem among them and had been ticketed for oblivion in the Soviet hierarchy, thanks to the machinations of Joseph Stalin, "the real fellow that is running the whole thing," as Will liked to say.

Although Duranty had written some favorable essays about the Soviets and their leadership, his ministrations couldn't bring Will together with Trotsky.

That was the greatest disappointment of Will's voyage, for he insisted, "I think if I had met Trotsky I would have found him an interesting and human fellow, for I never met a man I didn't like . . . after you meet people you can see a lot of good will in all of them . . ."

(Will uttered or wrote this tolerance maxim a number of times in his life. His willingness to apply such a saying to every prominent person he encountered, as well as to those with considerably less impressive credentials, underlined either his bad judgment, or a bland acceptance of the worst brigands, villains, and despots. More likely, Will found it to be a wonderful advertisement for himself, and a mechanism that could help him to meet anyone he wanted to meet, after he had given his assurance, ahead of time, that he would treat the person with kindness and forbearance.)

On the whole, however, Will saw enough of the Soviet Union and its people to develop a largely negative view of the events that were taking place there. He had managed to meander around without a guide—most unusual for such a prying character—although he did accept some supervision as he walked about the Kremlin.

"The whole idea is based on propaganda and blood," Will wrote, about the Soviet Union. He didn't think that much had changed since the czar had trampled on the masses. Nevertheless, he was amused to see people bathing in the nude in Moscow during a tenacious heat wave that summer. He told the writer George Seldes about this experience, as the two sat in the bar of the Hotel Adlon in Berlin, one of the great hotels of the world in the 1920s. Albert Boni, the publisher, eavesdropped on the conversation. "That would make the title of a book," Boni said. "Write it and I'll publish it." So the experience was transformed into a book, *"There's Not a Bathing Suit in Russia,"* a distillation, and not a very substantial one, of several articles that Will had written for *The Saturday Evening Post.* "I didn't get to see all of Russia," Will remarked, "but I did get to see *all* of some Russians."

On his return to London, before leaving for America, Will was still not in any mood to rest on his laurels. He immediately signed to do a movie, *Tiptoes,* with Dorothy Gish, half of the famous sister tandem. The film was about three vaudevillians who were having a hard time as they traipsed about England. Will volunteered that he was perfectly suited for the role. "All I have to do is act natural," he said. "I know how to play a vaudeville performer who isn't very good."

He worked on a bunch of travelogues that dealt with half a dozen European countries. Most of the lines that appeared on-screen were written by him, although they were hardly designed to break people up. Typical was this line: "In the Tuileries they've got the most beautiful gardens in the world . . . if a thing sprouted at home it would be a Senator . . ." Pretty lame stuff. But Will was dedicated to keeping busy.

Frustrated about having nothing to do at night while he was still in England, Will linked up with a musical revue produced by Charles Cochran, a man billed as the "British Ziegfeld." Will helped to make the revue a solid hit. He came on nightly for four weeks, delivering quips that often castigated the British for their odd manners, their inferior coffee, and their quirky nationalism. Postwar Britain, having suffered enough from its dreadful casualties on the Western Front, didn't need such provocation from this "insolent" American cowboy. As a result of his act, Will was scalded by a good part of the British press, although it wasn't clear whether he was being criticized more for his incessant gum chewing on stage than for his script.

Trying to make amends, Will ripped up a check given him by Cochran. Insisting that he had enjoyed himself immensely during the run, he said that under the circumstances, he couldn't possibly accept payment. The story of Will's payback was widely circulated in Britain. Cochran never denied it. It was good public relations for him and for Will.

While he was still in London, a catastrophic fire, costing the lives of forty-eight people, took place in a theatre in Dromcolliher, near Dublin. Shocked by the tragedy, Will at once wired the mayor of Dublin, offering to play a benefit for the bereaved families. The offer was promptly accepted, winning Will a nice send-off from the same members of the Fourth Estate who had previously questioned his charm and routine.

Before starting on his strenuous tour of Europe, Will had lunched one day with Adolph Ochs, publisher of *The New York Times*. An energetic southerner, Ochs became owner of the *Chattanooga Times* before he was twenty one years old. A dignified but exuberant man, Ochs was not considered a showman. Several years before his meeting with Will, he had suffered a nervous breakdown, which cut down on his daily work at *The New York Times*. Once he recovered, however, he was much engaged in pursuing new writers for the *Times*—thus, his lunch with Will.

Ochs was already familiar with Will's value to the *Times*, for the paper had run several articles by him. In addition, he had seen him on the stage and was a fan of his. While wishing Will well on his trip, Ochs promised that if Will stumbled across any interesting or newsworthy stories, the *Times* would be happy to pay his cable costs.

Never one to forget a promise, Will sent Ochs a collect cablegram in late July, (1926), informing him that Lady Astor would shortly be making a visit to the United States. "She is the best friend America has here," cabled Will. "Please ask my friend Jimmy Walker [mayor of New York] to take good care of her. She is the only one over here that don't throw rocks at American tourists. Yours, Will Rogers."

Ochs found the message amusing enough to run in a small box on the front page of the second section of the *Times*. Ochs also wired Will that he should keep sending him such pithy "takes." This kind of encouragement was all that energetic Will needed: For the rest of his stay in Europe, he kept peppering Ochs with his messages. The only time he didn't get his material off to Ochs was when he spent five days mountain climbing in the Alps and couldn't locate a telegraph office.

The trip abroad had been a success for Will, even though he joked about going home "broke." Traveling home first class on the *Leviathan*, where he experienced his usual attack of seasickness, Will had to be pleased with himself. On board the ship, he gave time and energy to raising over forty thousand dollars for the victims of a recent Florida hurricane. Learning that onetime Republican presidential candidate and former Secretary of State Charles Evans Hughes was also on the *Leviathan*, Will recruited him for the cause. At Will's urging, Hughes, a man of somber mien, delivered a light-hearted speech, and by the time the boat docked in New York, the two were carrying on like lifelong friends. They appeared together to greet the photographers and reporters who had gathered en masse to interview them at the end of the voyage—a ritual that enfolded every dignitary and celebrity arriving back in the States from foreign shores. At this juncture, Will was as well known as Hughes and, one could say, without hesitation, a good deal more popular. To the reporters, Will summed up his summer's sojourn: "America don't stand as good as a horse thief in Europe. The only way we would be worse with them would be to help them out in another war."

While Will had been hustling around Europe his tanned face, "with lip protruding like the point of a vulgar joke," made it to the black-bordered cover of *Time* magazine—a distinction usually reserved for presidents, politicians, and pompous businessmen.

Under the heading of "Prairie Pantaloon," the newsweekly ran a paean to Will, saying that his humor was "fearless, nonchalant and aggressively Western." The magazine went on to write that *"The New York Times* has called him America's Aristophanes, the New York *Herald* has hailed him as the successor to the famed Mr. Dooley (Finley Peter Dunne); Woodrow Wilson found his political roulades not only funny but illuminating. . . . When he first began to go about in society, Will said he had a lot of trouble finding out which were the servants and which the gentlemen. Then he found his clue—butlers had no braid on their trousers. After that he was able to distinguish the butlers. . . . Now his only trouble is to distinguish the gentlemen."

Awaiting him, too, was a telegram from the White House, inviting him to be an overnight guest in order to make his "report" to the president. Overwhelmed by Coolidge's offer, Will informed the president by wire that he'd be the only "non-office-seeker that ever slept in the White House . . . it'll be the first meal I ever had on the government and it's just my luck to be on a diet now . . . regards till somebody wakes me up."

Will had never thought that his daily boxed comments would play any permanent role in his career. But once he got back home, he found Ochs clamoring for more such dispatches. Many of Ochs's *Times* readers informed him that they liked Will's topical tidbits: They could read the pieces quickly over breakfast or on the subway, thus letting them start the day with a laugh and a catchy phrase or two.

Under the circumstances, it didn't take long for the McNaught Syndicate to latch on to a good thing. The syndicate sold the daily feature under the rubric *"Will Rogers Says."* Not long after that, over five hundred newspapers throughout the United States bought into it, giving Will a readership of close to forty million people—numbers that would have been unheard of for a writer only a decade before.

Under the agreement, Will began his daily box—the material was always presented in the form of a telegram—on October 16, 1926. By August 16, 1935, Will had complied with his deadline (filing time was 1:30 each day), without a break, for six days a week for nine years. No matter where he was, or what he was doing, or how he felt, Will was the reliable trouper. While baseball's Iron Horse, Lou Gehrig, of the New York Yankees, was putting together a good portion of his record-breaking 2,130 straight games during this period, Will was performing an identical feat—but with his typewriter. In fact, for 2,317 straight times Will never missed a deadline or a telegram. No journalist ever wrote at such an unfailing pace.

Betty remarked years later that Will's daily pieces, running from fifty words to less than two hundred, were his favorite chore. "His schedule was often overcrowded, and he would have been glad to drop the weekly article, but doing a daily wire, though it might sometimes be difficult, was never drudgery," she said.

Although Will often left the actual composition of his telegram until the last moment, he was able to concentrate fiercely in those crucial minutes before he had to file for the *Times*. It was usually his habit to rest his battered old typewriter on his knees, or on any other available support he could find, and just peck away at the keys, oblivious to anything that was transpiring around him.

If we are to rely on Betty's words, or on the words of friends and observers— as we must, of course—Will is said to have rarely retyped anything. He didn't employ carbons, he didn't bother to plunge into the dictionary to search for a proper spelling, and he was adamant about never asking questions about his tortured syntax and idiosyncratic punctuation. He just rattled it out. Sometimes he produced a bauble of clarity; at other times, it was tired text. More often than not, he hit home with his ideas and phrases.

There was never anything fancy about Will, in his use of either words or paper. His copy was usually pounded out on Western Union telegraph blanks, old memo pads, or hotel stationery. He distrusted "new words" and proclaimed that "old words" were his best friends. "You know the words," he said, "the minute that you see 'em."

Betty sometimes read the telegrams before they were sent off to the *Times*'s editors. She didn't always agree with either the themes or how they were stated. But Will was his own boss, a man operating a many-faceted creative machine right out of his Stetson. He refused to employ researchers to put cockeyed notions or misleading facts into his head and never put a gag writer (with one exception) on his payroll. Working with ghostwriters, who were already coming into vogue in the publishing field, was unthinkable to him—it would have been the worst kind of fakery. It's possible that he felt this way simply to avoid extra expense, but, more likely, it was his policy because he was stubbornly independent, the quintessential rugged individualist. He firmly believed that the best results could only be reached through his own efforts.

Will's random perceptions encompassed the whole world. This accounted for so much of his interminable running around, for he was constantly looking for what was going on, for what people really were thinking, and at how things worked or didn't work. He was determined to be authentic. He was being paid a good deal for his philosophical ramblings and had no desire to be a charlatan. Franklin D. Roosevelt, who became president on Will's watch in 1932, was very complimentary about Will's European odyssey of 1926. "Rogers's analysis of affairs abroad," said Roosevelt, "proved to be more accurate than any other I'd heard. He had an exceptional and deep understanding of political and social problems."

"He hopped around the country, like a cricket on a griddle," wrote Homer Croy. Indeed, there was a method to this mad pursuit of information. And the White House visit with Mr. Coolidge fit right in with Will's need for knowledge and fresh material—for almost everything, in fact, that happened in the country became instant fodder for Will's articles, lectures, and telegrams. For example, when Will arrived late at the White House, because his train from Philadelphia had been held up by an accident, he found Cal and Grace Coolidge already sitting down eating their supper. But Will wrote this way about it: "That's *real* democracy, the President and his wife waiting on dinner for me." It was a merry distortion of what actually occurred, but it certainly made for a better yarn.

Subsequently, when Will talked about his stopover with the Coolidges, he gave the impression that the president was sure pleased about his having been there. He threw in tidbits about the amiable chitchat, the cigars, and the jigsaw puzzles that were all part of the evening. He mentioned Mrs. Coolidge's knitting; Silent Cal's penchant for feeding two feisty dogs with a plate of table scraps; and the general homespun atmosphere that permeated the White House.

But in relating what transpired, Will was hard put to make any of it sound amusing. The reason, of course, was that Coolidge was as funny as a bee sting.

"The room in which I slept," said Will, "was big enough to rope a steer in it, with the biggest bed that I ever saw. I knew a lot of famous people slept in there at various times." In fact, Will was assigned to a small dressing room, where he did his sleeping in a single brass bed.

According to the legendary Ike Hoover, the veteran White House chief usher, Coolidge never had any intention of inviting Will for a return visit. Nothing really clicked between the two men, although it would have been hard to pick up such a negative conclusion from any of Will's quips.

Taking some time off before Christmas of 1926, Will had no idea of the surprise that was in store for him in his home community. While he spent a few unusually carefree days in Beverly Hills, members of the local real-estate board, driven as always by altruism, decided that their humble town needed a mayor. Others, besides Will, were eligible for this slot in this "town with two swimming pools for every Bible" (as Will put it), for any number of screen stalwarts (Leo Carillo, Doug Fairbanks Sr., Bill Hart, Richard Dix, Richard Arlen, etc.) could have graced the job. However, the leading citizens concurred that a mayor named "Honorable Will Rogers" would be ideal to improve Beverly Hills's public image.

Thus, Will was soon presented with a five-foot-long scroll that officially named him as the town's first mayor. The Los Angeles Fire Department band played "The Old Gray Mare" as Will took the oath, and the citizens turned out en masse for the formal induction ceremony, with banners proclaiming Will as "The Kiddies' Pal" and "The Dog's Best Friend." All the cops on the Beverly Hills payroll were there, too, to greet Will, for he had paid out of his own pocket for a handball court and a gymnasium for them. Surrounded by Betty, Will Jr., Jim, and most of the town's acting-lodge members, Will delivered his acceptance speech. "I'll be a moving mayor of a fast-moving town," he promised.

He added that he had never seen a mayor that wasn't comical: "As to my Administration, I won't say that I'll be exactly honest, but I'll agree to split 50-50 with you and give the town an even break. . . . I'm for the common people and as Beverly Hills has no common people, I won't have to pass out any favors."

Will had little opportunity to inflict any pet reforms on Beverly Hills, for in a few weeks the California legislature huffily ruled that his reign as mayor was illegal. According to the legislature, sixth-class towns such as Beverly Hills were obligated to make the president of the Board of Trustees the mayor. The honorable Will was thus deposed, almost as quickly as he had been imposed on the town. "Well, I ain't the first mayor that's been kicked out," snorted Will. "If Ida known Beverly Hills was a sixth-class town I wouldn't have taken the job!"

Will's uncanny ability to associate with famous people was helped along in 1927 by three transcendent events: Lindbergh's flight to Paris, Babe Ruth's accumulation of sixty towering home runs, and Jack Dempsey's long-count heavy weight championship battle with Gene Tunney. He had a knack of getting close to these personalities who dominated the news, and he made the most of it in his running patter.

Fascinated by almost all sports, with the exception of tennis, Will was a sucker for the highly romanticized gladiators and athletes of his time. There were enough people like Ruth, Ty Cobb, Bobby Jones, Red Grange, Knute

Rockne, Jack Dempsey, and Walter Johnson to keep his sports plate quite full. However, Will still considered that the flying men of his era, led by the enigmatic Lindbergh, were the true heroes of the nation.

From the moment that Lindbergh, or the Flyin' Fool (as he was called until that moment), took off at 7:52 A.M. on May 20, 1927, under a cloudy sky at Roosevelt Field on Long Island, Will felt his heart was in the heavens with him. While Lindbergh flew dangerously close to the Atlantic's waves, during his thirty three hours under a scudding sky, Will was spellbound by the feat. "No attempt at jokes today," he wrote in his telegram of May 21. "An old slim tall, bashful, smiling American boy is somewhere out over the middle of the ocean, where no lone human being has ever ventured before."

When Lindbergh completed his mission and gained near-hysterical world acclaim—and, as a result, became an overnight pop icon—Will was tongue-tied with admiration. (*The New York Times* got ten thousand phone calls, in eleven hours, about Lindy; and in the month after the flight, this man with "an old swimming-hole grin," as author J. C. Furnas described Lindy, received three-and-a-half-million letters!) Will now regarded Lindbergh as the chief catalyst in a drive to "sell" airplanes to a country that remained skeptical about their safety and practicality. To Will, Lindbergh ranked with Teddy Roosevelt as the greatest American of them all. He sensed that Lindbergh was a one-dimensional man who wasn't much interested in anything other than planes. But he still believed that the young flier possessed all of those characteristics that went into making the ideal hero—modesty, bravery, humility. Will managed to crack his usual jokes—"Lindbergh is the only man ever to take a ham sandwich to Paris"—but, for the most part, he was starry-eyed over the aviator. Even when getting to know Lindbergh at close range, Will's unstinted admiration didn't diminish. "He's the only man in the world that I'd stand on a soap box on a corner to get a peek at," Will said.

Shortly after the flight, Lindbergh attended one of Will's one-man shows, drawn perhaps by his knowledge of Will's feelings about him. Due to Lindbergh's presence, the crowd caused such a commotion that Will was forced to interrupt his act. Not until Lindbergh voluntarily left the theatre could Will continue. This demonstration caused Will to say that he hoped people would leave Lindbergh alone. But such importuning ultimately fell on deaf ears. Throughout the rest of his dramatic and tragic life, Lindbergh rarely was left alone by the public and the press.

Several months after Lindbergh's flight, Will was shooting some scenes in California for another of his silent films, *A Texas Steer*. A banquet in San

Diego, in honor of The Lone Eagle, was scheduled to take place at the same time, and Will was invited to make a speech. Of course, he jumped at the chance to meet his hero.

In a reception that was held before the banquet, Lindbergh was mobbed by movie people—one of the few times that they didn't resent taking a back seat to someone more deserving of admiration than themselves. Many in the crowd pressed forward in order to get close enough to Lindbergh to touch his suit, while others asked for autographs. Seeing the tumult, Will said that he guessed that Lindbergh rued the day he learned to write.

Taking his position on the dais to talk about Lindbergh, Will drew a gasp of astonishment from the audience when he opened by saying that he certainly didn't consider Lindbergh a proper inspiration to American boys. Lindbergh himself appeared rather startled at Will's words. Then Will instantly re-deemed himself: "It's just a lot of apple sauce, because if our boys tried to follow you they'd plunk right in the middle of the Atlantic Ocean. I don't want my boys tryin' to do the stunts that you've been pullin' off." The crowd roared with delight at Will's curveball, while Lindbergh was detected smiling at his new friend.

The next day, Lindbergh sent chills up Will's spine when he invited the Rogerses to join him on a trip to Los Angeles in his trimotored Ford plane. During the course of the flight, the plane became balky and tail-heavy, actu-ally causing Lindbergh some concern. Searching for the reason for the mal-function, Lindbergh took a look at the back of the plane. There, ten out of the plane's eleven passengers were huddled together, along with Betty and Will. Only one passenger was up front, aiming his camera at them. Lindbergh suggested that the passengers should scatter to the middle of the plane. Will was then asked by Lindbergh to join him in the cockpit. Seizing the oppor-tunity to explore Lindbergh's acumen and wit, Will asked, "How can you tell just where to land?" Calmly pointing below to some clothes hanging on a line, Lindbergh suggested that this was a good way to tell which way the wind was blowing.

"But suppose it ain't Monday?" asked Will.

"Then I just wait 'til it is," responded Lindbergh.

Since he continued to love to travel by air, Will was convinced that planes were the most expedient way of putting the economic future of the country on safe grounds. He already concluded that air travel was necessary for his own business and personal needs. With no regularly scheduled airlines tra-versing the country, Will would often squeeze into the cockpits of planes carrying U.S. mail. Dressed in every way like a pilot, with large goggles, a helmet, and a fleece-lined leather suit designed to keep out the chill, Will often found himself smothered by heavy sacks of mail. But this only added to the enjoyment and drama of the flight. He was content to pay for his passage according to his weight in terms of postage.

So fearless had Will become about planes that there were occasions when he chose to take unnecessary risks. He made the acquaintance of Blanche Noyes, the wife of pilot Dewey Noyes, who flew a mail route between Cleveland and Pittsburgh. Blanche was not yet an experienced pilot, although Dewey had taught her some of the fundamentals of the trade. Having done an engagement in Chicago, Will urged Blanche to fly him to Cleveland. Peering up at the leaden skies and watching snow pouring down at such a pace as to ice over the wings, Blanche told Will she didn't think it was advisable for them to take off. But Will was insistent: "Come on, little girl, you can do it. My next column is dated Cleveland. I don't want to kid anyone about it."

Blanche finally agreed. Battling through the raging storm, they landed in Cleveland without incident. But Blanche Noyes asserted that it was only with God's help that they had gotten through.

As the foremost advocate of flying in the country, Will seemed willing to take reckless chances. In future years he embarked on other foolhardy flights, suffering several close calls. Once he cracked up in a vacant Chicago lot, emerging luckily with only badly injured ribs. In some way he managed to keep the incident out of the press, never even calling attention to it in his daily telegram. But he continued to show not the least fear, whether he was flying with Lindbergh, Blanche Noyes, or anyone else who happened to be at the controls. One friend said about Will that he was so well and strong, so full of enthusiasm, that he almost regarded dying in a plane as a joke. Others who flew with him said that he was totally oblivious to adverse weather conditions and that he usually read himself to sleep. He showed scant interest in parachutes, once telling Eddie Cantor that "if a plane goes, I want to go with it."

Stopping off one day in a small town in Oklahoma, after one of his plane trips, Will met a young fellow named Gene Autry. A telegraph operator, Autry was plucking away at his guitar and singing along, using his own music, with a typically nasal country-singer's delivery. Will liked what he was hearing, so when Autry confided that he wanted to make a living through his music, Will encouraged him. "Get into the radio business," Will suggested. Years later, after Autry had become a big star on radio, and in cowboy movies, making enough money to become owner of the California Angels baseball team, he acknowledged that it was Will's enthusiasm for his talent that had given him his start.

Few places in the world in the 1920s gave Will more satisfaction than Mexico and its people. He had met many Mexicans in rodeos, often competing against them in roping contests, and he felt he understood them and appreciated that they had been badly treated by the United States. "We've always considered you a bunch of bandits," he said to the Mexicans, "and you look at us as one big bandit!"

In 1927, President Coolidge appointed his old classmate at Amherst, Dwight Morrow, ambassador to Mexico. Morrow was a well-to-do partner in the J. P. Morgan firm. Most Republicans greeted the appointment with pleasure, for they saw the move as enhancing Morrow's reputation in the next sweepstakes for the presidency. Rarely discussed in these circles was the fact that Morrow was close to being a chronic alcoholic. Despite his professed talents in dealing with people, Morrow also suffered from periods of absentmindedness. It turned out that such behavior was probably due to his intake of booze.

Will, like some others on the Democratic side of the aisle, had mixed feelings about Morrow's new job, but it had nothing to do with Morrow's frequent whiskey-induced fade-outs. It was Will's own streak of populism that caused him to distrust the nominee. However, when Morrow took up his post in Mexico City, one of his first moves was to invite both Lindbergh and Will to come down to Mexico on a goodwill mission—it was certain that the United States could use a touch of positive diplomacy in Mexico.

In order to win Lindbergh's approval for the venture, Morrow met first with the flier in his New York apartment. This turned out to be fortuitous for Lindbergh, for at this meeting he was introduced to Anne, Morrow's twenty-one-year-old daughter, fresh out of Smith College. A tiny, shy, intellectually gifted young woman, Anne was not much taken with Lindbergh at that first encounter, nor he with her.

Lindbergh decided to fly to Mexico, arriving there after Will was already on the scene. When he landed, a delirious mob of 150,000 Mexicans greeted Lindbergh, rushing the plane and threatening to tear both the vehicle and Lindy apart in their enthusiasm. Morrow asked the two famous men to join him on the American embassy's balcony, in order to give the throng a chance to see them together. Will nudged Lindbergh, giving him valuable stage instructions. "Smile, Lindy, smile," he suggested, as the crowd roared its approval.

It was not unusual that politically induced voyages such as this one often ended in disaster. There was fear, for instance, that the moody Lindbergh might prove to be unmanageable. But he was on his best behavior. It was Will who was something of a problem, for it was known that he sharply disagreed with Coolidge's policies about air transportation. In addition, he unleashed some dinner-table quips about Mexican corruption and the frequency of military coups in Mexico.

However, he soon got into the spirit of things, endearing himself to the Mexican public with his candor and charm. President Plutarco Calles regarded Will as a friend and laughed along with everybody else at Will's references to assassinated Mexican presidential candidates, of which the country had its share. On one dinner date with Calles, Will showed up late, unusual for him. When one of Calle's supporters charged that he shouldn't have kept the president waiting, Will explained his way out of his gaucheness: "Tell President Calles that I've been in Mexico only for a few days but I've found out that it's better here to stand in right with the soldiers than with the president."

On another occasion, when he faced Calles, Will held his hands up as a sign of surrender, much as he had done in his meeting with Mussolini. "I ain't a candidate for anything," he assured Calles, who laughed when Will's words were interpreted for him.

Before long, the Mexicans were affectionately referring to Will as "Guillermo Rodriguez." As he had done on his other travels around the world, he toured the country, constantly peppering people with questions, with the help of a wily interpreter named Jim Smithers. He never avoided associating with campesinos, and he attended a bullfight, even though he cared little for this type of bloody melodrama. He mangled the name of Mexico's volcano, Popocatepetl, but wherever he went he was greeted by cheers and hugs.

The Morrows originally thought that Lindbergh's own popularity would dwarf the reception for Will. But Will more than held his own. When he spoke at dinners or banquets, Will won the hearts of Mexicans by telling them that Americans didn't hate them, and that "I know you don't hate us." He kidded about Morrow's role in Mexico, saying that diplomats specialize in telling people things they don't really believe themselves. But then he praised Morrow by adding that the ambassador was an honest fellow who appreciated the fact that people have to be honest with each other in order to get along.

Will and Lindbergh were smash hits among the Mexicans, proving that Morrow had more of a flair for his job than Will suspected. But Will still paid homage to Lindy, and, in a wire to the *Times*, he wrote: "Morrow and I have resigned as Ambassadors in Mexico. Now there is only *one!*" The only untoward moment of the trip, as far as Will was concerned, occurred one day while he was touring a power plant: Suddenly the lights went out, sending Will scrambling to get under a nearby table. The former president of Mexico, General Alvaro Obregon, a brilliant leader of the revolution, assured Will that no bomb throwing was at hand. "The joke's on you," said Obregon. Embarrassed by his behavior, Will never mentioned the incident in any of his articles. (Ironically, Obregon was murdered not long after this episode.)

The relationship between Will and Lindbergh would remain close for the rest of Will's life. When they went up together in a World War I French plane that looked fragile, Will put the matter in a favorable light: "Falling in a plane with Lindy will be my only chance to be remembered."

In February 1932, Will visited with the Lindberghs (by this time Lindbergh had married Anne Morrow, who had obviously gotten over her original dislike of the flier). They were living in a house in Hopewell, New Jersey, in the Sourland Mountain region, twenty miles northwest of Princeton University. A month later, Charles, the first-born son of the Lindberghs, was kidnapped from an upstairs room of the house.

In his piece in *The New York Times,* the day after the kidnapping, Will recalled his happy visit and how Charles and Anne had enjoyed playing with their curly-haired baby. "His dad was pitching a soft sofa pillow at him as he was toddling around. The weight of it would knock him over. I asked Lindy if he was rehearsing his forced landings."

A following piece, written in great sorrow, emphasized how everyone in the land was centered on this "one thing." The greatest single kick, wrote Will, "that a whole nation got, outside of the signing of the armistice, was when the news had flashed that Lindbergh had landed in Paris. . . . The next one we hope and pray will be when this baby is delivered home."

But even as Will wrote these words, the baby was already dead. Two months after the kidnapping, the small body was found in a damp patch of woods in the neighborhood of the house, after Lindbergh had paid ransom money to an unknown kidnapper. Will's anger at the grisly event, expressed in his articles, lasted a long time. "A father that never did a thing that didn't make us proud of him," he said, of Lindbergh. "Why don't lynching parties widen their scope and take in kidnapping?"

The "crime of the century," as it was called, set off a torrent of publicity in the newspapers and on radio. It was without precedent in its constancy and magnitude. No day went by without a new lead, theory, or suspect being uncovered, or deflated, in the press. America's 125 million inhabitants had almost become one vast posse sniffing at the trail of the cold-blooded kidnapper. The incessant turmoil blighted the lives of the Lindberghs, causing them to seek out a place where they could be free of the badgering by reporters, photographers, police, con men, and well-wishers. They found such a haven on Will's sprawling ranch in California, where Will assured them, after his invitation, that nobody would bother or disturb them. "Charles and I appreciated the place, especially because it was so quiet and far away and protected that we felt completely private and free," Anne Lindbergh wrote to Betty, in thanks for the Rogerses' hospitality.

The Lindberghs had been staying for some weeks at the ranch when, on September 20, 1934, the police picked up Bruno Richard Hauptmann, a Bronx carpenter, born in Germany, who had been a machine gunner in the army of the Kaiser in World War I. At the time of his arrest, Hauptmann, who vigorously denied being guilty, had in his possession a twenty-dollar bill from the Lindbergh ransom.

"This whole thing is starting all over again," Anne Lindbergh said, with great remorse, to Will. He did his best to calm her, but there was little anyone could do or say that would bring tranquility to either Anne or Charles.

The Lindberghs remained at Will's ranch through the course of Hauptmann's trial, returning home only to testify in the case at a Flemington, New Jersey, courthouse. Hauptmann was convicted in 1935 and was executed the same year.

Lindy was not Will's only hero of the air—every famous aviator of his time became Will's friend. He knew Amelia Earhart, the first woman to fly the Atlantic, and also the first to fly solo across the ocean in 1932. He flew with Captain Frank Hawks. He flew with Billy Mitchell and stuck up for him through thick and thin. He got to know Wiley Post, another air pioneer of his era.

But indeed there were other idols of the 1920s that took to his fancy. He was amazed at the soaring home runs hit by Babe Ruth. During the 1927 season, the Bambino, making more money—$70,000—than any ballplayer ever had, showed he was worth every penny he could extract from the Yankees' owner, Colonel Jacob Ruppert. An unschooled, profane, wildly undisciplined man, but kindhearted and earthy, Ruth had an astonishing capacity for alcohol, hot dogs, and women. Will loved the big fellow. When he and Babe posed for pictures together, as they did whenever Will could make it to the ballpark, he was almost as pleased to be alongside the great slugger as he was to be pictured with Lindy.

Another legend of the Roaring Twenties was the swarthy, scowling, blue-jowled Jack Dempsey, whose name was synonymous with physical might all over the world. Dempsey had won the heavyweight championship of the world in 1919 by battering the awkward Jess Willard into a helpless hulk. Such brutal combativeness stimulated a national passion for prizefighting that culminated in Dempsey's two battles with the handsome, poetry-spouting Greenwich Village marine, Gene Tunney.

The first Dempsey-Tunney fight in 1926, before a screaming crowd of 120,000 in Philadelphia, saw Tunney take Dempsey's title away from him. The return fight in Chicago on September 23, 1927, included one of the classic moments in pugilistic history.

But before the two fighters even set foot inside the ring at Soldier Field, millions of words were written in a torrent of preflight flummery from the nation's most talented sportswriters, including Heywood Broun, Damon Runyon, Westbrook Pegler, Paul Gallico, Gene Fowler, and Grantland Rice. And Will, the nonsportswriter, was added to that list.

Much taken with boxers, Will had a particular affinity for Dempsey, based on Jack's early roots as a down-on-his luck hobo in Colorado, and also because of Dempsey's often-professed part-Indian heritage. When Dempsey set up his first training camp for Tunney in Saratoga, New York, Will was on hand as a fan and observer. Some even chided the forty-eight-year-old Rogers, suggesting that he should test Dempsey's power by sparring with him, just as Gallico had done before Jack's 1923 brawl with Luis Angel Firpo (Gallico was rewarded by being knocked down and bloodied by Dempsey, who didn't care to be a victim of such a journalistic stunt). But Will wanted none of it, for he treasured his straight teeth.

When Dempsey moved his camp to the Lincoln Field Race track in Chicago, Will followed him there, in the company of Illinois' governor, Len Small. The day Will was there, Dempsey failed to show up for his sparring session, but Will settled for kibitzing with the other hangers-on. He returned in the days immediately before the fight, becoming convinced that Jack was going to regain his title. But with over 105,000 people paying over $2,700,000 (the largest gate that had ever been recorded for an athletic contest), Tunney won the fight after ten hectic rounds—including the controversial long count in the seventh round, after Dempsey knocked Tunney down but failed to retreat to a neutral corner, (as the rule book required). The count over the fallen Tunney was thus delayed for several seconds by referee Dave Barry. After the fight, Will, who had never cottoned to Tunney's well-publicized preoccupation with William Shakespeare, George Bernard Shaw, Thornton Wilder, and Yale's William Lyon Phelps, said disappointedly, "Let's have prize-fighters with harder wallops and less Shakespeare."

Will also knew the preeminent college football coach in the 1920s, Knute Kenneth Rockne, a tough and tender immigrant from Norway, who guided Notre Dame to season after season of winning records. A great strategist, Rockne was, as well, a dynamic spiritual leader. He could give a pep talk that would rouse the birds out of the magnolias, just as Will could, so it was inevitable that they would hit it off. Following a Notre Dame victory over Army at West Point, Rockne treated his whole squad to a trip to the *Ziegfeld Follies*. Will, still starring in the show, was casually twirling his rope and casting out some commendatory comments about Rockne's Fighting Irish team, when he suddenly threw his lasso over the shiny bald pate of the famous coach. Much against his wishes, Rockne was pulled onto the stage, as the audience shouted encouragement. This started a friendship between Will and Rockne, which ended on March 31, 1931, when Rockne, like Will, an enthusiastic supporter of flying, was killed in the crash of a giant Fokker plane on the Flint Hills near Bazaar, Kansas.

Rockne's death at forty three was the biggest story of the year, as newspaper extras all over the country spread the sad tidings. Will's obituary about Rockne, in his daily telegram, echoed this widespread sadness: "We thought it would take a President or a great public man's death to make a whole nation, regardless of age, race or creed, shake their heads in real, sincere sorrow. . . . Well, that's what this country did today, Knute, for you. You died one of our national heroes. Notre Dame was your address but every gridiron in America was your home."

Strangely, what Will overlooked in his relationships with such personalities as Lindy, Ruth, Dempsey, and Rockne was that he was almost as great an institution in the country as they were.

14

The Ranch

espite his busy schedule, Will tried to be there when other people needed help. It was second nature to him, the only way he knew how to act. Eddie Cantor once said that he had learned the value of common sense and a love of America from Will. That love was best expressed by Will's activities on behalf of those people who had been hurt by the inequities and vagaries of life.

This side of Will was clearly demonstrated in the spring of 1927, when the Mississippi Valley was hit by the most tempestuous floods in its history. Thousands of people were left homeless, hundreds died, and damage ran into the millions, but the Coolidge administration was reluctant to summon federal help to salve the massive wounds: The president left it up to private agencies, including the American Red Cross, to provide aid. Will was distressed by this inaction, and he felt that a single rowboat could do more good for those caught in the floods than all the senators in Washington gabbing endlessly about the emergency.

Angrily, Will put his own talents and energy to work. He gave several benefits, while constantly urging his newspaper readers to open up their hearts and bank accounts on behalf of those whose lives and hopes had been crushed by nature.

"Look at the thousands of Negroes that never did have much, but now it's all washed away," Will wrote. "Don't forget that water is just as high up on them as if they were white. No matter what color you are you require about the same amount of nourishment." Although Will had been guilty, from time to time, of holding thoughtless, demeaning stereotypes about black people, he never was a racist. Certainly, when succor for Negroes was needed, he eagerly recommended that people forget color and social status.

These humanitarian activities were forced to come to a halt when Will was back on the lecture circuit in the little town of Bluefield, West Virginia. One morning, after getting out of bed in Bluefield, Will was seized with a searing bellyache. "I guess when you're in Bluefield you're tempted to think it's gunshot wounds," said Will, laughingly. But he didn't see a doctor at the time, trusting to his sense of invulnerability. "Nuthin' that a bowl of chili can't cure" was Will's cheerful refrain, even as he suffered.

When he experienced similar painful symptoms in Oklahoma and again in Beverly Hills, however, Betty wouldn't listen any longer to Will telling her that he was feeling fine. She insisted on calling in the family physician, who said that Will was a sick man, with gallstones, and needed an operation. A prominent California surgeon was enlisted and, in short order, Will was scheduled for surgery. The surgeon, Dr. Clarence Moore, was described by Will as "the most famous machete wielder on the West Coast." Although Will did put up pro forma resistance to the surgery, he must have been "hurting real hard," said Betty, if he acquiesced to the procedure.

Before submitting to the operation, Will asked Betty if she'd pinch-hit for him at Occidental College in Los Angeles, where he had been invited to speak. Betty knew that Will didn't like to disappoint people, so she consented to fill in. William S. Hart, once the king of all Western stars (dating back to 1914), was also enlisted to appear, and he was happy to help out.

Will felt as bad as he had ever felt in his life—but that didn't mean he'd miss his daily piece. On his way to the operating room, he literally dictated his next offering: "I'm in the California hospital, where they are goin' to relieve me of surplus gall, much to the politicians' delight . . . never had an operation before, so let the stones fall where they may."

After the operation, Will was so sick that his condition was considered "grave." Nonetheless, he put together another brief column. It read, simply:

"Relax, lie perfectly still, just relax." For a few days, anyway, Will followed his own admonition.

When he recovered, Will was asked to read the script for a movie called *The Texas Steer*. He turned down the opportunity, saying that half of the "fun of makin' pictures was not knowin' how it was all goin' to come out." However, he told the producer, Sam Rork, that he'd be pleased to make the movie, even if he had no desire to study the script ahead of time. The picture was to be directed by Richard Wallace—but in this instance, Will was not responsible for any of his own dialogue. That may have been the reason the picture was only a modest success.

The movie's plot centered on a straight-shooting Texas rancher (played by Will), who gets himself elected to Congress and journeys to Washington, D.C., to buck the stagnant system. Much of the film, which turned out to be Will's adieu to the silent screen, was shot on location in Washington. When the production troupe arrived there, Will was invited by the National Press Club to be the guest of honor at a star-studded reception. Many of the best-known legislators were on hand to hear Will, adding to the confusion as to who was there to listen to him and who was there to be *seen* listening to him. However, Will's recent illness didn't make a dent in his usual humorous put-downs. Upon being introduced as an "appointed congressman-at-large for the whole United States of America," Will shunned the designation—with a smile, of course. "That's the poorest appointment I ever got," he drawled. "I regret the disgrace that's been thrust on me here tonight. I have tried to live my life so that I would never become a congressman!"

The cast of *The Texas Steer* included Douglas Fairbanks Jr., then eighteen years old, and a double of his popular athlete-actor father, Doug Sr. (For years, Doug senior—who, in the silents, could leap off balconies, and race up long flights of stairs, with the same aplomb that Will had in handling his ropes— had been a close pal and neighbor of the Rogers family. Thus, Will had watched Doug junior grow up in the ménage of a world-famous Dad and a stepmother, Mary Pickford, who was known as "America's Sweetheart.") Doug junior's love interest in *The Texas Steer* was Ann Rork, the pretty, round-faced offspring of the producer. During much of the filming, Doug was forced to sleep on a park bench near the White House, because his incidental role in the movie didn't provide him with enough money to rent a hotel room. Working with Will proved to be memorable for Fairbanks. "He was a special person, with keen intelligence," Fairbanks recalled. "Watching this sometimes grumpy, but disciplined, funny man at work was really a learning process. In a way, he was like Charlie Chaplin, a sober and conscientious Chaplin. Comedy, as has been said, is a serious business, indeed, and Will was in that mold. . . . I was just a kid at the time, so Will scared me a little but I never did believe that nonsense about 'all I know I read in the papers.' No, Will was much smarter than that and liked to cover up the fact that he'd had a pretty good education."

In Fairbanks's recollection of *The Texas Steer*, he also cited the frequent short delays in shooting in order for Will to have a chance to "cogitate" about the comments that he'd integrate into his newspaper pieces each day. "Everything stopped for a few moments, while Will was thinking or pecking away at his typewriter," Fairbanks said.

With the coming of another presidential election in 1928, Will again warmed to the task of deflating the various candidates who were running. He still maintained that the entire process of nominating conventions was ludicrous. "There's nothing as useless as a delegate to a political convention, unless it's the man that he's a delegate for," he contended. Still, the process itself provided him with something to write and kid about. He viewed convention sites as noisy hippodromes, filled with sound and fury, signifying nothing. In 1928 the Republicans met in Kansas City, while the Democrats gathered in Houston.

From the beginning of the summer, Will didn't think the Democrats had a chance with Al Smith, or with anybody else, for most people felt the country was wildly prosperous. The uninhibited binge of the Jazz Age, in which almost everyone lived on credit and nobody took anything seriously—unless it was a beauty queen, a flagpole sitter, a gun moll, a sex scandal, or a sports hero—looked like it would go on forever. But in fact, Will hinted that things would not go on in this way indefinitely. As he tirelessly moved across America, he took a jaundiced view of Herbert Hoover's vapid campaign promise that there would be "two chickens in every pot and a car in every garage." Not for a moment did Will believe that spiel. Nor did he concur with Mr. Hoover's prediction that, "in accepting the Republican nomination for President, with the help of God, we shall soon be within sight of the day when poverty will be banished from the nation." What Will saw, instead, was a nation with an illusory feeling of well-being, "where the business of America was business" (Coolidge's maxim), and where nothing else was worth anyone's attention. The mass production of cars, telephones, refrigerators, washing machines, radios, and vacuum cleaners had moved the nation out of the horse-and-buggy era and into a never-never-land and that would, the Republicans insisted, benefit everybody. It was a fairy tale coming true, they insisted.

But Will looked at a recklessly soaring stock market, and untold swampy acres of Florida land selling for unthinkable rates, and figured that something was wrong. "I guess we don't have to worry about anything," Will said, wryly. "No nation ever was sitting as pretty. All we have to do if we want anything is to go out and buy it on credit. Perhaps some day we might have to pay for all this stuff."

Will's thinly veiled reservations about the state of America's economy came to the attention of Robert E. Sherwood, a recently successful playwright (*The Road to Rome,* 1927), and also the editor of *Life,* the humor magazine. Sherwood dreamed up the idea that Rogers should head up a maverick political movement that could be called the "Anti-Bunk party." Not only that, but Will would be the presidential nominee of such a party.

There was a mild precedent for Sherwood's notion, since in 1924, two Arizona delegates to the Democratic convention had supported Will. In addition, Will had received some write-in votes in the actual election.

However, Will was not moved by Sherwood's proposal. "This country hasn't quite got down to where it wants a professional comedian for president," he said. He admitted having an emotional link to the Democratic party but acknowledged he had never even bothered to vote.

Nevertheless, Will gladly played along with the joke, even contributing a slogan ("He chews to run") to his candidacy. He claimed that the offer to run struck him like a bolt out of the blue, leaving him dazed. Being dazed, he continued, would tend to make him a "splendid candidate." If elected, he promised, he would resign—which was more, he noted, than any other nominee had offered the American public.

Will went a step further by writing an Anti-Bunk platform and a number of campaign speeches that were dutifully published in Mr. Sherwood's magazine. Each piece earned him $500, not bad pay for a bunch of empty promises. "We want the wet vote and the dry vote," Will wrote. "There'll be more wine for the rich, beer for the poor and moonshine liquor for the prohibitionist." Sherwood often rewrote or expanded Will's copy, which was sketchy, much in the tradition of Will's daily pieces for *The New York Times.* This was unusual, for nobody had ever fooled around with Will's writing. However, Sherwood remained captivated by Will, at times comparing him with Abe Lincoln. In that regard, he was in good company, for Carl Sandburg, the Lincoln biographer, had registered similar praise for Will. "I've seen Will keep an audience in stitches for three hours," Sherwood said. "No other man in the world could have done that."

Many other admirers of Will happily threw their "support" to him: Eddie Cantor, writer Robert Benchley, and aviatrix Amelia Earhart promptly wrote glowing endorsements for him. Even the solipsistic gossip columnist Walter Winchell announced he was with him. (Winchell had once been a guest of honor at a dinner, and Will had showed up to praise him. "I'm here because I was afraid not to be here," explained Will, who was thoroughly familiar with Winchell's track record for vendettas.)

Right up until election day, the Anti-Bunk group prolonged its joke. Thousands of Rogers buttons, with his lop-sided grin plastered all over them, were given away. The only promise the candidate made was that he wouldn't make any promises. He also assured one and all that there'd be no "baby-kissin'," no passin' out of cigars or candies and no laying of cornerstones." This was the first time in history, Sherwood said, that a presidential candidate turned out to be *intentionally* funny.

Meanwhile, Will also pursued his real-life career, as a visiting journalist at the Republican convention in Kansas City. While flying from California to the conclave, Will's plane ran out of gas, causing it to flip over on its back. Fortunately, nobody was hurt. As usual, Will chose to make light of it. "I'm the first candidate ever to land on his head," Will joked. "Being a candidate, it didn't hurt me."

In the election, Hoover won a landslide victory over Smith, as Will had predicted. Again, Will picked up a substantial write-in vote. His Anti-Bunk backers claimed he actually carried the District of Columbia—but that amounted to the final spoof of the campaign.

Since Will was no longer able to spend much time in Oklahoma, where he still owned over sixteen hundred acres, and hundreds of steers, goats, sheep, and hogs, he started to focus greater attention on the ranch property that he had bought in 1921 in Santa Monica. At the time of the original purchase, Will had considered the investment as a hedge against potential reverses. For this very public man, the property was also considered a hideaway, and he meant to improve it, clear away the brush, grow things on it, build a polo field, and turn it into an enchanting retreat for his family and friends. Ultimately, he never really regarded it as a ranch, since it was not a profit-making venture. Rather, it became a place for him to unwind and enjoy the incomparable view of the Pacific Ocean and Catalina Island.

When Will bought the land, the 155 acres had been used primarily as a small vegetable garden cultivated by a Japanese truck farmer; the garden was located south of where the polo field was later constructed. At the time he bought it, Sunset Boulevard, then known as Beverly Boulevard, didn't extend as far west as the ranch, so he had to reach the property through a poor dirt path from the area of the Uplifters Ranch in the Santa Monica canyon. Although the property was indeed wild, remote, and almost impossible to reach when Will first saw it, he had a vision for it and carried it out. His boys, Jim and Will Jr., thought very little of the place. "I don't know how the hell we were able to get up there," said Will Jr. But both of them sensed their father's tremendous enthusiasm for the location. Will had told them that the city was moving westward, which meant that Beverly Boulevard would move westward with it. He underlined the fact that this was an unparalleled real-estate investment that would give the whole Rogers family lifelong security. The meld of high hills, gentle slopes, and flat mesas was just what Will had always dreamed of, Jim said. "It was the kind of place where he had just what he wanted, an area where he could play polo and ride horses to his heart's content. It just got too crowded in Beverly Hills for Dad and he wanted a place where he could get out."

At first, Will contemplated selling off small subdivisions of the land, but he quickly abandoned this plan. Instead, all during the 1920s, he kept adding to the property, so that it reached over three hundred acres in all. At one point he paid $120,000 for an adjoining eighty four acres. In developing the property, Will enlisted the services of Lee Adamson, a skilled civil engineer who was also his brother-in-law. When he wasn't around to direct things, Will mailed long, explicit letters to Adamson, detailing what he wanted done. Adamson took over from there, always heeding Will's caveat that the whole thing should be done "plain and ordinary."

Work went on constantly, including the burning of a vast native chaparral; teams of mules dug and cleared, as workmen camped out on the premises, throughout the day and night. Because of the inaccessible location of the ranch, the construction of the polo field represented a substantial engineering feat: Bulldozers, carryalls, and graders could not be used; instead, about 150 mules were recruited to pull fresno scrapers and to haul dump wagons. The animals managed to do the job fairly well, but when the field was completed, it was noted that the east end was some eight feet lower than the west. Hundreds of eucalyptus trees were brought on, in five-gallon cans, to provide shade. Jim Rogers helped to plant them by hand.

Because he loved horses, above everything else, Will built a barn on the property, even before he constructed quarters for his own family, explained Jonathan A. Dunn, a former California State Park Ranger at the Will Rogers Ranch. However, Will realized soon enough that he had to take care of the needs of his family, so construction of a two-story cottage, with bedrooms and a garage, got under way. The ranch's permanent barn, a large two wings connected by a tall rotunda, was purchased and transported to the ranch from the San Fernando Valley. In time, a rustic one-story cabin, with three small bedrooms and one airy living room, was added. With Betty's help, Will designed the cabin—another illustration that he was a hands-on person in all matters.

Curiously, there was no dining room—but that was due to Will's insistence that his family, friends, and guests eat outdoors whenever possible. Water and electricity were provided by the city of Los Angeles, the bills sometimes running over fifteen hundred dollars a month. Horse feed ran even higher than that. During Will's lifetime, there was never any gas at the ranch—the cost of laying the necessary pipelines would have been enormous, even for a man with Will's sizable bank account.

By late 1928, the Rogers family decided to leave their home in Beverly Hills (which was sold for $150,000), in order to make the ranch their permanent residence. The original weekend cabin now became the main living room and guest quarters.

The ranch was indeed a precious resource for Will. It helped to keep his sturdy body in good repair and was an important escape valve from the stresses of his nonstop life. When he was at the ranch, his policy was to exercise every day; otherwise, he'd go "down like a flat tire." He thought of it as stretching his muscles.

Visitors often commented on his devotion to roping and riding. However, he didn't like swimming and never installed a pool, the symbol of Southern California's easy living. Homer Croy and others recalled how Will used to welcome visitors to his ranch in his well-worn blue-denim overalls, white sweatshirt, and high boots. After a greeting, Will would spend most of his time in the corral on horseback, roping calves.

"Will told me once how he'd just been a guest on the big Hearst Ranch in Mexico," said Croy, "and how he'd seen a young Mexican do some fancy roping and he was trying to learn the twist of his wrist that made this Mexican great. 'I'd sure like to know how he does it,' Will said. He said he'd seen a lot of fancy ropers but none of 'em could give it the same flip that the Mexican did."

Curly Witzel, a stuntman and movie actor, told author Jim Garry that he had run into Will at a rodeo in Bakersfield. Curly was performing there at the time, and Will invited him to come back with him to his ranch, instead of having to camp out. Will told Curly he had a pen of steers and calves, and promised him that he and his friends could rope all week long at his place. "That's just what we did," recalled Curly. "About half a dozen of us. We put up there for a week and spent pretty much every day, all day, roping and working horses. Will would come out and join us for a little bit and rope a few head. There was a little steer that was getting chute-wise. He came out for Will and cut back to try and go behind him. It didn't seem to matter any way to Will. He just dabbled a loop back, as easy as you please, and picked up the steer's horns like that was a normal way of roping. He was just break-away ropin', not jerkin' 'em, and when he popped the rope off a little steer and rode back, he had that funny grin of his, like he was embarrassed about showing us all how easy it really was. We were all just sittin' there thinking' how thankful we were that he had gone into the movies, so that we didn't have to compete against him. The best any of us could have hoped for was second place money against him. And we were as good a ropers as there were going." For years, Jim Garry had collected tales and exaggerations that folks liked to share with each other about the Old West, but clearly, to Curly Witzel, Will's skill was no exaggeration.

In the late 1920s, Julian "Bud" Lesser's family summered in a house at the Uplifters Ranch, one canyon away from Will's place. Horse trails cut through the mountains and children living in the area were privileged to ride Uplifters horses to give them exercise between polo matches. "Fun on Sundays was to take the trail to Rogers' ranch a mile away to eat, while watching his polo matches," Bud Lesser recalled. "My father, Sol Lesser, who was an independent producer aligned with First National studios, knew Will only through industry connections, since Will was working for Fox. Our family was not among the usual group invited to the Rogers polo melees. Will did not know any of us kids, but since we rode in and we were horse people, we were always welcome." (At the time, Bud was a student at Los Angeles High School.)

"None of us were introduced to Will but since we were part of the landscape, Will and the other players didn't mind the audience. . . . The word 'melee' typifies the difference between the two ranches," Bud said. "The Uplifters polo field was grass, had baseball-type bleacher boxes, and the public was invited to buy tickets for Sunday matches. The matches were social events and visitors wore fancy clothes. Rogers' ranch was his home. In his huge living room he had a stuffed cow to practice his roping on. His polo field was all dirt and it had no bleachers. Viewers sat on horses. The matches were with his cowboy friends, some pickup polo players and macho movie people like Walt Disney, Big Boy Williams, Hal Roach, Darryl Zanuck, and Spencer Tracy. Will's polo style was what I'd call 'early Cherokee.' Instead of using the customary English saddle, he rode one of his cow ponies, in leather chaps mounted on a Western saddle complete with pommel. When he chased after the willow ball we could hear him yell and whoop as if he was heading off a cattle stampede. . . . During the usually dry California summers the galloping raised big clouds of dust, so the spectators often lost sight of the ball. But it was always a treat to watch the Rogers performance."

Will had a few close calls on the polo field. Once, when an opposing player cut in front of him, Will tumbled from his horse, causing the frightened creature to fall over on him. Fearing that Will might be badly hurt, actor Joel McCrea, one of the players that day, ran down the field to Will's side. By the time McCrea got there, Will was coming to. Gazing up at McCrea, he asked the young man "not to make an epic out of it." He then got up, shakily, remounted his horse, and rode off, insisting on continuing the game. "The way that Will treated that accident was the way he always treated life," said McCrea. "He was always all out, with little concern for matters like safety or longevity."

Despite his enthusiasm as a polo player, Will once informed the Internal Revenue Service that he wasn't too fond of the game. "I really took it up for what there was in it for me from a publicity angle," he wrote the IRS, in an attempt to have his polo expenses deducted for business reasons. This laughable bit of dissembling—for that's what it appeared to be—limns another side of Will: He was a cagey businessman, who knew the value of free publicity, which he expected to earn from his polo-playing image. Although the IRS eventually turned down the request, Will continued to play his hell-bent brand of polo on Sundays, always protesting that he could happily do without the game.

Fred Stone had never been as good at polo as Will was. Stone enjoyed the game—but he learned to enjoy flying even more. Unlike Will, who was content to be a passenger while most of the great pilots of the day did the work at the controls, Stone learned how to pilot a plane. He was so proud of his airmanship that he invited Will to join him on a flight from New York to Hagerstown, Maryland—the flight came off without incident.

In the late summer of 1928, Stone was preparing to open on Broadway in a musical comedy, *Three Cheers*. His daughter, Dorothy, would appear with him, as she always did, in a supporting role. Charles Dillingham was the producer. The show was well along in its rehearsals, with Broadway ready to welcome the father-daughter act, when Stone almost got himself killed in an air crash near Groton, Connecticut. Always in the mood for improvisation—whether in the air or on the stage—Stone had attempted a forced landing. Unfortunately, as he was preparing to land, weather conditions worked against him, and the plane went into a crazy spin and crashed. Stone's tongue was bitten in two; his legs were mashed; his ankle, thigh, and shin were broken; and he had a badly damaged rib cage. Placed in a full-body cast, Stone, whose career had largely depended upon his athleticism, refused to heed his doctors' advice that he have his leg amputated. They held out little hope that he'd ever be able to return to his normal livelihood.

Upon hearing the news about his closest friend, Will became distraught. In his daily piece for the newspapers, Will asked his readers to say a prayer for Fred. But he did something more than that—he at once volunteered to fill in for Fred in *Three Cheers*, until such time as Stone could rejoin the cast. "I'll just plug along," Will wired Stone. "I'll do the best I can with the part."

Fred replied that he was deeply grateful for Will's offer to pinch-hit for him, especially in light of the fact that Will would have to cancel his own lucrative lecture tour. "Bill, come on up and see me," added Stone. "I'm in a production of my own called Plaster of Paris. I'm the only one in the cast!"

A couple of weeks later, Will traveled to New York, where he began rehearsing to play what had been Stone's part—the monarch of a mythical kingdom, who goes to Hollywood. By the time that Will got through with his own interpretation of the role, it bore little resemblance to Stone's part. Never having rehearsed lines before, Will had a terrible time memorizing his part in such a short period. Although he wanted to fill in for Stone properly, he just didn't do it the way Fred would have played it.

The day before *Three Cheers* was set to open, both Dorothy Stone and Dillingham had misgivings about Will's inability to remember his lines. The producer was even tempted to postpone the opening. Although the show's plot had hardly more than the skeletal structure usually associated with innocuous musicals, Will did inherit several songs that Stone had been scheduled to sing. "That's as far as any man has ever gone for a friend," Will said, about his singing. As far as his lines were concerned, Will said he'd just do them his own way, just as he always had done in the *Follies*—he wouldn't be Fred, he'd just be Will. "If Fred were here, he'd be jumpin' around at this point," said Will, referring to a particular scene. "But I think I'll just stay where I am."

In *Three Cheers*, Will talked about almost anything that came to mind. It might be politics, sports, or the weather. It might be Herbert Hoover or the stock market. When the show opened on October 25, it featured all of Will's free-wheeling, obiter dictum monologues. But the audiences loved every moment of it and the play was a monumental hit—the box office hummed and the critics were utterly entranced by it.

"I'm afraid Rogers disorganized the show but as far as I'm concerned he can disorganize every show for the rest of his and my life," one New York critic wrote. Others said that Will's technique deserved serious study by all rival comedians. According to the critics, he was a master of pacing and timing. (Comedians of a later era, notably Jack Benny, assiduously tried to borrow this approach from Will.) Will's friend, Robert Sherwood, writing in *Life*, said that Will managed to give a different performance every night, which suited Sherwood just fine.

Will couldn't help being pleased by the response of the critics. Even Noel Coward, the ultimate sophisticate, wired Will to tell him how much he'd enjoyed his performance. In the long run, however, what gave Will his greatest emotional satisfaction was that he had been able to help out a friend in a crisis. Also, Dorothy Stone benefited, for she had never before appeared on stage without her father.

Although Will couldn't have predicted it at the time, *Three Cheers* marked his final appearance on Broadway. Following its New York run, the show hit the road in April 1929. On opening night in Boston, Will introduced Babe Ruth—then in the midst of another seasonlong assault on American League pitchers—who was in the audience. Secretary of the Navy Charles Francis Adams also received a nod from Will, with scarcely the audience reaction that the Babe received. "I'm now gonna introduce someone bigger than either of these gentlemen," said Will. Thereupon, a giant from the Ringling Brothers Circus stood up and took a bow.

The play had its final performance in Pittsburgh on June 1, ending this phase of Will's volunteerism. During the run of *Three Cheers*, Dillingham paid Will $5,000 a week, some of which Will shared with Stone. The press agent for the show, not content with spreading the word of Will's philanthropy, also tried to sell the story that Dillingham had given Will a blank check each week. There happened to be no truth to this tale—but press agents never stop trying.

Three years after doctors had predicted that Stone would never again set foot on a stage, he was back in *Ripples,* a musical. He went on to play a dishonest Kansas senator in *Jayhawker,* a work written by Sinclair Lewis, who had turned down a Pulitzer Prize for his 1925 play, *Arrowsmith.*

The cataclysmic stock-market crash of 1929 descended on the country only a few months after Will decided to end his run in *Three Cheers.* By that time, while the country was headed in a downward direction, Will ironically was headed upward, for another dimension had been added to his repertoire—the talking picture.

15

"I Was Never Sorry Movies Started To Talk"

It didn't please Will to have to say, "I told you so." But he had been hinting for months that America was on the wrong track. Now, the stock-market crash had proven his lugubrious assessment to be true. On black Thursday, October 29, Will happened to be in New York. "You had to stand on line to get a window to jump out of," he said, with asperity, "and speculators were selling space for bodies in the East River."

In short order, Herbert Hoover, the unsmiling engineer who had won the presidency in 1928 with 58 percent of the popular vote, and a 407-to-69 margin over Al Smith in the electoral college, became a symbol of hard times. "Poverty will be banished from the nation forever," Hoover had promised in 1928, but now his empty words were cause for harsh laughter. To Will, Hoover became "Doctor Catastrophe." In fact, when Hoover returned to Washington after a visit to a flood area, Will announced that "Bert is just resting between disasters."

Will had warned Eddie Cantor and other friends to get out of the stock market; instead, they compulsively stayed in it, up to their necks. Like millions of other Americans, Cantor thought the good times of the Jazz Age would never come to a screeching halt. "I'm not in the market," Will said to Eddie. "I get *my* money workin'." When Cantor lost practically everything in the crash, Will was there to bail him out.

With his country in pain, with millions of men joining the unemployment lines daily, and with millions of women and children bearing the harsh scars of hard times, Will knew he couldn't be flippant about the failings of the government. His caustic tone ceased. Instead, he became a compassionate cheerleader, as he tried to reassure "forgotten" Americans that things would soon get better. The country, he insisted, would weather the storm, even though its national anthem had become *"Brother, Can You Spare A Dime?"*

Rather than berate the mystified Hoover and his cabinet cohorts, Will chose to define what was happening by joking that "America was the only nation in the history of the world to go to the poorhouse in an automobile." By 1930 the wages paid out by Will's car-maker friend, Henry Ford, averaged less than a thousand dollars a year. Ford also cut salaries severely in the middle and upper brackets of his working force. When he announced, at the start of the depression, that he was initiating a seven-dollar day, Ford neglected to mention that employees were paid off in one department and hired in another at lower wages. At seventy, Ford had ceased being a miracle man in Will's estimate and in the eyes of many Americans. To fight the depression, Ford came up with the notion that "family gardens" could help workers grow their own food. Such folk remedies were dismissed as simplistic and naive. Feeling gratitude for Ford's having been a source of much of his material over the years, Will remarked, "Most people got no room for such a garden, so what Mr. Ford can do is put out a car with a garden in it. Then you hoe as you go."

In his efforts to bolster the general spirit, Will commented that "I haven't been buying anything myself, 'cause I wanted to give the other folks a chance to have confidence first." Even on an empty stomach, it was possible to break out in a smile at that witticism.

Through the dreary years of the Great Depression, Will spread his money around to any worthy cause that approached him. He was a liberal contributor to the Salvation Army and the American Red Cross, as well as to innumerable other organizations. He was making lots of money, but he gave away wads of the stuff almost as fast as he could deposit it in his bank account. This "one-man mission of mercy," as author Richard M. Ketchum called him, wore out his shoe leather and vocal cords on behalf of those who were in trouble and needed help. He traveled from one end of the country to the other, by rail, bus, car, and plane, raising money for hunger, drought, and earthquake relief. He gave out five- and ten-dollar tips to poor working folks who hadn't seen that kind of money in months. Theatrical associates and cowboy buddies, who once rode with him, were often the beneficiaries of his largesse. On one of Will's many journeys in this period, he again flirted with death in a plane crash, marking the third such incident within a few years. Going to a 1929 celebration in Dearborn, Michigan, honoring inventor Thomas A. Edison, Will's plane ran out of gas en route. Forced to return to Chicago, the plane turned over and Will was rudely tossed around, causing all of his ribs to be fractured. For some time, to alleviate the pain, he had to wear a girdle around his body.

Within the four most grueling years of the depression, when unemployment rose to over 13 million, among a population of 120 million, Will was as active as the White House was inactive. While Hoover's passive policy of "watchful waiting" resulted in little more than "the rich always getting richer, and the poor always getting poorer" (as Will put it), nobody seemed to have any panaceas for relieving the mass suffering. Will's personal reaction to America's grave situation was to keep scrambling around the land, to every city, town, and hamlet that wanted him. Although he often confessed that he didn't quite comprehend what was happening, he believed the federal government itself needed rescuing.

"You talk about this country being hard up," he said. "Every place thinks it's worse off than the other. The Red Cross, as usual, is doing heroic work, but it's the people that they can't reach, people that they've never heard of, people that are so far back in the woods that the rest of the world has almost forgotten 'em. Those are the ones I pity in this depression. I'm speaking of the Senate and the Congress of these United States. . . . It's almost worth this depression to find out how little our big men know."

Will Jr., then twenty years old, accompanied his dad on one particularly arduous benefit tour. For several weeks in the gloomy days of 1931, they teamed up with the "Blue Yodeler," Jimmie Rodgers, also known as the "Father of Country Music," to raise money in Texas, Oklahoma, and Arkansas, where economic conditions were unusually harsh. Hearing about Will's desire to play benefits in the area for the Red Cross, Jimmie volunteered to join him, since he was in awe of the "ambassador of wit."

From the start of the tour, on January 26, in San Antonio, the two men hit it off. Will began to refer to the team of Rodgers and Rogers as "the world's only yodeling rope throwers." The cooperation between them was striking, but it was rooted in their common concern for the desperate plight of farm families in the drought-stricken states of Texas, Oklahoma, and Arkansas. Rodgers had always been sorry for fellows worse off than he was, and the feeling, of course, was shared by Will.

"Some of my friends considered most hillbilly music cornball," Will Jr. recalled. "But I had all of Jimmie's records and played them on an old crank Victrola. Dad, of course, was a great admirer of his, so when they got together on the tour, it was a perfect mating. Sometimes Jimmie was too ill for the hard work of daily touring, flying, driving, arranging, talking, in and out of small hotels, so he sat it out."

Will was an inexhaustible performer, "the same old Will of the screen and the stage." However, one newspaper commentator noted that while Will always chatted amiably with the townsfolk in whatever community he had landed in, "he never gave away any comedy stuff. . . . Doubtless, he leaves that for the cash customers."

Naturally, Will never ceased to poke fun at powerful people. In San Antonio, as he stepped out of the plane, he was greeted by Mayor C. M. Chambers. "Welcome, Mr. Rogers," said the mayor, as he extended his hand. "I'm the Mayor of San Antonio."

"Well, sir," responded Will, "I'm glad to meet you *anyway*."

Generally, Will's good nature prevailed, regardless of where he was. However, in an engagement in Dallas, he was so annoyed at the meager crowd (1,966 people in an arena that could hold 5,000) that he openly grumbled about it onstage. He rubbed it in by remarking that many smaller cities had been more responsive. Backstage, he continued to berate the locals for their lack of charity, also managing to get in a dig at Mr. Hoover for having stated that "government relief established a bad precedent."

The San Antonio visit, the first of fifty stops in eighteens days, brought in $9,000 in receipts. The three-state itinerary, drawn up by Will himself, included stops such as Abilene, Wichita Falls, Duncan, Bartlesville, Claremore (despite its being a tiny place, almost $2,000 was raised there), Tulsa, Rogers, Hot Springs, Little Rock, and Texarkana. Although weather conditions were not always favorable—the troupe often got bogged down in mud due to steady rain—few benefits were postponed. In Fort Worth, over $18,000 poured in; in Oklahoma City, $10,000 was raised. There were times when Will doubled "the take" of a performance through his own matching contribution. He also devised a system of "fines" that he levied on notables. Even if such fines were uncollectible, Will's gambit shamed some of these people into "kickin' in." Not a single performer involved with the tour received a nickel.

They paid all of their own expenses, with gross proceeds being turned over to the Red Cross. In all, $225,000 was raised, a truly astonishing figure for those times. "People in America know the need is there. If they've got the money, they'll give," Will wrote in one of his daily telegrams.

In the midst of such misery, Will's own income had begun to rise to astonishing levels. It was calculated that he was paid nearly three hundred fifty dollars a minute to tell his jokes. His income had already reached nearly half a million dollars a year, even before he became the hottest property in the rapidly developing world of talking pictures. However, nobody ever bothered to total up the amounts of money that he blithely gave away to anybody who had a hard-luck story. Overall, Will had only had modest success in silent films. But with the advent of moviedom's new technology, which Will chose to call "the noisies," his popularity and money-earning ability rose to heights that he could never have anticipated.

Going back to the early 1900s, Edison and other scientists had spent much time trying to integrate sound with film images. By 1926, William Fox, formerly in the garment trade, and now the owner of a string of movie theatres, introduced the Movietone process, which recorded sound directly on film.

The 1926 film *Don Juan,* with John Barrymore, featured the recorded music of the New York Philharmonic, although there was no spoken dialogue in the movie. In 1927, forty-two-year-old Al Jolson, in blackface, crooned in the Warner Brothers production of a maudlin play, *The Jazz Singer.* This movie, with musical sequences, including some singing, and with dialogue (but without sound throughout), was recognized as the first talkie. At once, it turned the movie industry upside down, consigning the dead language of the silents to the scrap heap. The first full-length talkie, which rolled off the cameras in 1928, was *Lights of New York,* a Warners' Vitaphone production. As the motion-picture entrepreneurs then made the transition to the talkie, there was great anxiety about its potential and how it should be handled, artistically and commercially. The cost of wiring hundreds of theatres for sound was, in itself, enough to cause many first-rank producers to shy away from the new contraption. But the reality of *The Jazz Singer's* success (a two-million-dollar profit for Warners) was enough to send them scurrying for new plots, performers, and technicians who could profitably exploit the human voice.

Sadly, the coming of the talkies also meant the departure of a number of prominent silent-screen personalities. Many careers came to a grinding halt, as the shrill, squeaky, high-pitched, and gruff voices of many top actors and actresses simply didn't connect favorably with their on-screen images. For example, the virile personality of John Gilbert, the highly paid MGM hero of *The Big Parade,* as well as the on-screen and off-screen lover of Greta Garbo, became almost laughable when he delivered his lines. The "It" girl, Clara Bow, spoke a nasal Brooklynese that made fans forget her clear complexion and pepper-pot good looks. Douglas Fairbanks, Sr. was far better at climbing walls than he was at orating. Pola Negri, the dark-haired vamp with a heavy accent and Renee Adoree, Gilbert's co-star in *"The Big Parade"*; Mae Murray, Lew Cody and Colleen Moore became instant victims of the new medium. Chaplin resisted the talkies as long as he could, for the silent screen had been a perfect outlet for his herky-jerky, pantomiming movements. When he did turn to sound in *City Lights* in 1931, none of the actors, including him, did any talking; however, there was haunting music on the sound track.

"The whole business out here is scared cuckoo," Will remarked, about the turmoil created by the changeover. He wrote mockingly of all the actors running around Hollywood in a mad search for speech instructors, and he said that many who aspired to screen careers had suddenly discovered the word "enunciation," although he never spelled it properly.

Will had a right to be amused, for had he been a guzzler of champagne, he might have hoisted a glass or two in honor of those who had labored for years to perfect radio and now the talkies. The new setup was made to order for him, for he could now talk to his heart's content, be heard all over the country on screens, and get paid generously for it. "I was never sorry that movies started to talk," he said. Mary Pickford, the doyenne of silents, commented that the world was now topsy-turvy. Talkies should have come first, then silents, she insisted, for silents were the greater art. But she quickly adapted to the change, so successfully, in fact, that she won the second Academy Award in her first talking picture, *Coquette.*

Others also managed easily to make the transition to talkies. Gary Cooper, Richard Dix, Ronald Colman, Joan Crawford, Gloria Swanson, Lillian Gish, Adolphe Menjou, Wally Beery, Marie Dressler, Norma Shearer, John Barrymore, Paul Muni, Janet Gaynor, and Bebe Daniels, Jimmy Cagney, and Edward G. Robinson—they all did it with panache. The famed movie dog, Rin-Tin-Tin, had no trouble at all.

A long trail of hopeful actors from Broadway jammed the portals of Hollywood, already overrun with half-literates and sexy car-hops seeking fame, riches and haciendas with swimming pools. Some near-hysterical producers thought that by photographing Broadway plays in their entirety they could beat the new system, while chlorine-choked musicals (a transplant of the Ziegfeld Follies to the screen) rolled off the Hollywood assembly-line.

At 50, Will was an avuncular figure without typical-matinee-idol looks. His face was tan but weathered, with deep grooves at the side of each eye. His mouth was large and mirthful. His lower lip could have held a small puddle. His healthy shock of brownish hair was now tinged with gray, but his eyes always sparkled. His ears were as prominent as Clark Gable's, but he didn't have Gable's tomcat grin. His nose was bold, but not as formidable as Jimmy Durante's. He had the general demeanor of a common man, a self-elected representative of the world's underdogs. He was an "Aw shucks" guy at a time when uttering words like "To hell with it" would have made the church moralists bray from their pulpits. He projected a natural, relaxed, somewhat seedy look, although it's doubtful whether he was ever truly relaxed or casual. It was difficult to think of him without his shrugging, chewing, incessant mugging, and gesticulating.

The production chief of William Fox's talking-picture studio was Winfield Sheehan, who had studied human nature better than most. He was familiar with Will's career, and knew that his success in the silents had been limited. But he was confident that Will's voice, speaking words of goodness, truth, and integrity, would surely win a wide audience. Of the new cadre of personnel that Sheehan signed up for Fox, Will was considered to be the studio's most important acquisition. If Sheehan was looking for someone to play "just plain folks," Will was the man.

At the outset, Will was not too eager to embark on this tricky challenge. Having had a history of feeling anxiety whenever he was confronted with a new venture, Will's first reaction to Sheehan's proposal was to step back. "I've already had a bellyful of pictures," he insisted. But he didn't put up strong opposition. Among other things, Betty assured him he could handle it. He finally made up his mind, and signed up for four talkies, which would be shot over a sixteen-month period. The lordly sum was $600,000, or $150,000 for each picture. "If Winnie Sheehan and William Fox say this is OK, it goes for me," Will scrawled, next to his name on the contract, a departure from his usual verbal agreements.

To give him further reassurance, Sheehan's initial project for Will was a script by Homer Croy, who knew Will like the back of his own hand. Croy's original story, *They Had to See Paris*, was about an Oklahoma family that suddenly strikes oil, then takes off for Paris, where they try to marry their daughter off to a count. At first, Sheehan thought that Chic Sale or W. C.

Fields might be better for the part of the newly rich oilman, Pike Peters, but Croy convinced the producer that Will was ideal for the role. To buttress Will's confidence, Sheehan brought in Irene Rich to play Mrs. Peters. Miss Rich had been a "constant wife" to Will in the silents, so it was comforting for him to have her around again.

In *They Had to See Paris,* Rich enjoyed a lavish lifestyle in a French chateau. As expected, Will, as Peters, hated every moment of it. It was clear that he yearned for his home back in Oklahoma. A veteran director, Frank Borzage, was on hand to conduct the proceedings. He even succeeded in getting Will to "accept" a kiss from Rich. Such an event was momentous, since Will generally refused, out of a sense of propriety, to engage in amorous scenes that were now common fare in Hollywood films. After Rich planted a kiss on Will's cheek, he blushed like a schoolboy. "I feel like I've been unfaithful to my wife," he told a bystander.

When the movie was completed, Fox organized a well-publicized Los Angeles preview to exhibit the talking Will to the public. It was scheduled for September 1929, and it was decided that there should be a charge for tickets. Abashed by this action, Will refused to appear at the preview, excusing himself because of "the brigandage" of his sponsors. He even turned down publicity photos, as he ran off to Oklahoma, leaving the confounded Fox to wonder what was on his mind.

However, Croy saw Will's absenteeism more as a sign of his anxiety over the reception he would receive for his first talkie. Will needn't have been so concerned, for the movie won him high marks from critics and audiences alike. Within days, Will returned home from his temporary exile, with an embarrassed grin on his face.

Will tried to explain his absence from the preview by writing in his daily telegram, "I figured I better kinder take to the woods 'til the effects kinder blew over." With a note of studied humility, he added that "the picture had opened with no casualties. I've been practically forgiven for it. Wasn't bad enough to shoot or good enough to cheer."

Everyone who worked with Will on the picture, including Borzage, was intrigued with the way he had done his job. They said afterward that he was the ultimate improviser, to such an extent that half the time during the filming, he wound up in the wrong place—he meandered around the set in his own inimitable way, never bothering to note where he was supposed to be, or where Borzage wanted him to be. Ordinarily, this would have been a problem for the director, but Borzage assured everyone that there was no way he'd attempt to change Will's habits or idiosyncrasies. After all, Will's ad-libs were an improvement on Croy's script, a fact that Homer himself might have acknowledged. "Wherever Will is, that's where the scene's going to be played," Borzage proclaimed. "Whatever he says, we'll go with that, too."

The New York Times said that Will's role was the best one he had ever played. Others stressed that the talkies were obviously invented with Will in mind. Better than mere rhetoric, Fox's accountants said that *They Had to See Paris* made three-quarters of a million dollars.

The next step in the development of its newest talkie star had Fox casting Will in an all-star special called *Happy Days*. This was an eighty six-minute wide-screen presentation in which Fox trotted out Janet Gaynor, Charlie Farrell, Victor McLaglen, Warner Baxter, Georgie Jessel, Edmund Lowe, Dixie Lee, Betty Grable, J. Farrell MacDonald, and Walter Catlett. All of them played cameos in this junkyard of a movie, where the plot concerned a Mississippi showboat that is rescued from bankruptcy by a charity show. The picture did little to advance Will's career, helping only to fulfill his contract.

With a mixture of innocence and understanding, Will next played the proprietor of a Reno, Nevada, hotel, where women stayed prior to winning quickie divorces. The film was *Lightnin'*, a 1930 movie, in which a young man named Joel McCrea played the juvenile lead as Will's son-in-law. At the time, McCrea was just twenty four, and Will was fifty one, but the two hit it off immediately. Fresh out of Pomona College, in California, McCrea, a self-confessed greenhorn, badly needed guidance from someone other than direc-tor Henry King, and Will filled that role to perfection.

"By the end of the first day of shooting, I realized how much I liked this man," said McCrea. "The movie was shot in the high Sierras, on the border between Nevada and California, which made it thrilling to begin with. But when Will asked me if I'd like to ride home with him in his LaSalle, after the first day's work, that was even more thrilling. Will had seen me heading for the staff bus, so he called out to me, 'Wait, you ain't an extra any more, you don't have to ride the bus."

Will took McCrea into his circle of friends in a "no-sweat way." He in-structed McCrea about how to handle money, helped him out in promoting certain personal values, and in coping with people. Needing a five thousand dollar load to buy a good parcel of property near Thousand Oaks, McCrea was told by Will that he'd give him the money. When McCrea refused Will's offer on the grounds that it was a poor idea to borrow from friends, Will directed him to a bank in Santa Monica.

"There's a little English Jew in there named Strickland. Don't mention my name, but tell him your story," said Will. When McCrea visited the bank, Strickland got out a card and wrote "6 percent" on it. There was no mention of collateral, nothing like that. McCrea signed and got the loan, suspecting all along that Will probably had informed Strickland he'd stand behind the loan.

Will always called McCrea "Joe." "Joe, you're just like me," he told McCrea one afternoon. "You ain't very good-looking and you ain't a very good actor. Now these other guys I won't do this for, because they're already supposed to be good. But this is what I'll do. I say approximately the same things that are in the script. But sometimes I get an idea and I go on and make it a little better. Sometimes if I get tired of it and I don't think it's very good, I cut it short."

McCrea admitted that this technique could be a scary business for a young actor, accustomed to the security of the typed page. But Will also told him that when he was through talking, he'd nudge him. "Then you can talk," he advised McCrea.

"He helped me get the hang of his system right away," recalled McCrea. "His way of cueing probably also added an element of spontaneity that sure appealed to audiences. He came across as a fellow who wasn't acting. Basically, he wasn't. He was himself, saying what came into his mind."

McCrea and other actors who played in Will's movies felt that he didn't really change the story line by his ad-libbing. Some agreed that his extemporaneous lines were often better than the lines written by the professionals. In McCrea's case, he thought that Will's off-the-cuff comments made the characters more believable.

Will's presence on any set, according to McCrea, also tended to improve the behavior of others who were there. "He didn't preach one syllable, but attitudes towards foreigners, Jews, black people and America were always better with him around," said McCrea. "He did it just by example."

Will rarely went to church and took little active interest in religious matters. However, he made generous contributions to the Beverly Hills Community Church. "I honestly don't think any one religion is *the* religion," he said many times. "Whichever way you serve your God will never get one word of argument or condemnation from me."

Over the years that McCrea knew Will, he felt that his friend attempted to see the best in everybody. "But there *were* people he didn't like," insisted McCrea. This rarely-seen side of Will was dramatically displayed one time when McCrea and Will were sharing a latrine while waiting for shooting to start on a movie. "Will went way down to the other side of the latrine because he was shy about a lot of things like that," recalled McCrea. "I was the first to leave and Will was organizing to leave, when a man rushed in the door, then moved down towards Will, wanting his autograph. Since the man had nothing for Will to write one, he grabbed a sheet of toilet paper off the roll and asked Will to sign that. This made Will blazing mad. 'Get the hell outta here,' he shouted. When he got outside of the latrine Will was still seething. 'Can you believe a fella like that?' he asked."

In another 1930 film, *So This Is London,* directed by John Blystone, and again featuring Will's "reel wife," Irene Rich, Will played a country merchant who takes a trip to the British Isles. There his family meets a British lord called Hare. Will didn't have much affection for the British in the movie (such opinions were expressed occasionally in his columns), while Hare was equally hostile to the Yanks. However, Will's daughter, played by Maureen O'Sullivan (who later won renown as Tarzan's mate), falls in love with Hare's son, complicating matters. At the end, Will and Hare join in a conciliatory duet consisting of "My Country 'Tis of Thee" and "God Save the King."

O'Sullivan hadn't met Will before this movie assignment. But she quickly assessed him as a "sharp man, with nothing accidental in his behavior." One day she appeared on the set wearing tight-fitting slacks. That failed to win the approval of Will, for he didn't like women parading around in a such a way. When he made his feelings known about the matter, O'Sullivan concluded that Will thought "I was a fast young woman." His impression of her, she added, was that "I was not a traditional or proper person. It bothered him, causing me to think that if he ever said he never met a man he didn't like, he sure didn't care much for women!" (Will's reaction was not unusual in those days. As late as the 1960s, there were men who continued to harbor negative feelings about women in slacks.)

Proving to be prudish and old-fashioned, Will was equally as adamant about the role of women in society. In 1931, Irene Dunne, a versatile actress, starred with Richard Dix in *Cimarron.* On seeing the film, which was named the best movie that year, Will said she was the *only* woman for whom he'd ever vote for a seat in Congress. While ahead of his time in most political and social matters, Will was stuck back in the Dark Ages when it came to gender. In that respect, he probably shared the feelings of most of his fellow males.

Despite her mixed feelings about Will, O'Sullivan was cast again with him in *A Connecticut Yankee* in 1931, after Will had just finished a clinker called *Ambassador Bill.* In the latter, Will had joined Marguerite Churchill, Greta

Nissen, and Ray Milland, and he played another Oklahoma cattleman, who is appointed ambassador to a country whose king is exiled due to frequent revolutions. Will pleased the critics again. They said he saved the day with his rustic observations—but the film was sixty-eight minutes of fluff.

On the other hand, A Connecticut Yankee was a fine adaptation of Mark Twain's book, and was the second time Will had appeared in a literary classic (he had played Ichabod Crane in the silent version of Washington Irving's Legend of Sleepy Hollow). Yankee proved to be a major financial success, and in the trade it was known as a colorful romp. Conked on the head by an accidental blow, Will dreams back to the days when maidens were fair and knights were bold. In his fantasy, he gets to lasso a knight of the Round Table. At the finish, he saves himself from the stake by accurately recalling an eclipse that had occurred several hundred years before he was born.

Scarcely attempting to change his accent for the part, Will sounded like what he was, an Oklahoma cowboy. Needless to say, that added to his appeal. But another actress in the movie, Myrna Loy, reacted to Will much as O'Sullivan had. She thought he embraced stuffy Victorian attitudes.

"He was a rascal who liked to tease me," recalled Loy, who played Morgan LeFay in the film. "Around the studio he had that innocent, corny way of his. When I tried to seduce him in the movie, they tinted the scene somehow so that he blushed. His face actually turned red on-screen. He was shy and was supposed to be." (Will's ranch covered much of the property above Loy's Rivas Canyon house.)

In the 1931 movie Young As You Feel, Will played the owner of a meat-packing business, who meets the saucy Gallic star, Fifi Dorsay. A victim of a swindler, Fifi escapes total ruin, with Will's help. Meanwhile, Will's two playboy sons swear to reform themselves, as Will makes the ultimate sacrifice: He persuades Fifi to return to her husband, thus chalking up another mark on his platonic scoreboard.

By the end of 1932, Will had hurdled to ninth place among moviedom's top box-office stars. His salary had jumped to two hundred thousand dollars per movie, as he worked out a six-picture deal with Fox in which he would get $1.2 million. His own progress in high finance contrasted sharply with what had befallen Flo Ziegfeld. The producer's health was failing; he was continually badgered to pay back taxes; his bank account was dwindling; and his career appeared to have reached a dead end.

Regardless of this bleak scenario, Ziegfeld plunged ahead with grandiose plans for a first nationwide radio show, "The Follies of the Air." It was planned after Ziegfeld, Eddie Dowling, and orchestra leader Al Goodwin had put their heads together to come up with a viable format. The premiere half-hour broadcast was presented on April 3, 1932, and the show ran for 13 weeks, through June 26. Ziegfeld rounded up every available star who had worked for him, including Will, Ruth Etting, Billie Burke, Paul Robeson, Helen Morgan, and Fannie Brice. Although he never fancied himself a performer, Ziegfeld also appeared on the show. Like a good trouper, he rallied his strength to utter a few words—but it was Will's words that touched the difficult maestro. "Every man that flies that ocean from now on will always be an imitation of Lindbergh," Will said on the air, "and every musical show that is produced is just an imitation of Ziegfield." (Will continued to mangle Flo's last name.)

His ego bolstered by the general response to the radio show, Ziegfeld then staged a revival of *Show Boat*, the production that had set New Yorkers to cheering in the halcyon year of 1927. The new version opened at the Earl Carroll Theatre on May 19, 1932. With Robeson singing "Old Man River" as nobody had ever sung it before, *Show Boat* was actually judged to be better than the original. It was certainly a temporary boost to Ziegfeld's morale.

Unfortunately, by late June, Ziegfeld became desperately ill with a lung ailment. He tried to prevent the news of his sickness from being publicized, but those close to him, like Will, knew he was sinking. As Ziegfeld's medical bills soared, Will helped to pay most of them. In the first week of July, Ziegfeld left for the West Coast on a private railroad car paid for by his sister. Two of Will's children, Mary and Jimmy, went along to lend a hand. Once in California, Ziegfeld took advantage of Will's hospitality, spending considerable time at his ranch. However, Billie Burke rented a home in Santa Monica, where she thought her husband might have an easier time recuperating. Soon Ziegfeld took a turn for the worse. On the evening of July 22, 1932, he died, bankrupt, at the age of 65. His passing was front-page news all over America. That night, Will took Billie and Patty, Flo's daughter, to his ranch, where they could mourn privately. He attended to the details of the funeral; broke the news to Eddie Cantor, who was shattered; and quietly paid for all expenses relating to Ziegfeld's burial. His eulogy at the St. Athjanasius Episcopal Church brought tears to the eyes of a crowd of close friends and associates.

"Our world of make-believe is sad," said Will. "He picked us up from all walks of life. He led us into what little fame we achieved. He remained our friend regardless of our usefulness to him as an entertainer. He brought beauty into the entertainment world. . . . The profession of acting must be necessary, for it exists in every race and language . . . so good-bye, Flo, save a spot for me, for you will put on a show some day that will knock their eyes out."

Will's affection for Ziegfeld was surpassed only by his loyalty to the man. His son Jimmy remarked after the funeral that "no two men lived who had greater, deeper respect for one another. My dad didn't have that feeling with any other people he worked for."

The tiny, curly-haired Shirley Temple was now Fox's reigning child star. Not since Jackie Coogan had stolen scenes from Charlie Chaplin, in the early 1920s, had any moppet captured the hearts of Americans the way Shirley did. On the Fox lot, there had been talk that the studio was set to pair Shirley and Will in a picture. Since both of these Fox players had popularity credentials that promised a box-office bonanza, it seemed inevitable that they'd be brought together in a major film. The word was that, as the depression worsened, Shirley and Will had kept Fox from going bankrupt. In 1934, Will was second only to Marie Dressler as a box-office draw, and the next year, he surpassed Dressler. But Shirley, zoomed to the top herself in 1935. Only Amelia Earhart and Eleanor Roosevelt were more popular American women than Shirley was in the early 1930s.

Will and Shirley met for the first time in December 1932, at a money-raiser being held at the Fox Criterion Theatre in Santa Monica, a typically gilded palace of the 1930s. The Unemployed Citizens League was the beneficiary of the event, and Will had been invited to take over as master of ceremonies at the halfway mark. He cracked his usual topical jokes, with a special application to the Hollywood community. Then Shirley, barely five years old, pranced on with her dance routine, in a flowered skirt, white pumps, and barelegged. The audience, enchanted with the youngster, cheered her, causing Will to summon her back for an encore. When the two went backstage after the show was over, Will, with some embarrassment, asked Shirley, "What's your name again?" She answered, "Shirley Jane Temple, and this is my mommy. What's yours?" By the next year, Shirley had become famous enough for Will to remember her name.

Shortly afterward, Fox commissioned Alberto Vargas, a Peruvian painter, to create a mural for their executive dining room. At a special reception celebrating the work, Will was again the MC. He looked over at Shirley, with a grin, acknowledging that "she's the greatest squawkie entertainer in the world today." Pointing his finger at her, he added, "But she's still only pint-sized. Shirley, you're lucky your teeth can grow back, mine don't!"

The last get-together Will had with Shirley occurred when he was on a break from shooting *David Harum* in 1935. He took the opportunity to saunter over to a neighboring set, where Shirley was hard at work on *Baby, Take A Bow.* They got into a friendly, earnest conversation, and Will confided to her that they might be acting in the same film after he returned from a planned trip to Alaska.

"Where's Alaska?" Shirley inquired. Will carefully arranged several chips of wood on the cement floor so that they roughly represented the outline of the United States. "Here's where we are," he said, poking his finger at California on his improvised map. "And here's where Alaska would be." Shirley nodded her appreciation of the quick geography lesson.

In the memoirs that Shirley wrote many years later, she said she liked Mr. Rogers because he was "outgoing, accessible, and natural." She found him attractive, even though he wasn't good-looking. "His speech had an appealing cadence and he laughed a lot," she said.

In a sequel to *They Had To See Paris,* Will acted in *Down To Earth* in 1932. It wasn't a robust hit, yet it afforded Homer Croy another chance to make some money as the writer of the script. That was enough to assure Will's participation in the venture. In 1932's *Business and Pleasure,* based on a play by Booth Tarkington, Will was up to his old traveling tricks again. This time, he played a business mogul from Oklahoma who visits Syria to pry loose some secrets that might be of help in his razor-blade business. In the process, he draws a few hearty laughs by getting involved with a fortune-teller—of course, no female, however seductive, could cause him to stray.

Too Busy To Work, his last film in 1932, saw him playing Jubilo, a hobo intent on finding a man named Burton, who had run off with his wife and daughter many years before, while Jubilo was off to war. By a twist of fate, ordained by Fox, Will winds up as a handyman in Burton's home. Never revealing himself to his daughter, Jubilo manages to straighten out her love life, while also tending to his wife's grave. The critics regarded this as a "charming Rogers outing," helping to buttress Will's growing appeal.

The next year, Will made *Mr. Skitch,* with the poker-faced comedienne Zasu Pitts, and Rochelle Hudson. (The latter was a fixture in several of Will's films, adding the pristine touch that was so essential to the portrayal of women in his movies.) Will and Zasu played a hard-working farm couple from Missouri, who had been forced off their land because of their inability to pay off a mortgage. After a series of incredible events, everything comes up roses in the end. Some felt this was Will's weakest movie up to this point. But he remained relaxed about the matter, which was one good reason why he was so successful at what he was doing.

Basically, Will kept playing Will Rogers in one part after another. He continued to ignore the scripts that were handed to him by directors, still preferring to get the gist of the plot, then extemporizing from that point on. Each day, when he arrived on the set, he always had a cheery "Good mornin'" for all hands. From that moment on, he enjoyed himself immensely. Incontestably the most popular person on the set—except when he was antagonizing a Maureen O'Sullivan or a Myrna Loy with his strict fashion preferences—Will was rewarded by management with a ridiculously lavish dressing "room." It was a Spanish bungalow that had a couch, fireplace, private bathroom, and huge closets; since Will had an almost nonexistent wardrobe, the closets remained empty most of the time. He paid scant attention to the luxury of his private quarters, so when crowded tour buses stopped at his bungalow, he usually wasn't in it.

Instead, he preferred using his LaSalle car—which he drove to work himself—for occasional catnaps, often on the running board. He also found that he got better inspiration for this daily telegrams by sitting in the backseat of his car, with his all upper-case-key typewriter resting precariously on his lap. All manner of provisions—"a cuckoo's nest," as Croy described it—cluttered the backseat, as Will banged out his column. Surrounding him were playing cards, spectacles, old newspapers and magazines, ropes, telegraph blanks, apple cores, banana peels, and books. For lunch, Will usually would bring along a sandwich from home. If he chose instead to eat in the studio commissary, he'd gulp down his bowl of chili. Those who might join him at his table would invariably have the tab picked up for them by Will.

When the time came for him to act, he ignored props, such as funny hats, multicolored shirts, or other fancy clothes. "I'm only funny with ideas," he insisted. Makeup for his face was out of the question. He was always prompt in arriving and was also a stickler for a 4:30 P.M. departure time.

A bucolic novel by Philip Stong provided him with his next vehicle, *State Fair*, in 1933. Directed by Henry King, it was just under an hour-and-a-half long and featured some of Fox's most prominent players: Janet Gaynor, the dollface of *Seventh Heaven* (one of the silent era's most popular movies); Lew Ayres; Sally Eilers; and Victor Jory and Norman Foster—they represented a load of highly paid talent in this pleasant tale. The main character in the movie actually was Blue Boy, a prize boar with outsize tusks and a mean disposition. Going to the Iowa state fair with this animal, Will hoped that Blue Boy would be selected as the best in the show. When Blue Boy turned out to be a winner, Will realized his dream. The romance in *State Fair* was carried off by Ayres, a reporter with a way with women—he went for Gaynor. Foster wound up with Eilers.

During the shooting of *State Fair*, King warned Will that he should be very careful when he was around the truculent Blue Boy. But Will reassured the director that he knew full well how to handle hogs of all kinds (he may have had some people in mind), and that he was confident that Blue Boy wouldn't give him any trouble.

One day, nobody could find Will on the set. They finally located him sleeping next to Blue Boy in a pen that was specially constructed for the hog. Stretched out alongside Blue Boy, with his head propped against Blue Boy's distended belly, and his Stetson pulled down over his eyes, Will appeared at peace with the world—and certainly with Blue Boy. Will may have been pretending to be asleep. But Blue Boy wasn't faking. At any rate, Will proved his point with King.

When *State Fair* was completed, a Fox supervisor asked Will if he'd like to take Blue Boy home with him. Sure will make good eating for the whole Rogers family, the official suggested. Will mulled it over for a moment, then said that he appreciated the offer but just couldn't do it. "I just wouldn't feel right eatin' a fellow actor," he concluded.

Until *State Fair*, Ayres had never played in a movie with Will. He had already achieved considerable renown for his impressive role in Erich Maria Remarque's *All Quiet On The Western Front*, a 1929 antiwar film. To many, the image of Ayres, as Paul, a German foot soldier, reaching out to touch a butterfly at the film's conclusion, was unforgettable.

The handsome young Ayres, from Minnesota, experienced a "sense of awe" working with Will. "Many of us were moved by him," said Ayres. "He never got excited and seemed to be so wise and strong. Most of us envied him. He made you fascinated by what he had to say, and had the insight and capacity to win people over. At the time we made the movie Will was older than my father, so I was somewhat shy around him. I did go to his home as his guest but he never became a close friend. Perhaps he didn't have many close friends. But he did have many admirers."

One reviewer, commenting about Will's performance in *State Fair*, summed him up this way: "He is what Americans think other Americans are like." In almost all of his roles, Will affirmed old cultural pieties, fighting an unending struggle against bullies, tyrants, liars, and hypocrites. Sometimes he was called on to travel beyond the confines of his own village to challenge the deceitful ways of the outside world. Other times, he was the street-corner sage who played the mentor for ingenuous young couples that badly needed a few pearls of his simple wisdom. Whatever role he played, Will succeeded easily in the pursuit of such images. To the folks at Fox, his wily, horse-trading personality was just what they had ordered. The country was getting its dose of Will's disarming manner—or "improvisational naturalism," as writer Ethan Mordden called it—and never seemed to tire of it. He belonged to a vanished age, a world most Americans once took for granted, added Mordden.

However, there were also acerbic critics of this effortless display by Will. One of the most severe was Dwight Macdonald, who constantly ranted about "middlebrow culture." Macdonald began his assault by suggesting that there was a limit to the detachment of art from present-day realities. "At a time when the American farmer is faced with ruin," grumbled Macdonald, "when the whole Midwest is seething with bitterness and economic discontent, a movie like *State Fair* is an insulting "Let 'em eat cake" gesture. The vaudeville rusticity of millionaire Will; thus Hollywood embodies the farmer. There is no excuse for the cheerfully trivial tone of the whole thing, the studied avoidance of anything more serious in the life of the farmer than whether his hog will win the state championship. . . . The movie is about as earthy as the gingham overalls in a musical comedy number. . . ."

Attacks on Will were not limited to his movie portrayals. A Socialist newspaper, *The American Freeman,* charged that Will was misusing his daily role as a columnist. "He likes to pose as home folks but the truth is he's a millionaire," said the publication. "He's never written a sentence in support of a worker or striker. He's never spoken a sentence that doubted the divine justice of the capitalist system. Many of his wisecracks reveal a hidden sympathy for the Fascist type of demagogue. The great Mark Twain was a real humorist who wasn't afraid to utter truths about the mountebanks of religion, politics and militarism."

Although Will didn't reply to this ideological battering, he did show sensitivity to those who chided him for continuing to say nice things about Mussolini. As late as 1933, having Mussolini obviously in mind, Will averred, "Dictatorship is the best government in the world, provided you have the right dictator." When the chief editorial writer of the *San Diego Union* reminded him that Mussolini was a despot, Will countered by saying that Franklin D. Roosevelt had more power, at any time, than Mussolini, but that Americans seemed to be tickled to death about that.

To those who openly suggested to Will that he shouldn't meddle in politics or other serious matters, but should stick to his insubstantial one-liners, he could be surprisingly brusque. Frequently, he knocked out letters of response to those who had criticized him, thus revealing, perhaps for the first time, a thin-skinned, spiteful side that few of those close to him ever saw. Once he angrily challenged an editor of a small northwestern paper to a one-on-one debate on foreign policy, after the editor had acknowledged that he read a magazine called *Foreign Affairs*. "When a magazine can learn him foreign affairs," growled Will, "I want to tangle with a guy like that."

Will occasionally argued with the editorial policy of *The New York Times,* where his daily quips took up space. Since many of his wisecracks were directed at foreign countries, there were those who accused him of being xenophobic. The sudden rise in Will's ego and blood pressure could have been attributed mostly to his ceaseless, enervating travel, and to the incessant demands on his time and energy. He wasn't young enough, or resilient enough, to brush off the sniping directed at him. And as things got worse in America, and people became angrier and more intemperate, Will indeed became a convenient target.

By the early 1920s, director John Ford had won a reputation for movies about America's pioneer days. In 1931 he directed a superb talkie version of Sinclair Lewis's *Arrowsmith,* with Helen Hayes playing the lead. For some time, he had told Fox that he was eager to direct Will in a movie. The studio finally accommodated Ford's desire by matching him with Will on *Dr. Bull,* in which Will played a small-town doctor who worked to mend his community's ills, of which there turned out to be many. It was a downbeat yarn, reflecting Ford's dark, morose perspective on life. The only upbeat part was Will's pursuit, in his diffident way, of the local widow, Vera Allen.

Born and raised an Irish-Catholic, of the old-fashioned kind, Ford was a tough, hard-drinking fellow who liked his performers to fit neatly into his own mold. Typical of this type were Harry Carey and J. Farrell MacDonald, both perfect Fordian heroes. Will was not exactly in that category. Yet, when Ford stressed sentiment—which some critics insisted he did in excess—Will became most compatible with his director.

At times, the relationship between Will and Ford became stormy, although the two men had a great fondness for each other. There were occasions, for example, when Will tried to give Ford instructions on how to direct and how to develop certain scenes. Not taking, such behavior kindly, Ford would stomp off the set, only to return to find that Will had actually taken over the directing chores. Then Ford's temper might flare again. But that didn't stop them from working together in other movies. Since Will was generally a surrogate for justice in Ford's pictures, he liked playing such roles and managed to smooth things over in the long run. (After Will died, Ford continued to wear a hat, with a funny hole in it, that Will had given him as a gift.)

In *Handy Andy,* in 1934, Will was directed by David Butler, with a cast that also included Peggy Wood and Robert Taylor. The black-haired Taylor, regarded as one of the handsomest men ever to appear in films, was making his debut as a leading man. Once again, Will played a small-town, homespun type—a druggist whose wife (Wood) nursed high-society aspirations. She forces Will to sell his store to a large chain, then gets herself involved in a social whirl, including a flirtation with a gigolo. During *Handy Andy,* Will appears in a Tarzan suit and is thrown into jail. In the end, however, he gets both his store and Peggy back, with the latter being properly chastened.

The picture was notable chiefly for the number of nonhumans that appeared. "It was an animal picture, with actors," laughed Will, referring to the six kittens, one Great Dane, one cat, and twenty-four pigeons that were employed in the movie. Displaying his usual tricks, Will ad-libbed throughout the movie, often breaking up the cast. "He never made a change in dialogue that didn't immensely improve the script," Wood said. "I didn't bother to look at my lines until an hour or two before I was supposed to speak them, because Will was likely to speak lines a scenarist never thought of, often making me change my dialogue. So I just waited and heard what Will had to say, then tried to fit the script's dialogue into it." Like most actors had done in the past, whenever Will did his extemporizing, they changed their own lines to accommodate his changes.

When Will went on to make *David Harum* in 1934, with James Cruze as the director, he played a small-town banker living in upstate New York in the 1890s. Cruze could stage-manage optimism as well as any resident Hollywood director. What he constructed in *Harum* certainly appeared to make a statement about the state of the economy in the past and in the present, the 1930s. Will was supposed to represent the common sense of most Americans—he reassured everybody in the little town of Homeville that things, in the natural course of events, would get better. It was an inherently smug message that could send critics like Dwight Macdonald running for the exits. The role called for Will—a nonsmoker—to smoke a pipe. (At one point he became so ill that the production was delayed.) As a confirmed bachelor and horse trader, Will (Harum) confronts a parsimonious deacon, with whom he makes a number of bad deals. Noah Beery and Evelyn Venable supported Will, as did Stepin Fetchit, the black man from Key West, Florida, who had the burden of depicting shiftless, slow-moving characters.

Fetchit was not the only actor in that era who was called on to fulfill white Hollywood's patronizing stereotype of the American Negro. There were other blacks, too, who played obsequious maids who carried feather dusters, or hired hands whose eyes popped out of their heads when they confronted black cats. A social distance on-screen was maintained between the white actors and the black actors. That included Will, who was never heard expressing disapproval of such portrayals. Perhaps it was too much to expect from a man whose family had been slaveowners, and who had come from a parochial southwestern background. The plots in these movies were basically hokum, as were the dreadful racial stereotypes in regard to whites as well as blacks. Years after his acting career was at a standstill, Fetchit, having been accused of debasing his race, tried to explain what moviemaking was like in the thirties. "People don't understand what I was doing then, least of all the young generation of Negroes. Hollywood was more segregated than Georgia," he said.

Never a "camera hog" in any of his movies, Will was content to let others show off their faces and talent, for he liked to see them get credit for what they did. In *David Harum*, there was a scene shot at Fairmount Park Racetrack in Riverside, California, in which Will rode in a horse race against Charles Middleton. When Cruze kept putting Will in the foreground during the shooting, Will realized that this was not fair to Middleton; so he asked the director to give Middleton a break. "You won't ever be able to see him in the movie," he told Cruze. Thereupon, Cruze complied with Will's wish to feature Middleton more prominently.

Arguably, the best movie that Will ever made, from a box-office and an artistic view, was *Judge Priest* in 1934. For this film, Ford was back at the directorial helm, although hardly in complete control of Will. The movie offered a slice of life in a small Kentucky town at the start of the twentieth century, and was roughly based on several of Irvin S. Cobb's short stories. It was only proper that Will was able to exploit Cobb's material, for Will's newspaperman-friend was one of the few people who could compete with him when it came to exchanging mutual insults.

Judge Priest had a formidable cast, with Henry B. Walthall, Tom Brown, Fetchit, Hattie McDaniel, Charlie Grapewin, Anita Louise, and Rochelle Hudson. Judge Bill Priest, played by Will, steps down from the bench to defend a local war hero. The role echoed that of Dr. Bull, yet Priest was less irascible. The plot was said to be an evocation of the ghosts of Cobb's boyhood. However, when Will attempted to make a strong antilynching plea (such a scene was actually shot), it was excised in the final take. Obviously, at that time, the studio didn't choose to engage in such humane politics. In one scene that again perpetuated stereotypes, Fetchit was fast asleep in the courtroom. Judge Priest, directing that Stepin be awakened, said, "If anyone's gonna sleep in this courtroom, it's gonna be me."

The veteran actor Walthall benefited considerably from his association with Will in *Judge Priest*. In the final sequence of the movie, Walthall was featured prominently—which was due to Will's efforts. Will stood on the sidelines, feeding Walthall cues, "practically effacing himself to give Walthall a better opportunity to enjoy center stage," Cobb wrote of the incident. The result was that Walthall, who had previously been reduced to playing very minor roles, was awarded a fine contract on the strength of his acting in *Judge Priest*.

As America's number-one entertainment provider, Hollywood had wisely learned to celebrate itself, beginning in 1927, by holding an annual awards ceremony. In 1927, such silent films as *Wings, Seventh Heaven,* and *The Way of All Flesh* won top picture awards, thus setting the stage for the future spotlighting of the event. By 1934 the presentation of Oscars became the most widely publicized moment of the industry's season. That year, on the night of March 16, the Academy Awards were bestowed in the Fiesta Room of Los Angeles's Ambassador Hotel, with Will, fresh from his appearance in *State Fair,* (a Best Picture nominee), serving as the genial host.

Holding his head down, as usual, Will began by saying, "This looks like the last roundup of the ermine. I got my courage to come here and talk to you highbrows and brains of the industry after I read recently that Sam Goldwyn lectured at Harvard. In person, too. I understand now that Harvard's writin' back, 'Will you please send us the English version.'"

When it came time to the pass out awards, Walt Disney, tapped for his popular cartoon, *Three Little Pigs,* came to the podium with his head swathed in bandages. Will explained that Disney had been injured in a polo match at the ranch, when "I also got whacked over the head with a mallet."

As the audience held its collective breath, prior to Will's announcement of the winner of the Best Director Oscar, he opened the envelope and purred: "Well, well, what do ya know. I've watched this young man for a long time, saw him come right up from the bottom, I mean the bottom. It couldn't have happened to a nicer guy. Come up and get it, *Frank!*" Whereupon Frank Capra, director of *Lady for a Day*, leaped up from his seat and bolted for the platform. "Over here, over here," Capra yelled at the operator of the spotlight. But instead of the spotlight falling on Capra, it landed on another Frank—Frank Lloyd, the director of *Cavalcade*. It was Lloyd, not Capra, who then raced to the dais, where he was embraced by Will. (In his autobiography, Capra admitted that this episode was "the most shattering of my life. . . . All my friends at the table were crying." However, the next year the academy made amends to Capra by honoring him for *It Happened One Night.*)

Nobody believed that Will had purposely set up Capra for such an embarrassment—the entrapment of the poor fellow was indeed inadvertent. *The Hollywood Reporter* and the *Los Angeles Times* thought that the affair was carried off brilliantly. It was Will, despite the Capra caper, who won the lion's share of praise. "He imbued the whole thing with a cheerful spirit," said the *Times*. (In future years, the ceremonies would be hosted by such notables as Conrad Nagel, Georgie Jessel, Irvin S. Cobb, Bob Hope, Jack Benny, Jimmy Stewart, Robert Montgomery, Agnes Moorehead (the first woman who acted as host), Dick Powell, Paul Douglas, and Johnny Carson, but few were as amiable and relaxed as Will was in the role.)

Will's workload at this stage was formidable. Between his daily telegrams, his lectures, his movie commitments, his radio engagements, and his charity endeavors, he had more than enough to command his attention and energy. Yet he compulsively accepted a bid to play the lead role of Nat Miller—a newspaper publisher in a small town—in a 1934 stage production of *Ah, Wilderness*, one of Eugene O'Neill's less-mordant plays. Performances began in San Francisco, then went on to Los Angeles, where the play gained first-rate notices and ran for ten weeks.

For a while, the play, and Will's role in it, gave him a good deal of pleasure, despite the fact that he was obligated to pay close attention to the lines written by O'Neill. "I had my troubles readin' 'em, much less learnin' 'em," Will remarked. Betty was convinced it was the best sustained performance he had ever given, while O'Neill himself gave Will the notion that he was portraying Miller to perfection. Mary Rogers, who was beginning a season of summer stock in Maine, wired her father that he was doing just fine—and so was she.

However, unexpected storm clouds suddenly gathered when a local clergyman protested Will's appearance in such an "immoral" enterprise. After accompanying his teenage daughter to see the show, the clergyman angrily wrote to Will that he had left the theatre in a huff, upon hearing Will, as Miller, deliver a lecture to his sixteen-year-old son on the theme of physical relations with a woman. Will was shocked by this reaction, for he had originally judged O'Neill's play about small-town New England to be excellent family entertainment. Within days, he quit the production, saying he wanted no further part of it. "I could never again utter those words, even in the dark," he announced. In addition, he turned down Fox's offer to do the *Ah, Wilderness* movie. (Eventually, O'Neill's opus was filmed by MGM, with Lionel Barrymore as Nat Miller.)

Will's movies continued to rack up large box-office numbers, although Fox's finances were in a precarious state (the company lost over nineteen million dollars in 1932). He was even more active in going before the cameras in 1933 and 1934, although his fees per picture were reduced from a high of $187,000 to a low of $88,000. This hardly placed him near penury, for he remained one of the highest-paid people in the country. He earned more from each movie than the president of the United States earned in a year, so he could have said, as Babe Ruth said, in signing for $80,000 a year to play for the Yankees, "I had a better year than he did."

Will's next movie, *Doubting Thomas,* a 1935 adaptation of George Kelly's Broadway play, was a comedy about a blundering amateur theatrical troupe. The picture depended largely on scenery falling apart and actors flubbing their lines. One of Will's favorite directors, David Butler, was on hand again. *In Old Kentucky* and *Life Begins at 40,* also 1935 releases, both rated three stars in *The Film Guide,* and were directed by George Marshall. *In Old Kentucky* was notable for the presence of the remarkable Negro tap dancer, Bill "Bojangles" Robinson, who had shared a stage with Will in earlier theatrical productions. "Will got me into any number of scenes that I wasn't written in for," Robinson once said, underlining Will's penchant for being supportive of his fellow actors.

Life Begins at 40 boasted such character actors as Slim Summerville, Jane Darwell, and Sterling Holloway, and, as the romantic leads, Richard Cromwell and Rochelle Hudson. As a small-town newspaperman, Will befriends Cromwell, who has been framed on a bank-robbery charge. The subplot features the town bum (Summerville), who is chosen by Will to oppose a mean-spirited bank manager (George Barbier) for mayor. Cromwell turns out to be innocent, while Barbier's son is found guilty of the robbery. The movie was regarded as surprisingly contemporary; yet it also had Will playing his usual role: the embodiment of decency and integrity fighting the most palpable villainy.

Mickey Rooney, already making his name as an energetic child star (rivaled only by Shirley Temple in that category), won his chance to act alongside Will in 1935 in *The County Chairman*. The movie was set in a rural county of Wyoming, circa 1880, with Mickey playing a local youngster named Freckles. Will was the county chairman trying to elect his partner (Kent Taylor) district attorney; oddly, Taylor's future father-in-law was the rival candidate. Although the plot was thoroughly predictable, *County Chairman* served once more to fulfill Will's basic credo: *"Never act in a movie that parents wouldn't permit their own children to see."*

During the filming of *County Chairman*, Mickey, a fourteen-year-old squirt, was complimented by Will for his "professionalism"; after the first day of shooting, Will informed Mickey that he handled himself very well. At the time, Mickey was certain that Will had never heard of him. "I think he was probably wondering how this tough little kid born in a Brooklyn rooming house could have such self-assurance," said Mickey.

"You sure know all your lines," Will told Mickey, "and you don't interfere with mine. You know how to have fun with the script and I can tell you that your performance makes mine better."

(In later years, Mickey, while playing Will's father in *The Will Rogers Follies*, on Broadway, summed up his experience with Will: "What the hell kind of relationship could I have had with a man forty years older than I was! But he didn't intimidate me at all. Mainly, I remember him as a Gentile version of Mort Sahl.")

The last of Will's three pictures that John Ford directed was *"Steamboat 'Round the Bend,"* a gentle fable about a salesman (Will) who becomes captain of a steamboat that wanders up and down the Mississippi River. Made in 1935, *Steamboat* proved to be Will's final movie.

The Sacramento River in California wasn't exactly the legendary Mississippi. But that's where Ford chose to shoot the movie. Will's role—that of Doctor John, who sells a cure-all from his steamboat—pivots on his attempt to prove the innocence of John McGuire, soon scheduled to hang for murder. Will pursues the one witness who can save McGuire's skin; he does it out of his fondness for Anne Shirley, who is McGuire's sweetheart.

In a mad race against time, Will and Shirley are forced to burn everything on board the steamboat, including a wax figure collection, in order to speed down the river before the hanging takes place. Essentially, that was the plot that emerged in the movie. But when Cobb joined the cast (as Cap'n Eli, Will's rival), at the start of the shooting, Ford asked, with gentle sarcasm, if either one of them had the slightest idea of what the hell the story was about.

"I don't for one know," said Will. "Somethin' about a river, ain't it? Well, where I was raised they don't have any rivers to speak of, so you might say I'm a stranger here myself."

"I thought so," said Ford, gruffly. "Have you had a chance to glance at the script?"

"Been too busy ropin' calves," Will responded, mocking his guilt. "Tell you what, John, you sort of break the news what this sequence is all about and I'll think of a line for Cobb to speak and then Cobb'll think of a line for me to speak. In that way there won't be no ill felin's or heart burnin's and the feller that can remember what the plot was about—if there's any plot by then—gets first prize, which will be a kiss on the forehead from Mister John Ford." Cobb, hired by Ford, at the insistence of Will (who had told Ford it would be "great fun for everyone"), said, years later, that that was precisely the way the movie was shot. "As heaven is my judge," he said. "And Ford sat by as solemn as a hoot owl."

Movie producers, looking to save money, didn't offer a day of rest on Sunday. Under an unrelenting California sun, Will was the most willing worker on the *Steamboat* lot, even on Sunday. He did his takes and retakes, never murmuring a word of protest. In addition, he always found time to retreat to the river bank, where his car was parked, in order to pound out his latest daily report for the papers. More than one hundred feet away, you could hear the battering of the keys on Will's portable. "It sounded just like a brewery horse with a loose shoe running away across a covered bridge," recalled Cobb.

One afternoon, when Will was so fatigued that the lines in his face betrayed him, he still insisted on visiting an old companion, Buck McKee, who had worked with him in vaudeville thirty years before. He had learned that McKee had set up living quarters in a tiny ranch not far from the movie lot, but that he was too shy to come to the set to see him.

"He's a real oldtime cowhand," Will told Cobb. "He's got legs on him like a set of horse collars. But I ain't too shy to go see him."

When they met, the two couldn't stop gabbing about old times. This only served to remind Will of how sad it was that vaudeville had faded away. "We were glad to play in it," mused Will. "It had real class in those days."

On the final day of the shooting of *Steamboat,* Will dropped in at the studio to say good-bye to other members of the large cast, including Cobb. "Come on out to the ranch," Will implored his old pal. "We'll get on a couple of broncs and ride up the trail to the top of the canyon." Will was aware that Cobb's Falstaffian physique wasn't much built for riding. "I love to see you in the saddle. You do such humorous things on a horse and you ain't deliberately trying to be funny, neither, if I'm any kind of judge," laughed Will.

Cobb had an urge to go; yet he knew that Will probably preferred being alone, roping calves in his corral, rather than poking along a mountain trail with him. "I got something else to do," Cobb said.

"Better change your mind, old-timer," Will said. "This picture's done and I'm fixin' to go away and we might not get together again for a spell."

This was the last time that Cobb would see Will alive.

Steamboat 'Round the Bend won rave reviews. However, Ford hated the movie. He was convinced that Fox ruined the picture with its final cut of the film. As far as Will was concerned, *Steamboat* proved that he wasn't slipping at the box office—which, some suspected, might have been the case.

16

Political Adventures

Vaulting to the top of the talkie industry in the 1930s, in a rumpled business suit that had replaced his usual cowboy garb, Will was right up there alongside other screen icons—from Wally Beery, who never bothered to tuck in his shirt, to the irrepressible Shirley Temple.

Still, despite all of his renown, Will refused to ignore the real world in which he lived. He appreciated the fact that he was one of the few fortunate ones, a millionaire in a time of endless lines of unemployed. As the black clouds of misery hung over the country, Will was much taken with the charismatic new leader, Franklin Delano Roosevelt. A Democrat with a voice charged with conviction and strength, FDR had become a hero of the radio age. He spoke in arch, cultivated tones, with a pronounced Harvard accent— qualities that normally would have given Will ammunition for sly ridicule. Recognizing that this was a crucial moment in American history, Will refused to be sour or malicious about FDR, although he had openly expressed disgust at the ineptitude of President Hoover.

In the summer of 1932, during the worst period of the depression, thousands of World War I veterans descended on Washington. They came from

across the country, many with their wives, children, pets, and all their possessions. In their hands they carried certificates that called for a bonus that was to
be paid by their government in 1945, in return for their war service. Out of
both jobs and luck, these men asked for immediate payment of their bonus
money. They believed they were entitled to collect a legal debt and had
marched to Washington to claim it.

But Hoover was appalled at this squatter's battalion, bunked down in their
rude shelters and stinking tents along the banks of the Potomac, in a marshy
field called the Anacostia Flats. He considered them a threat to the republic
and to proper sanitary conditions. After Congress grudgingly agreed to give
them their fare to return home, they were denied the bonus payment. Many
took the fare and went home, but some twenty-five hundred stayed to continue their angry protest.

After the police attempt to evict the remaining veterans caused bloodshed,
Hoover summoned the army to maintain law and order. The army's chief of
staff, Douglas MacArthur, moved the miserable men from their ramshackle
homes, at the point of bayonets and guns. "They are a bad-looking mob
animated by the spirit of revolution," charged MacArthur. "They threaten the
institutions of our country." He thought their presence could lead to an
"insurrection."

Some spoke out bitterly against the expulsion. Representative Fiorello
LaGuardia, of New York, wired Hoover: "Soup is cheaper than tear gas and
bread better than bullets in maintaining law and order in these times of
depression, unemployment and hunger." The frequent Socialist candidate for
president, Norman Thomas, called Hoover's action a "bad case of nervous
irritation, mixed with fear."

In admitting that he disapproved of the bonus march, Will played politics
on the issue—a reaction, among officeholders, that he had often criticized.
However, he conceded that the veterans had as much right to put pressure on
Congress as any other group of lobbyists had. They were a welcome change,
he added, from those paid to talk in behalf of others. But it was the general
behavior of the veterans that most impressed Will: "These veterans hold the
record for being the best behaved of any 15,000 hungry men ever assembled
in the world. They were seeing our government wasting thousands and
millions before their eyes, and yet they remained fair and sensible. Would
15,000 hungry bankers have done it, 15,000 farmers, 15,000 preachers? Just
think what 15,000 club-women would have done to Washington even if they

wasn't hungry. . . . It's easy to be a gentleman when you are well fed, but these boys did it on an empty stomach."

Will had been an early celebrant and admirer of Roosevelt's, going back as far as 1928, when FDR had put Al Smith's name in nomination for president for the second straight time at the Democratic convention. "This fellow Roosevelt," said Will, "would have gone pretty far in the Democratic party himself but he had this act all perfected and don't like to go to the trouble of learnin' somethin' else."

When FDR won reelection as governor of New York in 1930, Will predicted, without reservation, that "the Democrats just nominated their president yesterday." There were those who tended to scoff at Will's crystal-gazing efforts. After all, wasn't Will the same fellow who had said such nice things about Mussolini? And didn't he once say that "those rascals in Russia may have some very good ideas"?

Walter Lippmann, the political columnist, never thought much of FDR—"a man of first-rate temperament and second-rate intellect," he had written. Even Al Smith, whom FDR called the "Happy Warrior," headed up a stop-Roosevelt movement, accusing his former booster of hypocrisy.

But Will wasn't having such talk about Roosevelt. He consented to address the 1932 Democratic convention in Chicago, "to kill some time and act the fool." Fully confident that FDR would be the Democratic nominee, Will announced that, in his view, the Democrat nominated (and that meant Roosevelt) would become president, "if he lives until November."

Of course, Will hadn't considered the possibility that he himself might get the Democratic nod! On the second ballot, which had Roosevelt ahead with 677 ¼ votes, the Oklahoma delegation, refusing to support FDR, deserted "Alfalfa Bill" Murray and switched its 22 votes to another "favorite son," Will Rogers. (Will quipped that he might have swapped these votes with FDR for a cabinet post.) Damon Runyon, ordinarily a commentator on the sports beat, tried to convince FDR's backers that Will wouldn't grab the nomination from him. "Rogers makes more money at his own racket," he explained.

Runyon was right. On the fourth ballot, FDR was nominated. Glued to the radio in Albany, New York, where he had been listening to the wrangling among his fellow Democrats, FDR at once hopped a plane to the convention. Realizing that Roosevelt had just broken a precedent, Will bragged that the move "gave aviation the biggest boost it ever had."

Will Jr., then a freshman at Stanford, shared a room with his dad during the

1932 convention. It was an unusual arrangement, for the two rarely got to spend much time together. In this instance, young Will also acknowledged that he was hardly able to get any sleep because his father was on the phone with all sorts of people, famous and otherwise, during the night. During daylight hours, he acted as a buffer for his father, against all those people who wanted to talk to him. On one occasion, an old, white-haired man in a threadbare sailor suit approached Will, and Junior tried to fend him off. However, the man turned out to be the well-known Lincoln biographer, Carl Sandburg, and Will was delighted to see him. Later that night, Will invited Sandburg to his hotel room, along with the comedian Groucho Marx, to engage in a session of singing and guitar playing. "Groucho is an ideal musician," cracked Will. "He can play but doesn't bother."

In the election that fall, FDR, facing "the same old vaudeville team of Hoover and Curtis," as Will put it, got some additional help from Will. On the night of September 23, as the campaign heated up, Will introduced FDR before a roaring capacity crowd at the Hollywood Bowl. Will said he was just "overawed" at being asked to introduce Roosevelt. "I'm wasting no oratory on you tonight," he said to FDR. "You're just a mere prospect. Come back when you are president and I'll do better."

In many ways, Hoover's campaign was pathetic. He was full of personal hurt—his face was puffy, his manner resentful. "Many people have left their jobs," he said, in a stunning faux pas, "for the more profitable one of selling apples." This remark came back to haunt him. In some places in the country, he had become so unpopular that it was unsafe for him to campaign. So, a fleet of limousines was provided for him by Henry Ford, who still regarded Hoover as a good president. But, according to Will, Ford himself was "no longer a miracle worker." (However, after FDR began his first term in office, Will still showed vestiges of his old loyalty to the auto magnate. "You can take the rouge from female lips, the cigarettes from raised hands, the hot dogs from tourists' greasy paws, but when you start jerking the Fords out from under the traveling public, you are monkeying with the very fundamentals of American life," he said. After a dispute between Roosevelt's NRA and Ford, Will declared that "Ford will do better by labor than anybody else.")

A dire warning from Hoover—that, after an FDR victory, "grass would grow in the streets of America and weeds would overrun millions of farms"— was scornfully rejected by the disaffected voters. "Gosh, you can't get grass to grow on your lawns," Will chided. On November 8, FDR won by an overwhelming margin. In the electoral college, he topped Hoover by 472 to 59; in the popular balloting, FDR ran ahead by over 7 million votes. Pleased with FDR's victory, Will offered a brief capsule of advice to the new president. "Your health is the main thing," he told the president, now badly crippled after twelve years of his battle against polio. "Don't worry too much—and don't forget that a smile will look like a meal to us." Will was already familiar with FDR's boundless optimism, which was reflected in the easy, radiant grin that was capable of setting off sparks in people's hearts.

On Inauguration Day, March 4, 1933, standing bareheaded on a raw, windy morning, FDR asserted, in ringing tones, that "the only thing we have to fear is fear itself—nameless, unreasoning terror which paralyzes needed efforts to convert retreat into advance." The reaction among the shivering thousands in front of the Capitol was electric. To millions listening at home on their radios, the words were galvanic and inspiring.

To Will, FDR's coming to power was a happy day for America. "They got a man in there who is wise to the ways of Congress, wise to our so-called big men," he said. "The whole country is with him. Even if what he does is wrong, they are with him, just as long as he does *something*. If he burned down the Capitol, they would cheer and say, 'Well, at least he got a fire started, anyhow!' We have had years of 'don't rock the boat.' Go on and sink if you want to, we might just as well be sinking, as like we are." Will was especially pleased that FDR tried to rally the country with his "fireside chats," which showed "public speakers what to do with a big vocabulary—leave it at home in the dictionary."

But as Roosevelt fought the Great Depression, two men appeared as obstacles: They posed a threat to democracy and to the stability of FDR's administration. One of these men was Senator Huey Long, a flamboyant Louisiana demagogue, who acted the role of a clown, even though he proposed various economic nostrums to solve America's problems. To many observers Long—the "kingfish"—was a home-grown, ruthless tyrant, who specialized in staging one-man filibusters against the evils of concentrated wealth.

But Will didn't seem to regard Long with the same jaundiced eye as FDR did. Will even seemed amused by his tactics: "Imagine ninety-five Senators trying to outtalk Huey Long. They can't get him warmed up." When Long battled against a banking-regulation law, Will actually doled out praise: "Sometimes Huey gets so close to the truth that Wall Street is on the verge of calling him a menace."

During one of Long's all-night filibusters, Will remarked: "Huey pulled the biggest and most educational novelty ever introduced into the Senate. He read 'em the Constitution of the United States—a lot of 'em thought he was reviewing a new book." Watching Long perform at the Democratic convention in 1932 Will marveled at his speaking prowess. "By golly," he said, "he made a good speech today. He won his own game."

FDR preferred to view Long in a much different light. He feared that Long had the makings of a dictator and might even have gotten there, had not the "New Deal come along with a sensible program." FDR thought that Long might join forces with Father Charles E. Coughlin—the rabble-rousing radio priest, from the Shrine of the Royal Oak in Michigan—to exploit an imperiled middle class. Coughlin, compared to Jesus Christ by some of his followers, also made a bid for power by reaching out to the fervent anti-Semites. FDR's New Deal soon became the "Jew Deal" in Coughlin's speeches, for which he had audiences as large as the popular radio program "Amos 'n' Andy" had.

Sensing that Long's "share-the-wealth" program was winning a receptive audience throughout the country, FDR, ever the wily manipulator, put forth his own plan, designed to secure a wider distribution of wealth. But what FDR was prescribing wasn't far removed from what Long had been preaching for years. Recognizing that FDR had coopted the "Kingfish's" recipe for recovery, Will wrote: "I sure would like to have seen Huey's face when he was woke in the middle of the night by the president, who said, 'Lay over, Huey, I want to get in with you.'"

Oddly, although Will's olfactory senses could usually sniff out phonies from a mile away, he never closely examined Huey and Coughlin—and he more than mildly accepted their ranting. Will, as a matter of fact, caught on to a dictator, who was an ocean away, faster than he realized the dangerous potential of Long and Coughlin in his own country. For, shortly after the emergence of Adolf Hitler as Germany's paranoid führer, Will shrewdly judged him as a "guy trying to copy the Ku Klux Klan. . . . He's got Germany like Al Capone has Chicago." (Will once actually visited Capone in prison, spending several hours chatting with the mythic gangster. When he left Scarface Al, Will admitted that he was quite taken with him. However, he wrote sharply in his column: "There was no way I could write about Capone and not make a hero out of him. What's the matter with an age when our biggest gangster is our greatest national interest?")

To get a closer look at Hitler, Will tried to arrange an interview with him while he was visiting Europe. But bad weather disrupted a planned flight to Berlin in 1934; so the chance for Will to put the American public on further notice about Hitler's ambitions went by the boards.

Will remained pretty close to FDR, missing few opportunities, in the beginning months of Roosevelt's reign, to praise him generously. In February 1934, Will was invited, along with Betty and Mary, to the White House for a reception presided over by Eleanor Roosevelt. The mixed bag of guests included two formidable members of FDR's cabinet—Secretary of State Cordell Hull and Postmaster General Jim Farley—as well as the acid-tongued Alice Roosevelt Longworth, Teddy Roosevelt's daughter. One observer at the scene said that "Will held the floor part of the time, making it one of the most amusing evenings I've ever spent. . . . Will Rogers *is* Will Rogers, nothing else. . . . Under his commonness is one of the nicest people in the world." FDR wasn't the least bit shy in flattering people to their faces, even though he was often critical and deceitful behind their backs. But he was amused and impressed by Will. If Will were the one fellow that the American public, in its time of distress, respected and believed, then FDR wanted to have him on his side. That didn't mean that Will didn't issue some typical barbs toward FDR. He did. But he also made sure to balance the needling with words of high praise: "That bird has done more for us in seven weeks than we've done for ourselves in seven years . . . he's the Houdini of Hyde Park." The country should give FDR all the authority he wanted, Will added, even "if it's to drown all the boy babies, for the way the grownups have acted, he'll be perfectly justified in drowning any new ones."

It wasn't long before the advocates of big business and the Wall Streeters, types that Will found objectionable, opened up at "that damned cripple in the White House." FDR, they charged, really stood for Franklin "Deficit" Roosevelt. Such foul blows were to be expected. But the sheer meanness of some of these attacks was more than Will could tolerate. Although he was aware that FDR was perfectly capable of fighting back against the "economic royalists," Will suggested another approach: "Let these rich old boys practice their own brand of rugged individualism; then after one full year of the stuff if there's not more people rugged than there is unrugged, the rich guys lose."

Like everybody else, Californians were singing "Brother, Can You Spare a Dime." If anyone needed further proof of the universality of hardship, there was the case of the future Pulitzer-Prize-winning novelist, John Steinbeck. Living in a small cottage in Pacific Grove, California, Steinbeck wrote of his personal miseries: "I couldn't afford postage on the manuscripts I was sending out. . . . Without dough you couldn't have a tooth pulled. . . . We pooled our troubles and our pleasures."

By January of 1934, many Californians in the Democratic party were looking for a savior. They urged Will to run for governor of the state. He was honored by the thought, he said, but promptly nixed the offer. "I'd rather be a poor actor than a poor governor," he responded. With Will being out of the running, the Socialist author and muckraker, Upton Sinclair, took up the challenge. For years, Sinclair, a fifty-six-year-old idealist born in a Baltimore boardinghouse, had been exploring the social evils that he believed were destroying the country.

Sinclair's 1906 book, *"The Jungle,"* a stark exposé of Chicago's meatpacking industry, was soon followed up by his works on coal, steel, and the Sacco-Vanzetti case. As a result, Sinclair won a reputation as a writer who had great empathy for the underdog. However, one critic said of him that he knew how to write about underdogs but had never met one.

Ready to confront the emergency situation in California—where half a million were out of work, and triple that number were on private charity and relief—Sinclair came up with his EPIC (End Poverty in California) plan to cure the state's ills. After Sinclair—to the amazement of most people—won the Democratic primary, shock waves traveled all across the state. These reverberations reached all the way to FDR in the White House. For once, the crafty politician didn't know which way to turn—whether to endorse Sinclair or not.

Red-baiting reached its peak in the rancorous campaign that followed. On the Republican ticket, Frank Merriam, regarded by his foes as the "bald nincompoop," faced Sinclair. Herbert Hoover, a resident of the state, claimed that the fate of California rested on the coming election and on the defeat of Sinclair. Earl Warren, the Alameda County District Attorney (and later the governor of California), predicted that the Communists were about to walk off with the state. A shrill signal went out to the big-business interests: that Sinclair had to be crushed.

Led by MGM's Louis B. Mayer—who despised Sinclair—and by Mayer's adjutant, Irving Thalberg, and with an assist from movie-czar Hays, Hollywood's movie studios set out to make certain that Merriam would win. Extensive political advertising was utilized for the first time in an effort to defeat Sinclair.

However, many in the acting and writing fraternity of Hollywood, including James Cagney, Chaplin, Robert Benchley, Irvin S. Cobb, Groucho Marx, and Gene Fowler, joined Sinclair's ranks. Sinclair also declared that Will was with him in his fight. But Will remained uncommitted.

"Upton's a darn nice fellow and plum smart, and if he could deliver just some of the things he promises, he should not only be governor of the state but president of all of them," Will said. But there was no official endorsement. While almost everyone in Fox's hierarchy blasted Sinclair on a daily basis, Will kept teasing him, much like a deft prizefighter flicking light blows on a foe's head, then retreating from closer contact. Having access to the airwaves on a regular basis—after signing a contract with Gulf Oil, in 1933, for seven nation-wide broadcasts (the announced amount for Will's services was $50,000, all of which he turned over to unemployment relief efforts, half to the American Red Cross, and the other half to the Salvation Army)—Will had any number of opportunities to endorse Sinclair unequivocally. But he never did. In 1934 he was on the radio every Sunday night for twenty-four weeks but he did little more than crack jokes about the EPIC candidate. Invariably, he'd fall back on his bewhiskered maxim: "I tell you, folks, all politics is applesauce."

One time, he begged off by saying that he "never made any endorsements for governor of any state, not even of Oklahoma." Another time, he said that since he made a living by joking about the governor out there (in California), "it might be best that Sinclair gets elected." Will Jr. openly backed Sinclair but his old man didn't. "Dad kept telling me not to be critical of Merriam," recalled Will Jr.

At this juncture of Will's career, it wasn't certain whether he preferred radio over the movies or stage work. The main flaw in radio, as far as Will was concerned, was that there was always a cutoff point stringently dictated by time pressures. While you were in the middle of telling a joke, the clock could run out on you. The other negative for Will was that a fellow could never really tell how he was doing with an audience. Under instructions from the producers, studio audiences could erupt in false laughter. So how was one to tell how he was really doing with the vast unseen bleacher crowd out there, tuned in on the radio? While performing on the stage, an actor could get feedback from an immediate, honest reaction. But that wasn't true on radio.

Will managed to solve the time problem by installing an alarm clock at his side. When the contraption went off, it was the signal for him to call a halt, "whether I'm in the midst of reciting the Gettysburg Address or the Declaration of Independence." On any one of these broadcasts, Will might have said something positive about Upton Sinclair, but he never chose to do so.

Another escape hatch for Will from California politics was the trip around the world that Will took (as a second honeymoon) with Betty, Bill, and Jim in 1934. Mary, now making her own career on the stage, might have joined them but was too occupied with summer theatre in Maine. By being so far removed from America—whether he was in Honolulu, Japan, Russia, Siberia, the British Isles, Hungary, or Finland—Will was able to divorce himself from the doings in California. Now known fondly in almost every part of the world as "America's ambassador without portfolio," Will received last-minute instructions from FDR. "Don't you go and jump on Japan," the president said to him. "Just keep them from jumping on us."

At the beginning of the trip, while the entourage was en route to Hawaii, Will was informed about the bloody demise of the notorious bank robber John Dillinger (known as Public Enemy Number One). A posse of G-men had shot Dillinger to death as he emerged from a third-run movie theatre in Chicago. In his column the next day, Will wondered just "what picture had got Dillinger. Hope it was mine." It wasn't. The film was *Manhattan Melodrama,* with Clark Gable.

When Will was asked, toward the end of his trip, if word had reached him that the Democrats had nominated Sinclair, he acknowledged that he had found out about that in Siberia, "where they send all the rich men in Russia. In America we send them to the Senate." As Will and Betty sailed for home on the Ile de France in mid-September, he observed, uncomfortably, that things had been awfully quiet in Europe, "not much war talk." That led him to believe that "one would probably soon break out."

Throughout his trip, Will remained on his good behavior. He emphasized, wherever he went, that he brought "no goodwill in his suitcase." Nations, he said, are fed up with bearers of goodwill. "All they want is to be left alone, let 'em work out their own plans and their own salvation, the same as we do. There's not a nation in the world that wants war."

These words, issuing from Will's mouth, sounded like his usual brand of common sense. Yet, they also revealed an inherent isolationism. Coming from a man, who, in his constant travels, had always made the nations of the world seem closer together, they were indeed paradoxical.

One event that Will kept close tabs on, even while he was away, was the progress of the two baseball pennant races in the National and American Leagues. There was a dogfight that summer in the National League (ultimately, St. Louis won), while in the American League, the Detroit Tigers, led by their manager and catcher, Mickey Cochrane, appeared to be heading for victory.

Will had always been a fervent baseball fan, going back to the late teens. He had continually referred to the game in his spoken and written remarks. In the mid-twenties, when two of baseball's foremost outfielding icons, Ty Cobb and Tris Speaker, were accused of betting on games that had taken place several years before, Will stood up for Ty and Tris: "I've known 'em for fifteen years and if Cobb and Speaker have been selling out all these years, I would like to have seen 'em play when they weren't selling." Ultimately, Commissioner Landis exonerated both Cobb and Speaker of the charges of either fixing or betting on ball games. However, the smell lingered on for some time.

Will's pals in baseball were legion, ranging from the embattled John J. McGraw to Babe Ruth and now to Dizzy Dean, baseball's nonstop talker. One of Will's frequent companions at the ballpark was also the inscrutable utility catcher, Moe Berg, who played for five teams from 1923 until the late 1930s. The brainy Berg adored newspapers as much as Will did, and was known for handling a half-dozen foreign languages better than he could hit major-league pitching. Once, when Berg sat next to Will at a game, Will turned to him and said, with a wink: "Moe, let's turn the town pink—let's step out tonight with two exciting verbs."

Casey Stengel, too, had been a favorite of Will's. When Casey huffed and puffed his way around the bases for a game-winning, inside-the-park home run in the 1923 World Series against the Yankees, Will was there to cheer him on. "I never saw a man run faster than that, unless he was running from the sheriff," Will said. The two men got along famously, even if Casey's incessant, word-mangling monologues rarely matched the clarity of Will's "Aw, shucks" dialogue.

With the emergence of the dirty-pants, rambunctious St. Louis Cardinals Gashouse Gang in 1934, Will was eager to watch the Cardinals perform in the upcoming World Series against Detroit, so he made it a priority to be back in the United States in time for the October games. He would visit the ballparks in Detroit and St. Louis, not only as a fan but as a paid newspaper observer. The right-handed pitching ace of the Cardinals was Dizzy Dean, who often boasted he had been born in three different states, including Will's own Oklahoma. In the summer of 1934, Dizzy was as big a story in the country as the Dionne quintuplets, who had been born in Canada. Soon after the birth of the quintuplets, it was rumored that Will was slated to play the role of Dr. Allan Roy Dafoe, the small-town doctor who had delivered the children; the movie was supposedly high on the Fox agenda.

"I wanna go watch Dizzy," said Will. "He's full of personality, so boastful. But he does it in a kidding way. I think he's the most natural ballplayer since Babe Ruth." Will wouldn't have gotten an argument on this from the garrulous Dizzy, who quickly returned the compliment: "There ain't nobody like Will since old times."

Will arranged to sit in Henry Ford's private box when the Series opened at Navin Field in Detroit on October 2. Ford doled out $100,000 to obtain broadcast rights to the Series, although Will thought he was plain daffy to do such a thing. "Maybe Mr. Ford ain't worried 'cuz he's the richest man in the world," said Will, "but I think those Dean boys must have him plenty worried." Dizzy had a brother named Daffy, who also won a bunch of ballgames for the Cards that year.

The day before the Series began, Will went to a rehearsal of a new play called *Jayhawker*, which featured Fred Stone. Will thought it was sort of curious that the play was written by Sinclair Lewis. "Not to be confused with Upton Sinclair," he kidded. "When I get home I guess I'll have to take care of him." Will's ambiguous feelings were still apparent when it came to Sinclair.

Promising to declare his stand on the gubernatorial race (once he got back to the ranch, where presumably he could commune with his better nature), Will set out to enjoy himself at the Series. He occupied one of the best seats, surrounded by a cluster of celebrity faces. Comedian Joe E. Brown, an avid fan, was on hand; so was George Raft, who played bad guys on the screen and was a gambling pal of Leo Durocher, the Cards' slick-fielding shortstop. Actor Bill Frawley was there to see if "Dean was for real." Henry Ford was there, of course, sitting close to Father Coughlin—a matchup made in heaven. And over in a corner of Will's box was his friendly little rival for box-office receipts, Shirley Temple.

On the first morning of the Series, Will sat down to breakfast with the Dean boys at Detroit's Book-Cadillac Hotel. It was hard to tell who was having more fun, Will or the two country pitchers. Watching Dizzy eat as though he were a lion, Will stuck to a glass of grapefruit juice because he was trying to keep his weight down. "Seems to me," he marveled, "that only opera singers and cotton pickers can eat that much."

Before each game, Will appeared in the Cards' locker room, bantering with Dizzy and exchanging punch lines. He showed up *after* each game, too, reveling in the up-and-down depression Series that had the nation glued to its radios. In the final and decisive seventh game, on October 9, Dizzy and the Cardinals galloped off with a one-sided 11-0 victory, highlighted by a rousing brawl between Ducky Medwick of the Cards and the Tigers' third baseman, Marv Owen. Medwick had slid into Owen with his spikes high, thus precipitating the ruckus. When Medwick trotted out to his left-field post, the enraged and frustrated Detroit fans greeted him with a barrage of food and garbage. The game was held up for twenty minutes before Commissioner Landis ordered Medwick out of the game, presumably on the grounds that a player shouldn't be forced to succumb to rotten food.

Sensing the importance of the story, after the game, Will rushed to visit with both Medwick and Owen. Acting like a little boy, he boasted that he was "the only fella in the world that talked to both fellas in the dressing room right after the fight." Then he posed with Dizzy, who, decked out in a pith helmet, rubbed it in by waving a rubber Tigers' doll in the photographers' faces. "What did I tell ya, Will," he chortled. "I knew I'd whip them Tigers." Between Dizzy and Daffy, they won all four games the Cards needed to take the Series.

Later that winter, Will appeared with Dizzy on the dais at the New York Baseball Writers' dinner. Looking over at the pitcher, who never had a shy moment in his life, Will assured him that he was worth every cent he could get by bargaining with Cards' management. "I know that for a fact, son, and so do you," Will told him. At the time, Dizzy was making less than twenty thousand dollars for a 30-and-7 season, not much more than Will picked up for one of his radio broadcasts for Gulf Oil.

Will and Dizzy remained in the headlines for months, helping people to forget their empty stomachs and wallets. Shortly after the Series, Dizzy was quoted as saying that "a lot of folks that ain't saying ain't, ain't eating." But some years later, Dizzy, who didn't do much recanting, did recant. "I didn't say that stuff about 'ain't,'" he said on a radio show. "It was really my old friend, Will Rogers, who said that."

With the business of baseball being finished for the year, Will went back to California and its own brand of zany politics. When he arrived in Santa Monica—where he figured he'd get in a little riding, polo, and lassoing—Will found that all anybody wanted to talk about was Upton Sinclair. A small newspaper in San Francisco published a rumor that Will was about to plunge into the campaign by encouraging a write-in vote for himself. Such a ploy, if true, would have certainly taken votes away from Sinclair.

Will vigorously denied the tale but a few days later, he posed smilingly, for a picture with Frank Merriam on the Fox set of *The County Chairman*. Did that signify that Will supported Merriam? the reporters inquired. No, he insisted. As author Greg Mitchell has written, Will then fell back on a comparison of his own situation with that of the Hearst newspapers. "They're goin' to wait 'til it's all over, then write an editorial about it," said Will, quoting Hearst's tepid instructions to his editors. With a few days to go before the election, Will said that most people who paid any attention to such matters thought that Merriam was going to win.

"But I'll tell ya," said Will, "this old Sinclair has throwed such a scare in these rich folks, they won't stop shiverin' 'til this whole thing is over." He pointed out that even if Sinclair won, he wouldn't be able to do much of anything. "But he's sure put wrinkles in brows out here that won't be out for years," Will added.

Right until election day, Will kept mum about his endorsement. He didn't even bother to vote, firming up his reputation as the most political nonvoter in the state. When all the returns were in, Sinclair had 900,000 votes. But that wasn't enough to win, for Merriam corraled 1,100,000 (A third candidate pulled in 300,000 votes). In an enigmatic postmortem, Will declared that if Sinclair "had had more money in his pockets, he would have been elected." Then, reducing the whole matter to a joke, he suggested that Sinclair should debate Huey Long during halftime at the Rose Bowl on New Year's Day.

17

The Last Flight

ny normal person would have been exhausted from the grueling pace that Will set for himself. At fifty-five years of age, his body was beginning to show wear and tear from a stunning series of commitments that he had pursued for almost twenty years.

His eyes weren't as sharp as they used to be, so he wore glasses more often. His legs weren't as sturdy; his fingers on the old portable weren't as supple. He often fell asleep early in the evening, even as he perused his beloved newspapers while sitting up in bed. His columns were now more rambling, fragmentary, and free-form than ever, often expressing nostalgic feelings about "the good old days" and "good old pals." He could get more defensive about criticism, while the crowds of common folks who besieged him for autographs began to represent more of an annoyance than an ego-boosting pleasure. He had never sought anonymity, but fame now had its penalties.

He became more philosophical about life: "We're only here for a spell and then pass on, so get a few laughs and do the best you can. Live your life so that whenever you lose, you're ahead." Being true to his own axiom, the way

Will lived his own life put an accent on free-wheeling, selfless generosity. "He constantly signed checks at the Beverly Hills Bank of America to down-and-out actors, who sometimes turned down extra jobs because they were getting extra pay from Will for doing nothing," Eddie Cantor remarked.

Will Jr. had always known his father as being filled with energy and vitality. As a little boy, Junior would be roused from his sleep by his dad. "Get up, son, let's ride those horses!" Will would say, shaking the boy. But now, Will Jr. found his father increasingly nervous, restless, and anxious, which caused his mother to express some concern about him. Like other members of the family, Will Jr. believed that his father was continuing to take on too much for himself, as he approached middle age.

Another certain sign that Will might have been feeling more fatigue than he was willing to acknowledge was that he had hired an assistant to help him edit his column and to come up with gags. In his early years, this would have been unthinkable, for Will prided himself on his ability to write and think without outside intervention.

The assistant was a young comic and cellist from Chicago named Morey Amsterdam, who met Will in Los Angeles, where Will was making one of his many Community Chest appearances. "There was one dirty dressing room and one toilet on a floor that looked as if it were about to cave in," recalled Amsterdam, about their first encounter. "So I stuck a sign up over the toilet saying, 'If you're constipated, flush first. It will scare the crap out of you.' " Will meandered by, took a look at the sign, and thought it was pretty darn funny. He asked who had written it, and within a few days, Morey was assisting Will with his column.

When Will used one of Amsterdam's quotes—"The beset thing about telling the truth, as opposed to telling lies, is that you don't have to remember it"—Morey knew that he was having more success in his new job than he had anticipated.

In January 1935, Will was awarded a ten-picture, $1,100,000 contract with Fox, which should have pleased him enormously. It was completed with the usual handshake, still true to Will's tradition. His landholdings, which were now substantially increased over his original land purchase, provided him with more than the measure of security that he and Betty had always sought. The now-swollen ranch property also was the one place where he would get a rest from his tumultuous public life.

"His career was never brought into our home," Betty wrote. "Over the family dining table, there was always more talk of the afternoon's polo or calf roping than of the theatre, radio or movies. . . . It often seemed to me that I had four children, instead of three, and that Will was the greatest child of them all."

In order to further relieve Will of prosaic pressures, Betty could always be relied on to pay all the bills, attend to daily tasks around the ranch, and take care of other money matters. She also served as Will's agent and manager, scheduling his bookings and constantly trying to make the place more comfortable.

For the children, the ranch represented something a bit different from what it did for their father. Will Jr., who, on growing up, had become an admitted "city slicker," found the ranch claustrophobic, an isolated backwater place, where there was little to do if one didn't care to spend time around horses. Mary, pursuing her theatrical career, was inclined to feel the same way about the place. However, for Jim, who loved horses and the outdoors as much as his father did, it was a heavenly spot. He spent most of his free time at the barn or on the polo field. Being a true "chip off the old block," Jim was closer to his dad than either Will Jr., or Mary were.

Will tried, whenever possible, to compress his moviemaking schedule of three films a year into the first six months. That would leave him the other six months for roaming around the ranch and for traveling. He still looked to the air when going places, even though he wistfully remarked occasionally that the best way to travel was probably to get into a car and tour the country in a catch-as-catch-can manner. It seemed that he wanted to slow down a bit, to alter his pace somewhat, to smell the roses. Yet there was that inevitable restlessness cropping up that would send him running off to somewhere in the world, to see places and people that he'd never seen before.

As the summer began in 1935, Will wrote that "we are living in great times. A fellow can't afford to die now with all of this excitement going." Unfortunately, much of the "excitement" was of a decidedly negative quality. One-third of the U.S. workers—some twenty million people—were still standing on breadlines, in spite of FDR's strenuous and innovative reform efforts. Mussolini invaded helpless Ethiopia, as the world watched in silence. The Japanese, in their expansionist mood, glared eagerly at Peiping. Hitler's German government issued its infamous Nuremburg laws, depriving Jewish citizens of all of their rights. Bruno Richard Hauptmann went on trial for the kidnapping of the Lindbergh baby. Oliver Wendell Holmes died at the age of ninety-four, leaving a legacy as the Supreme Court's great dissenter.

The bright side of the picture found FDR fighting a successful battle to get his Social Security program enacted. Further, people danced merrily to the latest craze, the rumba, while George Gershwin's opera masterpiece, *Porgy and Bess,* made its debut. In a symbolic gesture, a button was pushed in the White House on May 24 to celebrate the lighting up of Cincinnati's Crosley Field for the first night game in baseball history, while Babe Ruth's playing career ended in a bombastic "last hurrah," as he hit three home runs for the Boston Braves against the Pittsburgh Pirates. And the S. S. *Normandie* sped across the Atlantic in 107 hours and 33 minutes, for a new record. But what Will liked most was Pan Am's inauguration of a Pacific air service from San Francisco to Manila.

Having finished the shooting of *Steamboat 'Round the Bend,* Will told Homer Croy that he might like to spend some time as the world's first "flying reporter." This quixotic plan had him buying his own plane and basing it in London, from where he would run off to all of the world's hot spots. "When I knock around that way," Will said to Croy, "my newspaper stuff gets better."

Will even gave some thought to booking passage on Germany's *Graf Zeppelin*—the state of the art in dirigibles—and floating up the coast of Africa. The fact that Will had never set foot on a zeppelin didn't discourage him one bit. He had been sold on air travel—of any kind—since that day twenty years earlier, in Atlantic City, when he had paid five dollars for a trip on one of Glenn Curtis's "flying boats." But he hadn't heeded Charles Lindbergh's advice to take up parachute jumping, and to stay out of single-motor planes at night, for Will never learned how to use a chute, and often flew after dark on anything that stayed glued together.

Perennially listening for news that one of his many pilot friends was about to embark on an adventurous trip to "somewhere," Will ran into Wiley Post, one of the most celebrated airmen in the world, in Los Angeles. The two had originally met ten years earlier, when Post flew Will to a rodeo in Oklahoma. Now there were rumors in aviation circles that Post was contemplating putting together an air route between Alaska and Russia. Curiously, a couple of years earlier, Will had received a letter from an Alaskan, informing him that he should pay a visit to Alaska because it offered some of the finest big-game hunting in the world. Hunting had never had much appeal for Will, for he shied away from shooting animals and, unlike others who had his frontier roots, he wasn't an aficionado of guns. However, he was now fascinated by the prospect of taking a look at what remained a largely unexplored, rugged area. From the moment he had received the letter, he filed the idea in the back of his mind. Now, with some time available for hitting the road again,

Will seriously thought about accompanying Post on his journey, if Wiley would have him.

In June, Will signed off for the summer in a message to his vast radio audience. "Everybody is tryin' to save the country," he said. "Only they're tryin' to do it in different ways, and it's too big, the country is too big, for all of them put together to spoil, anyhow. So good-bye, I'll see you in the fall."

Wiley Post was born in Saline, Texas, in 1899, making him twenty years younger than Will. When Wiley was a little boy, his father, an itinerant farmer, moved the family to Oklahoma. Wiley developed a fascination for planes, from the first moment that he gazed at one of them as it crossed overhead when he was fourteen. He promptly gave up farming and took a succession of jobs, first with a flying circus, where he risked his life as a parachute jumper, and then as a roughneck in the oilfields. In the latter job he suffered an injury that would not only mark him for life, but also establish a dramatic persona for him: A man working alongside Post with a sledgehammer accidentally caused a steel chip to hit Wiley flush in his left eye. The eye became infected and couldn't be saved. At first, Post used a glass eye, but when he continued to get headaches flying at high altitudes, he was convinced that the glass replacement was the root of his troubles. So he substituted an eye patch, which in time became a symbol of his heroic image. It identified Wiley in much the same way that Will's familiar cowlick identified him.

After Wiley was awarded $1,800 as compensation for his injury, he bought a damaged Canuck plane with this money. Coddling his purchase like a newborn child, Post reconditioned the plane and went barnstorming in it. He was forced to work hard on his depth perception, which concerned him, and anyone who chose to fly with him. But in short order, he won his wings as a commercial pilot and became recognized as one of the most fearless pilots in the business. He charged passengers $2.50 for a ride and gave flying lessons for $3.00.

Forced to accept a full-time job because of meager earnings, Wiley became the personal pilot for an Oklahoma oilman named F. C. Hall. By 1930, he achieved a measure of instant fame by winning the Los Angeles-to-Chicago Bendix Trophy. A year later, Hall sponsored Post and an Australian navigator, Harold Gatty, in an around-the-world flight in a Lockheed Vega plane named *Winnie Mae.* The two men accomplished the feat in a record-setting eight days, fifteen hours, and forty five minute, winning headlines, a clamorous reception in New York City, and an awestruck comment from Will: "Post and Gatty are making this world of ours look like the size of a watermelon."

But Wiley wasn't satisfied with such a trivial pursuit. He wanted to try the same world route *alone.* He did just that two years later, when he successfully made his solo trip in under eight days, astounding other members of his dangerous profession. The fact that he had flown by himself, just as Lindbergh had six years earlier in his flight to Paris, added to a mystique that quickly grew around him. When he then went on to become the first man to fly in the jet stream, while experimenting with high-pressure suits that could be worn in high-altitude flying, he became known not only for his bravery, but for his scientific know-how.

Despite these achievements, Post had his detractors and enemies. There were those who were envious of him and insisted that he wasn't very smart, just damned lucky. Others were put off by his feisty personality and stubbornness. None of these qualities bothered Will, who was totally won over by Post, as he always had been by other glamorous pilots of his time. When Post approached Will about writing an introduction to his book coauthored with Gatty, *Around the World in Eight Days,* Will jumped at the chance.

After Post decommissioned the *Winnie Mae,* he set out to build his "dream plane," a red, silver-striped monoplane, which would be specially designed for long-distance flying. Working in a hangar at Burbank's Lockheed Airport, Wiley jigsawed the parts of his hybrid aircraft. It included the fuselage of a Lockheed Orion, with a 550-horsepower Pratt and Whitney Wasp engine and a long Serius wing. The propeller was a three-bladed Hamilton standard, and there were compensating tanks, one on each wing. Post's link with the *Winnie Mae* was still so strong that he installed several of its flight instruments in the new plane. In the course of completing the construction of his unconventional plane, Post was often visited by Will, who was fascinated by the whole process, although he was not adept at mechanics; nor did he quite comprehend exactly what Post was trying to do.

The Lockheed Company had reservations about the hodgepodge manner in which Post was assembling his plane. But when Wiley applied for a "restricted license" to operate it, the Bureau of Air Commerce gave its consent, but with a caveat: that only one pilot and two qualified crew members could fly in it. It was dubious that Will was "qualified," for outside of his inordinate enthusiasm for flying, he wasn't particularly knowledgeable about the planes in which he flew.

As rumors swirled about the future trip that Post had scheduled, he took off with Will on a flight to New Mexico, where they stayed at Waite Phillips's ranch. Will spent most of the time looking over Phillips's cattle, while Post fished and tinkered with his plane. Post concluded that the nose area of the craft might be too heavy, so he added some scrap iron to the tail. In a column written from the ranch, Will denied that he and Wiley were headed for Siberia. It was unclear where they were going, and Will couldn't provide anything definite for Betty, either.

Once he got back to California, early in the summer, Will stayed in close touch with Post by phone. In Seattle, Wiley decided to have heavy pontoons installed on the plane, instead of conventional landing wheels. This move hinted strongly that Wiley was headed for Alaska, where the weather was poor and icy landing conditions dictated a switch to pontoons. Even at this stage, Will hadn't firmed up his plans to accompany Post. But the lure of a trip to such a vast, uncharted land became too attractive for Will to turn down, especially with Post at the controls. The fact that Betty continued to have misgivings about flying over Siberia was weighed by Will in his final decision to go. However, he knew that she would always make concessions to his wishes. If there were anything that Will desperately wanted, Betty would invariably go along with it.

"Will wanted me to want him to go," Betty wrote later. "If he felt that I wanted him to go or to do something, he was always happier. So I tried to be happy about this, once he made up his mind to go."

Although Will was superstitious about some matters, he consented when Betty asked him to have a will prepared. She knew by this time that he had decided to make the trip, even though he hadn't said it in so many words. On August 3, Will joined with Betty in signing a one-page will, in which all of his property was left to his wife. Two friends—Ewing Halsell, an Oklahoman; and Eddie Vail, a neighboring rancher—happened to be at the ranch at the time, so they served as witnesses to the signing of the simple document.

On the Sunday morning before Will left to join Wiley for their odyssey, Will rode around the ranch with Betty. They talked of new things that needed to be done on their property, new trails to be built. They stopped briefly to look at the new log cabin that had just been constructed in a canyon back in the hills. That was where they could seek more privacy when there would be guests at the ranch. Will seemed disappointed that they hadn't been able to spend any time alone there together.

Betty picked up on this quickly. Why not postpone the trip for a few days, so they could stay there, she suggested. But Will shrugged her off. "No, let's wait 'til I get back," he said, quietly.

That afternoon, Will packed two small bags, rejecting almost everything that Betty had laid out for him. He liked to travel light, and managed to do that if Betty didn't interfere. It was too late, too, for her to try to interfere with his travel plans. But she kept walking in and out of the room, drawing Will's attention to her. He sensed what was on her mind.

"Hey, Blake," he said, "ya know what I just did? I flipped a coin." She said that she hoped it had come out tails.

Within a half-dozen hours, Will would be flying off with Post. But a rodeo called "Tex Austin's World Champion Riders and Ropers" was in Los Angeles that night, at Gilmore Stadium, and Will just couldn't stay away from it. After all, he knew so many of the men in the show, old-timers who got a kick out of swapping doubtful stories with him before the performance. Before leaving for the rodeo, Will had dinner with Will Jr. and Betty. Then they all left for Gilmore Stadium, on a summer night that was cool, even for California.

"I missed the hot sunshine and the hot smell of cattle and I missed the friendly clouds of dust kicked into your hair, into your eyes and into your lap," Betty wrote, of that evening at the rodeo. "But Will was having a good time. Sitting there in a box under the floodlights, I watched him grin and wave to the contestants, as they rode by on the tanbark. . . . As the evening wore on, they came over to shake hands with Will, standing around to talk a little. . . . Someone gave Will a little wood-and-paper puzzle while we sat there and it never left his hands. Quite unconsciously, he toyed with it throughout the evening. It was a mannerism that I knew so well, and which was so much a part of him. His restless hands could never stay still. . . . When the show was over, I saw him stuff the puzzle into the pocket of his coat. The printed program went there, too."

Will had always collected everything that was connected to his life: theatre programs, restaurant bills, toothpicks, dinner or banquet cards, pencils, addresses of friends, old newspaper clippings, pictures of his family, ticket stubs. His pockets were a veritable potpourri of trinkets, souvenirs, and reminders he had scrawled for himself.

"We drove after the show from Gilmore Stadium to the airport," continued Betty. "When we got there the waiting room was crowded, so we slipped outside to talk until the plane [an eleven-o'clock flight to San Francisco] was ready to go. Then we said good-bye, and with his overcoat flung over his shoulder and a roll of midnight newspapers under his arm, he got on board. The plane taxied down the field, turned around and in a second or two came back for the takeoff. As the ship nosed up I caught a fleeting glimpse of Will through the window—and I stood looking up at the red and green lights of the plane until they disappeared into the darkness."

Arriving in San Francisco, Will attended to his passport, then proceeded to Seattle. Once there, he met an annoyed Post, who hadn't yet received the set of pontoons that he had ordered. Being equally impatient as Will, Post impulsively decided to use a couple of pontoons from a Fokker plane that were available. After the installation of the pontoons, Post took the plane up for a trial spin and became aware that the craft still tended toward nose heaviness. The nonexpert, Will, also took a look and agreed that the pontoons appeared "awful big," which might have made a less zealous flier more wary. But Wiley quickly brushed off any reservations that Will might have had. His response was to tell Will to ride as far aft in the plane as possible, thus compensating for the load being carried up front in the nose. Post would occupy a single seat in front, alongside some of the baggage.

An outside chance that Mae Post, Wiley's wife, would join them as a third passenger was rejected, principally because Will had argued against her presence. Will figured that it was going to be a grueling trip, with lots of camping out in the wilderness—conditions too harsh for a woman to endure. Once again, Will's double standard, when it came to women, was apparent: As far as he was concerned, women were essentially gentle creatures, who didn't belong in mannish slacks or on rugged excursions with Wiley and him. "Alaska is no place for a lady," Will said to Mae Post. (Curiously, he continued to refuse to grant interviews to women journalists.)

On August 6, early in the morning, Will and Wiley took one last glance into the cabin of their plane, threw two cases of chili into the rear, and "took off like a bird" for Juneau, Alaska. As they flew over the brooding Alaskan wilderness, Will was enthralled by the scenery below. But this didn't mean that he didn't get in his usual sleeping time, for he had an uncanny ability to fall asleep, wherever he happened to be—even hunched in the back of Wiley's plane, he had no trouble dozing off.

After reaching Juneau, they were forced to remain there for several days because of poor weather conditions. This gave Will a chance to visit with his old friend Rex Beach, who lived in Juneau. For hours one night, Will and Rex talked about everything under the sun, until Wiley fell fast asleep listening to the two old friends. Beach kept reminding Will to be careful, and Will responded that he trusted Post to do the right thing. "Amelia Earhart told me that Wiley's the greatest pilot in the world," Will informed Beach.

Post told Will that they would fly to Dawson, in the Klondike region, and to Fairbanks, before going to other places in Alaska. The probability was that, after making these stops, they would move on to Siberia. It wasn't a carefully planned or structured itinerary, and Will preferred it that way. He cherished the idea of spontaneity—just picking up and taking off—especially in an area that fascinated him. He already loved the natives, the little villages, and the animals, particularly the reindeer and the caribou herds that ran loose wherever they went.

Before taking off for the Yukon, Will made sure not to forget Betty. He bought a red fox fur, had it boxed, and then mailed it to her from the Juneau post office. He wanted her to have a remembrance of his trip, even though the package could not possibly arrive in her hands before he returned home.

Word had reached Dawson, then the capital of the Yukon Territory, that Will and Wiley were headed that way, so the B Division of the Royal Canadian Mounted Police was alerted. When the plane set down on the river in front of Dawson, William E. "Ted" McElhone, a twenty-six-year-old recruit in the RCMP, was among those on hand to greet the travelers. McElhone later recalled how fifteen of the Mounties, including him, played hosts to Will and Wiley that night, in their barracks, after a hearty supper of moose meat. This was the type of audience that Will appreciated, as he regaled his new friends with stories about his vaudeville days and his meetings with American presidents. Will never failed to tell his reliable anecdote of how he made Calvin Coolidge laugh, in order to win a bet with Irvin S. Cobb. The story went over well with the Mounties in Dawson, just as it had with hundreds of other audiences.

After leaving Dawson, Will and Wiley flew to Yellowknife, in the Northwest Territories. They stayed there for a couple of days, then moved on to Fairbanks, where Wiley had the chance to meet up with an old friend, thirty-two-year-old Joe Crosson, from Minneapolis, Kansas, who had a reputation in Alaska as the finest bush pilot around. Crosson looked over Wiley's plane and expressed the opinion that it appeared somewhat heavy in the nose. Then they swapped stories for a while, and then Crosson invited Rogers and Post to join him in a flight to Anchorage in his own plane. As they soared close to Mt. McKinley, at 20,320 feet—the highest point in North America—Will marveled at the sight. In several of his columns (which were not neglected during the trip), Will exclaimed about the transcendent beauty he was witnessing. "Pictures don't near do the scene justice," he said. Will never took pictures himself and rarely carried a camera—it was the sort of thing he was trying to get away from.

The following day, Crosson shepherded the two men to the Matanuska Valley, where several hundred Americans had recently settled in hopes of living off the land. The landing strip there was barely approachable but Crosson was an expert at grinding his plane to a stop. As the famous occupants of the plane stepped into the cold air, the Matanuskans greeted them as if they were running for office. Questions were fired at Will. One person asked him how he was feeling. "I came to look around, not to report on my health," he replied. A small group standing at the side of the plane attracted Will's attention. "Where are you boys from? Anybody here form Claremore?" Will asked. No, there were no folks there from his hometown. The two travelers were then conducted on an inspection tour around the area, which was in dismal shape. But Will was kind enough not to make any disparaging comments about the Matanuska Valley's state of disrepair. Instead, he cracked jokes and soon had the crowd laughing along with him. "We're gonna get a polo team on this Matanuska project," he quipped. "That's about the only thing the Democrats haven't done for this colony."

As they climbed back into Crosson's plane, a local cook rushed up to them with a plate filled with cookies. Will took a huge bite out of one of them, and expressed his delight. "They're real good," he said. "But I'll toss 'em out if we can't get off the ground!"

Once they were in the air, Will asked Wiley where they were going next, and Wiley told him that their destination would be Barrow, a primitive fishing village some three hundred miles inside the Arctic Circle. (Barrow had an Eskimo population of four hundred, and nine whites.) Dr. Henry W. Greist was in charge of the Presbyterian Mission and Hospital in Barrow, which he had run for over seventeen years. Will was agreeable to this upcoming adventure, for he knew about Greist and he wanted to pay a visit to Charles Brower, who had spent half a century in the area as a trader and whaler. Brower was the type of personality who could make good copy for the pieces he was filing from Alaska. A native New Yorker, Brower was something of a stabilizing influence in a region that was almost totally disconnected from civilization. He was often referred to as a "Daniel Boone sort of person, who wouldn't be happy unless he could find a frontier to live on." Men like Brower and Greist (the latter was the only doctor for miles) were, in Will's mind, true pioneers performing unnoticed, thankless work that the average person would shun. In talking to such people, Will liked to try to figure out what made them tick.

The region they were now headed for was the wind-tormented Arctic tundra—endless miles of a freezing, treeless environment, where mail perhaps got through about four times a year, and then only if the ice broke up.

On August 15, Will again thought of family matters, as preparations were made to fly to Barrow. Mary was still acting in summer stock in Skowhegan, Maine, playing the lead in *Ceiling Zero*. (Also in the cast was Keenan Wynn, the son of Ed Wynn, the comedian who had often been on the stage with Will in the *Ziegfeld Follies*; and an up-and-coming performer named Humphrey Bogart. In the play, Mary's father loses his life in a plane crash.)

After knocking out his latest column, Will composed a telegram for Mary; he then asked Joe Crosson if he'd be kind enough to send both pieces from the telegraph office in Fairbanks. The telegram read this way:

GREAT TRIP. WISH YOU WERE ALL ALONG. HOW'S YOUR ACTING? YOU AND MAMA WIRE ME ALL THE NEWS TO NOME. GOING TO POINT BARROW TODAY. FURTHEST POINT OF LAND ON WHOLE AMERICAN CONTINENT. LOTS OF LOVE, DON'T WORRY. DAD.

There was probably no more forbidding or barren stretch of land anywhere than in the five-hundred-mile area from Fairbanks to Barrow. If a plane went down somewhere in this wild region of mountains, snow, and ice, that would simply be the end of it, for any chance of emerging alive from an accident or of even being found, would be poor. (On Post's first around-the-world flight, the *Winnie Mae* had made a forced landing and was damaged near Flat, but that was on the Yukon River in central Alaska.)

Heeding Crosson's admonition, Post decided not to take off for Barrow with a full tank. Instead, he planned to fly to Lake Harding, some fifty miles away, where a full tank could be taken on, under more favorable circumstances. But the weather ahead of them was so bad, according to radio reports issued by the U.S. Army Signal Corps weather station in Barrow, that Post delayed taking off. With the visibility reported to be less than forty yards, and a thick fog, even the restless Post was discouraged from putting his plane in the air. They lingered for a day or so in Fairbanks, with Will catching up with his column and his sleep, while Wiley, itchy to get going, just roamed around. Although the weather reports remained miserable, Post still wanted to fly. Will didn't react much differently—relying on Post's instincts, he wanted to get moving, too.

Crosson advised Post to wait for some pronounced improvement in the weather. But Wiley said that they could always turn back if the weather didn't get any better. In addition, he said that he always flew in Alaska by keeping the ground in sight. So the two men got into their little plane and, in the half-light of the Arctic afternoon, headed for Barrow. Stopping at Lake Harding, Wiley loaded up with a full supply of gasoline. However, instead of waiting for a further weather report from Barrow, Post took off immediately. If he had gotten such a report, he would have learned that the weather was still so bad—dense fog, low clouds, constant rain—that only a fool would have attempted to fly through it. (Brower, the supposed king of the Arctic, later said that these were some of the foulest conditions he had ever seen in the region.)

Skirting the coastline to the northwest and flying blind, Post was forced to confront the storm that he had chosen to ignore. Trappers and herders in the area heard the plane overhead, near Smith's Bay, about sixty miles east of Barrow. Trying, under such conditions, to pick out tiny, isolated Barrow was next to impossible, so Post had to circle overhead several times. The chief result of such a maneuver was a loss of fuel. By this time, Post figured he had probably overshot his mark.

Suddenly, late in the afternoon, as Will insouciantly tapped out his column, while being crammed in the rear of the plane, Post pointed to a break in the cloud cover. In a few minutes, he set the plane down on a patch of water known as the Walakpa lagoon, some sixteen miles northwest of Barrow. Will spotted a group of Eskimos fishing nearby on the shore and Post taxied the plane over to them. The two men then climbed on the pontoons and struck up a conversation with Claire Okpeaha and his wife, who, as luck would have it, had been a teacher in Dr. Greist's Sunday-school class. Claire still didn't do very well with English but his wife had benefited from Greist's instructions.

"Which way to Barrow?" Will asked.

Claire's wife gave hand directions, indicating that they were about ten minutes from their destination. Will couldn't resist asking the Eskimos what they were fishing for. The answer was seals, giving him another item for his column. Then, in his friendly way, he waved to the Eskimos, the last audience he'd ever have, in a career that had begun in the Indian Territory.

After Wiley and Will climbed back into the plane, Post taxied to the end of the lagoon to prepare for his takeoff. The motor was revved up with a roar, the plane moving across the surface of the water at a quickening pace, and the pontoons carving a long spray behind the craft. The plane lifted off, veering sharply to the right, presumably in the direction of Barrow. As the plane reached a point some fifty feet in the air, its engine sputtered, then went dead. With its nose down, the plane dropped, flipping over onto its back, a dead weight. One wing broke off from the fuselage, which split open like a sliced watermelon. Suddenly, all was silent, as a film of oil spread slowly over the water's surface. Will and Wiley had died instantly, in the crushing of twisted metal and wood.

The Eskimos, who, only moments earlier, had been Will's communicants, watched the whole episode with horror. Claire now approached the wrecked plane, moving as close as he could, but his shouts were met by nothing but the sound of the wind. He told his wife that he must inform the people of Barrow about what had happened, and he set out at once to run sixteen miles through shallow lakes, bogs, and mud. Five hours later, he arrived at Barrow's only store. Exhausted and frightened, Claire told the government agent, Frank Daugherty, what he had seen. Daugherty hadn't the slightest idea who was in the plane, or where it had come from. He speculated that it might be a Russian craft that had lost its way, or a private plane of Americans hunting in the area.

A rescue party was assembled by an army sergeant, Stanley Morgan, who was in charge of Barrow's weather station. Morgan, Daugherty, Charlie Brower, and several Eskimos, including Claire Okpeaha, crowded into two launches, which were loaded up with medicine, food, blankets, and heavy Arctic clothing. It was then that Claire described, as best he could, what the men in the plane looked like. "One man's big, with tall boots," he said, "the other man's short, have rag over sore eye." Aware of Will's and Wiley's presence in the region, Morgan sadly concluded that they must have been the passengers in the plane, since Claire's words fit their description.

By the time that the launches got back to the site of the crash, Will's broken body had been removed from the wreck by the Eskimos. His left arm was smashed, his forehead had caved in, his scalp was detached; the long bone of his right leg had a compound fracture. It appeared that, at the moment of impact, Will might have been standing up.

In his pockets, there was $770 in cash and $2,040 in traveler's checks. The little puzzle, which he had been given on the last night he had spent with Betty, was still there; so was a photo of Mary, clipped from a newspaper. There was also a pencil stub, a rodeo program, a pair of eyeglasses, a pocketknife, a magnifying glass, and a two-dollar Ingersoll watch that was still running when it was found. Wiley's solid-gold watch had stopped at 8:15 P.M.,

Oklahoma time. His body, wedged between the engine and the pontoons, had to be extricated by Dave Brower, Charlie's son.

Will's portable typewriter, while a bit beaten up, was still intact. In the roller was the third page of Will's last weekly article, including his comments about leaving Fairbanks. The piece included Will's nickname for the plane, "Post Toasty," and a sentence about a gun case that Wiley had brought along on the trip. "I don't hunt or shoot myself," Will had written.

A water-soaked bag—containing other writings scheduled for Will's future columns—was also located in the demolished plane. "The backbone of the Arctic is a dog's backbone," Will had written, referring to Balto, a legendary dog of the North, and to Mickey, "a great bear dog." The last word in the piece was "death."

As word of the tragedy spread, Will's family—none of whom were at home on the ranch—received news of his death. Betty, accompanied by her sister, Theda, had gone to Skowhegan, Maine, to see Mary in *Ceiling Zero*. When the manager of the theatre, where the play was being presented, drove up to Betty's cottage and began speaking in low, confidential tones to Theda, Betty thought something had happened to Jim, who was then on a cross-country auto trip to New York. But then Theda quietly told Betty that Will had had "an accident." At that moment, all of Betty's misgivings and premonitions about Will's trip were sadly realized. The planes that Will loved, without reservation, had proven his undoing.

When Will Jr. got the news, he was working in the engine room of a Standard Oil tanker in San Diego, on a summer job. Jim finally heard about it when he arrived at the Gotham Hotel in New York. In North Haven, Maine, Charles Lindbergh was informed of his friend's death by the Associated Press. Immediately, he phoned Juan Trippe, president of Pan American World Airways, for whom he had been working as a consultant, and asked if Trippe would help bring the bodies home; Trippe was quick to oblige. Lindbergh then made a second phone call, to Betty, the only call that she accepted that day.

Choosing to be with his two friends on their final air trip, Joe Crosson piloted the plane containing their remains. The first stop was Fairbanks; then he went on to Juneau, then to Seattle. The last leg of the trip to Los Angeles was made in a Pan Am plane. When Crosson disembarked, with darkness descending on California, he looked haggard from his sorrowful 3,500-mile journey. Meanwhile, Wiley's body was placed on board a plane headed for Oklahoma City, where services would be held for him.

On August 22, there was a simple funeral service for Will at the Wee Kirk O' the Heather, attended by his family and friends, including Fred Stone, Eddie Cantor, and Stepin Fetchit. Since Will had not professed his allegiance to a particular church, it was a nondemonimational service. And since so many people wanted to say farewell to him, the family consented to having his casket lie in state at Forest Lawn Memorial Park in Glendale. There, a crowd estimated at up to seventy-five thousand waited under a broiling sun to pay their last respects to a man they regarded as a personal friend. At the Wee Kirk O' the Heather, floral arrangements were made around saddles, lariats, spurs, and chaps; and John Boles, a romantic leading man in films, with an operatic voice, sang "Old Faithful."

Several days after the funeral, the famed Hollywood Bowl, in the center of the film colony, was the site of a public service for Will. The bowl, nestled in a natural amphitheater, was filled with thousands who gathered to mourn Will's passing. Prior to that time, few deaths of public personalities had had the impact on Americans that this double tragedy had. Tributes and remembrances came from all parts of the globe: From the Soviet ambassador to the United States, to President Roosevelt, to singer John McCormack, to hard-boiled editorial-page writers, to cabinet members, to the "little guy in the street"—the words of praise were recorded.

FDR said that "Will was an old friend of mine, beloved by all. He showed all of us how to laugh." Columnists rolled out their elegant phrases. The sportswriter Grantland Rice, as beloved in his own trade as Will was in his, picked up on Will's words—"I'm off somewhere in a red bus"—that he had uttered before embarking on his ill-fated trip. Rice wrote: "Off somewhere, with a ghostly rope and a cheerful grin, and wherever his roving feet may fare, I know they'll like him and take him in, and ask why he was away so long; . . . where most of the best have gone before, to find new roads and another song, and sail their ships to a newer shore."

The *New York Sun's Sun Dial* printed a poetic eulogy that occupied almost an entire page: Here it is, in part:

> Cowboy humorist
> Apostle of horse sense,
> Court jester to a nation,
> Envoy of the world,
> The beloved philosopher
> Dead in the murky tundra
> The friend of millions,

Companion of all men. . .
Hoboes and potentates
Saw more clearly through
Your rural logic
You went smiling because
Under the cap and bells
Was a fine courage
It took you from ranch
To the big cities
From tent show and
Vaudeville to stardom
From obscurity into
The hearts of all men
Dead?
Not to us, Will
But alive and smiling
Chewing away and twisting
That old lariat
Forever and forever,
Down through the ages. . .

Stories in the press ran for weeks, and, more often than not, on the front pages, as Americans pondered the loss of this man. He had entered into their homes and lives, there was no mistaking it. He had appealed, in his quirky way, to the mighty and the meek. He was no battle hero; no disease-conquering doctor or scientist; no handsome devil of the screen or stage; no job-creating industrialist; no silver-tongued politician. He fit under no ideological umbrella or label. Yet he had struck a common chord among millions.

If Post had perished alone, he would have earned major headlines and obituaries, for he had carved a reputation as a daring figure in an occupation experiencing a startling transition. He was, indeed, admired greatly for his role.

But Will had seemingly touched people all over the world. His sweetness of character, uninhibited generosity, down-deep common sense, and infectious story-telling had made him a universal favorite. He was fondly thought of as someone who never put on airs or fancy clothing. "Just as common as old cornbread," a cowboy on the streets of Claremore said about him after his death. Others said, "Just folks, as pleasing as an old shoe," Most people thought he was one of them, and they liked the idea that he represented them as the quintessential American.

Although mildly skeptical about the future of mankind, at a time of pervasive distress, Will still retained an optimistic faith in his country and in ordinary people. He might have sometimes sounded like Voltaire's Dr. Pangloss, when he insisted that America was the best of all nations. But he seemed to believe this—and Americans seemed to believe him. Like St. Francis, "he was a lover not of mankind at large, but of men as individuals," wrote *The New York Times* in 1931.

Will earned enormous amounts of money, at a time when many people didn't have enough in their pockets to pay for their next meal. But he gave lots of it away, often to anyone who would ask him for a handout. He kept few records of his goodwill and charity, for he didn't believe in making a fuss over such matters.

He was terribly sentimental and good-hearted, yet he showed little open emotion toward members of his own family. Public displays of affection simply weren't his style. He playfully criticized innumerable public figures but probably would have been a failure as an elected representative, for he lacked the toughness, single-mindedness, and drive for power that are endemic in politicians.

By the common consent of his two sons, Will Jr. and Jim, Will never was as funny in private as he was in public. "He didn't have many jokes to tell when we brought home bad grades or got tickets for speeding," Jim once remarked. But, said Will Jr., "Did did what was natural to him. He didn't pay much attention to what people might think about him. He was perfectly at ease with everybody, just a terribly civil man, with charm and wit. And even though he knew or had associated with almost every famous person of his time, he wasn't a name-dropper."

In the words of *Life* magazine's Roger Butterfield, Will Rogers lived "for fun, for friendliness, and for his family and his country."

Appendix A

Postmortems

Over the years, a number of theories have been advanced to the cause of the air crash in the Walatka lagoon. Exactly what happened will never be known. But on one thing, almost all observers have agreed: The oversized pontoons created an imbalance in the craft, making the plane much too heavy in the nose. This, combined with sudden engine failure, caused Post to lose control of his aircraft.

Why the engine failed has also been the subject of speculation. Some said the engine cooled off during the time that Wiley and Will chatted with the Eskimos. Others suggested that the plane simply ran out of gas, a theory that gained support from the fact that there was no gasoline found in the tanks, following the crash, and none on the surface of the lagoon. The sudden sputtering of the motor, before the plane took its fatal plunge, adds credibility to this notion.

Another theory that has been offered was that, as Post was taxiing down the lagoon on the takeoff, the plane's pontoons collided with a submerged sandbar. However, scant credence has been given to this idea; similarly, little attention has been paid to the suggestion that Will actually drowned in the two or three feet of water that flooded the plane.

After studying the matter with Joe Crosson and others, Dr. Greist concluded that the plane, after flying for several hours in the fog, ran out of gas. Since the plane was equipped with two gas tanks, the pilot had to watch vigilantly so that when one tank ran low, he could turn on the hand control that switched on the other tank. Dr. Greist felt that Post did become aware of the situation—but too late: He tried, but failed, to turn on the hand control when the plane was probably less than fifty feet from the lagoon's surface. Wiley just couldn't pull the plane out of its dive at that point.

In any case, whatever happened to Post's judgment, and, thus, to his plane, Will's life abruptly ended when he was still at the crest of his restless career. Every indication pointed to his continued popularity and to his ability to continue to earn large sums of money. At the time of his death, he was, by any standards of the period, a wealthy man. Indeed, in the last year of Will's life, he made over a half-million dollars from his movies, syndicated writing, and radio broadcasts.

"I don't buy anything that I don't understand," he often explained. This policy meant that he never invested in stocks, but preferred to put his money into life insurance and U.S. bonds. All of these holdings, bequeathed to Betty, provided her with well over a million dollars. The sprawling Santa Monica ranch, representing the real estate that he had always fervently believed in, was worth millions. In 1944 the ranch was given to the state of California by Will's children, just as seventeen acres of land in Claremore were donated by Betty, in 1938, to the state of Oklahoma, to be used as a memorial for Will.

After Betty died in 1944, her body, Will's body, and that of their infant son were brought from Los Angeles to Oklahoma and were placed in the Claremont Memorial, Claremore's granite museum. The museum rests on a promontory of the reddish hills there, a site that Will, years earlier, had chosen as the place for his home, after his retirement. Looking like a rambling ranch house, it is visible from the Will Rogers Highway (Route 66) and houses countless possessions of Will and his family, including letters, notes, recorded radio broadcasts, movies, Indian relics, and other memorabilia that Will had a penchant for collecting.

In the central lobby of the museum stands a life-size bronze statue of Will, sculpted by Jo Davidson—a duplicate of the one that is a fixture at the Statuary Hall in Washington, D.C. Thousands of people file by every year to look at Will's hunched figure, with his hands typically resting in his pants pockets, and a sly smile creasing his face. Although Will declared that memorials should be living things, such as hospitals and colleges, instead of cold heaps of stone, he probably would have liked the Claremore museum.

Following Will's death, his children pursued varied careers. Mary Amelia Rogers, recalled by her friends as a flapper in her style, but a bright lady, appeared on the stage and in the movies. She was a strong-willed woman: If Will tried to discourage her from joining him in the acting business—and it is said that he did—he did not succeed. "I don't want her choosing a profession where education plays no part," he said, jocularly. But Mary refused to listen to his message.

Two years before Will died, Mary acted in a movie, *My Weakness*, employing the name of Mary Howard. She wanted to be judged on her own talents, rather than as the daughter of a famous man. However, on the stage she used her own name. Although she made a number of movies in the 1930s, Mary was never a top star, usually settling for second leads in B movies. Her brief, unhappy marriage to Walter Brooks, the stepson of Douglas MacArthur, ended in divorce in 1952. After that, she spent many years living outside the United States. She died in Santa Monica in December 1989, at the age of 76, from complications associated with cancer.

Will Jr., admittedly never as devoted to horses and the outdoors as his brother Jim, was a graduate of Stanford University, where he took a degree in journalism. Considerably more politically oriented than Jim, he was tied to the Democratic party, while Jim regarded himself as an independent. In 1942, when he was thirty one years old, Will, Jr. ran for a House seat as a Democrat from Southern California. When the army called him during his campaign, his wife, Collier, and some of his friends took up his cause, helping to win him the seat. Two years later, he resigned, joining the army as a tank commander. He was wounded in the Battle of the Bulge, winning a decoration for heroism.

When World War II was over, he ran for the Senate as a Democrat, losing to William F. Knowland, a rock-ribbed conservative Republican. However, he had better luck running Harry Truman's presidential campaign in Southern California in 1948. During the 1950s and 1960s, he appeared in two movies based on his father's life. He played Will, to whom he bore a striking physical resemblance.

From 1935 to 1953, he was publisher of the *Beverly Hills Citizen*, which had a pronounced liberal predisposition. During this period, he also became actively involved in trying to help Jewish refugees in Palestine, in defiance of

British restrictions. For two years in the late 1950s, he was hired as the host commentator on the "CBS Morning News." In 1967–1969, he was an assistant to the federal commissioner of Indian affairs; he also once headed the California State Park Commission.

He and his wife (who died in 1976) adopted two boys, Clem and Carlos. Clem, a Navajo Indian, has worked for the Bureau of Indian Affairs as chief of security on the Papago Reservation in Arizona. In July 1993, after a series of health setbacks due to heart trouble, strokes, and hip surgery, Will Jr. committed suicide near his retirement home in Tubac, Arizona. He ended his life with a gun, a weapon his father had shunned.

Jim has spent most of his life as a rancher in California. For a while he acted in some of Hal Roach's cowboy movies, but it wasn't his milieu. His wife, Astrea, died in 1987. He lives in Bakersfield, California, and has two sons, Charles and Ken, and a daughter, Bette.

Appendix B

More Wit and Wisdom

During his lifetime Will spoke, wrote and repeated thousands of jokes, one-liners and puns. Following are some of the most memorable:

❖ ❖ ❖

"We are the first nation in the history of the world to go to the poorhouse in an automobile."

❖ ❖ ❖

"Heroing is one of the shortest life professions there is."

❖ ❖ ❖

"There's no more independence in politics than there is in jail."

❖ ❖ ❖

"A mother and a dog are the only two things that show eternal love."

❖ ❖ ❖

"Do you think the pilgrims would have let Indians land, the way the Indians let the pilgrims land?"

❖ ❖ ❖

"California always did have one custom that they took seriously. That was in calling everything a ranch. Everything big enough to spread a double mattress on is called a ranch."

❖ ❖ ❖

"Everybody is rushing to go somewhere where they have no business, so they can hurry back to the place where they should never have left."

❖ ❖ ❖

"A Democrat never adjourns. He is born, becomes of voting age and starts right in arguing over something and his first political adjournment is his date with the undertaker."

❖ ❖ ❖

"The question of the world today is not how to eat soup, but how to *get* soup to eat."

❖ ❖ ❖

"When the boys were coming back from overseas and parading every day, why didn't we let them sit on the reviewing stands and make the people march those fifteen miles."

❖ ❖ ❖

"Alaska voted one Ku Klux away up there. Can you imagine a man in all that snow and cold with nothing on but a thin white sheet and pillow slip?"

❖ ❖ ❖

"There was so many men being nominated that some of the men making the nominating speeches had never even met the man they were nominating. . . . I know they had not from the way they talked about them."

❖ ❖ ❖

"Mussolini could run this country with his eyes shut. In fact, that's the way our Congress has been running it."

❖ ❖ ❖

"I'm for the common people and since Beverly Hills has no common people, I'll be sure to make good."

❖ ❖ ❖

"This would be a great world to dance in if we didn't have to pay the fiddler."

❖ ❖ ❖

"My idea of an honest man is a fellow who declares income tax on money he sold his vote for."

❖ ❖ ❖

"My epitaph: Here lies Will Rogers. Politicians turned honest and he starved to death."

❖ ❖ ❖

"Every time Congress makes a joke it's law and every time they make a law it's a joke."

❖ ❖ ❖

"Spinnin' a rope's a lotta fun, providin' your neck ain't in it."

❖ ❖ ❖

"One day there was four innocent people shot here in New York City. That's the best shootin' ever done in this town. Hard to find four innocent people in New York."

❖ ❖ ❖

"Lord, the money we do spend on our city government. It's not a bit better than the government we got for one-third the money two years ago."

❖ ❖ ❖

"The income tax has made more liars out of the American people than golf has. Even when you make one out on the level, you don't know, when it's through, whether you're a crook or a martyr."

❖ ❖ ❖

"If you read the fine print before you sign, what you get is an education. If you read the fine print after you sign, what you get is experience!"

❖ ❖ ❖

"Americans are the most generous, kind-hearted people on earth as long as they're convinced not one dollar of it is going for taxes."

❖ ❖ ❖

"I'm the only man who came out of the movies with the same wife he started with."

❖ ❖ ❖

"Everything is funny, as long as it's happening to somebody else."

❖ ❖ ❖

"I've never been a member of any organized political party—I'm a Democrat."

❖ ❖ ❖

"Mothers, when you see your baby picked up by someone nowadays it's either by one of two men—a kidnapper or a politician."

❖ ❖ ❖

"England has the best statesmen and the rottenest coffee in the world."

❖ ❖ ❖

"More people should work for their dinner, instead of dressing for it."

❖ ❖ ❖

"Ninety percent of the people in this country don't give a damn. Politics ain't worrying this country one-tenth as much as parking space."

❖ ❖ ❖

"I'd rather be the one to pay too much than the man to charge too much."

❖ ❖ ❖

"He [Coolidge] didn't do anything, but that's what the people wanted done."

❖ ❖ ❖

"The United States never lost a war or won a conference."

❖ ❖ ❖

"Every time a woman leaves off something, she looks better. But every time a man leaves off something, he looks worse."

❖ ❖ ❖

"If a man makes a speech he takes a chance on saying a damn fool thing and the longer the speech the greater the thing."

❖ ❖ ❖

"I'm only an ignorant cowpuncher but there ain't anybody on earth, I don't care how smart they are, ever gonna make me believe they'll ever stop wars. We ain't as smart as the generations behind us and they tried to stop them and haven't been able to."

❖ ❖ ❖

"Don't worry if a man kicks you from behind. It only proves you're ahead of him."

❖ ❖ ❖

"Congress is going to start tinkering with the Ten Commandments just as soon as they can find someone in Washington who has read them."

❖ ❖ ❖

"Once a man holds public office he is no good for honest work."

❖ ❖ ❖

"Congress is so strange. A man gets up to speak and says nothing. Nobody listens, then everybody disagrees."

❖ ❖ ❖

"Englishmen are the only race of people that never travel just for fun."

❖ ❖ ❖

"Rome had Senators. Now I know why it declined."

❖ ❖ ❖

"Everybody is trying to find out what's the matter with movies. If they ever do find out they will ruin the business."

❖ ❖ ❖

"You know that everybody is ignorant, only on different subjects."

❖ ❖ ❖

"You can't say civilization don't advance because in every war they kill you in a new way."

❖ ❖ ❖

"Communism is like Prohibition. It's a good idea but just won't work."

❖ ❖ ❖

"A comedian can only last till he either takes himself serious or his audience takes him serious."

❖ ❖ ❖

"Politics is so expensive that it takes a lot of money to even get beat with."

❖ ❖ ❖

"It takes a strong man to remember what country he is representing when the wine and flattery start flowing."

❖ ❖ ❖

"It looks like the only way you can get publicity on your death is to be killed in a plane. It's no novelty to be killed in an auto any more."

❖ ❖ ❖

"A politician is not as narrow-minded as he forces himself to be."

❖ ❖ ❖

"Corruption and golf is two things we might just as well make up our minds to take up, for they are both going to be with us."

❖ ❖ ❖

"We shouldn't elect a president; we should elect a magician."

❖ ❖ ❖

"If all politicians fished instead of spoke publicly, we'd be at peace with the world."

❖ ❖ ❖

"I'd rather be right than Republican."

❖ ❖ ❖

"Every time a lawyer writes something, he is not writing for posterity, he is writing so that endless others of his craft can make a living out of trying to figure out what he said; 'course perhaps he hadn't really said anything, that's what makes it hard to explain."

❖ ❖ ❖

"Diplomats are nothing but high-class lawyers—some ain't even high class."

❖ ❖ ❖

"When you get into trouble five thousand miles from home you've got to have been looking for it."

❖ ❖ ❖

"A Columbia Professor wrote a book in 15 hours and won a prize. That's a good thing. The quicker the authors write them the quicker they can get to some useful work."

❖ ❖ ❖

"There is nothing interesting in an actor but his act and you can get it at the box-office price."

Index

271